## DATE DUE

|  |  |  |  |
|---|---|---|---|
|  |  |  |  |
|  |  |  |  |
|  |  |  |  |
|  |  |  |  |
|  |  |  |  |
|  |  |  |  |
|  |  |  |  |
|  |  |  |  |
|  |  |  |  |
|  |  |  |  |
|  |  |  |  |
|  |  |  |  |
|  |  |  |  |
|  |  |  |  |
|  |  |  |  |
|  |  |  |  |
|  |  |  |  |
|  |  |  |  |
|  |  |  |  |

# PIERCED BY MURUGAN'S LANCE

ELIZABETH FULLER COLLINS

# PIERCED BY MURUGAN'S LANCE

Ritual, Power, and
Moral Redemption among
Malaysian Hindus

ᴍᴍ

NORTHERN ILLINOIS UNIVERSITY PRESS

DEKALB 1997

© 1997 by Northern Illinois University Press
llinois University Press,
is 60115
ates using acid-free paper
eserved
∞

ing-in-Publication Data
Collins, Elizabeth Fuller.
Pierced by Murugan's lance : ritual, power, and moral redemption among
Malaysian Hindus / Elizabeth Collins.
p. cm.
Includes bibliographical references and index.
ISBN 0-87580-223-0 (clothbound : alk. paper). —
ISBN 0-87580-574-4 (pbk : alk. paper)
1. Hinduism—Malaysia. 2. Tamil (Indic people)—Malaysia—
Religion. 3. Thaipusam. I. Title.
BL1164.3.C65 1997                96-52671
294.5'36'095951—dc21
CIP

# CONTENTS

## ACKNOWLEDGMENTS

My debt to the community that has nourished my thinking is immense. Many of my best ideas come from my mentors, Hanna Pitkin, Alan Dundes, Nancy Chodorow, George Hart, and George De Vos. Stanley Brandes patiently listened as I developed my ideas and gave me encouragement to go on. In conversations with Lee Grossman, I began to understand why I was fascinated by ritual vow fulfillment and how the stories that Murugan's devotees told me could be understood as narratives showing the meaning(s) of their acts. I also thank the many friends and colleagues—Joanna Goven, Dan Avnon, Emily Hauptman, Dennis McEnnerney, Jill Frank, Pat Boling, Meta Mendel Reyes, Jackie Stevens, Brian Wiener, Ivan Strenski, Susie Sutch, Vijaya Nagarajan, Linda Hunt, Steve Howard, Diane Ciekavi, and Celeste Friend—who read various parts of the manuscript, listened to my stories of Thaipusam, and asked probing questions.

Without the devotees of Murugan, who told me stories and answered my endless questions, this book would not have been possible. Sometimes it took me a long time to understand what they were trying to tell me, and I thank them for their unfailing courtesy and interest in my project. I also thank Mr. V. Ramachandran, Headmaster of the Ramakrishna Mission in Penang, who tried to teach me to wrap my tongue around the fluid melodies of Tamil. My discussions with him were crucial in my coming to an understanding of the traditions that Tamils brought from India to Malaysia. Sharlini Sankaran provided invaluable support with Tamil. Many other friends in Penang also contributed to this book— Bob and Pat Seward and Hung Wah and Lim Chin Lam deserve special mention. Kristina Youso's help with editing was invaluable.

This book has been a collaboration from the very beginning. My children, Emmons, Nicholas, and Claramarie Collins, have given me their love and encouragement. I dedicate the book to them. Michael Leaver, Nancy Tingley, Henry Ginsburg,

## ACKNOWLEDGMENTS

Joanna Williams, Linda Hess, Elaine Craddock, Alison Keith, Maureen Katz, Tyrell Collins and Bob Conway, Joe and Claire Fischer, Maya and Gary Matkin, Eric and Cathy Crystal, and Dick and Judy McGinn have given me unstinting support throughout the years of completing this project. My deepest thanks to all of you. To those I have forgotten to mention, I apologize. As is always the case, my debt to the people who have made a difference in my life is too big to acknowledge fully.

# PIERCED BY MURUGAN'S LANCE

# THE POWER OF MURUGAN'S LANCE

*Vel, vel, vadi vel.*
*Vel, vel, vetri vel.*
*Vel, vel, vira vel.*

*[Lance, lance, beautiful lance.*
*Lance, lance, victorious lance.*
*Lance, lance, lance of courage.]*

The chant praising the leaf-shaped lance of Murugan, son of the great Hindu deities Shiva and Parvati, resounded through the early cool of a tropical dawn. On the grass-covered field, enclosed on three sides by buildings owned by the municipality of Penang, small groups of worshippers clustered facing a small and very old temple of the goddess Mariamman. Surrounded by relatives and friends, the devotees of Murugan who were to fulfill vows to him on this day could be distinguished by simple yellow loincloths or saris of cotton. We watched as each devotee arranged an offering of flowers, incense, sacred ash, limes, coconut, and a pot of milk in front of a *kavadi* (wooden arch), which served as an altar. The kavadi, which was typically decorated with a picture of Murugan and peacock feathers or crepe paper, consisted of an arch that would be carried by the devotee on the day's pilgrimage.

The priest, who had come a week earlier to invite us to the temple of Mari-amman for the ceremonies scheduled as part of the celebration of Thaipusam, approached through the crowd. He, with several other *pujaris* (non-Brahmin priests), had been moving from group to group to perform the ritual initiation for vow fulfillment. He nodded silently to the companions of a young man who stood quietly in an attitude of prayer, head bowed and hands clasped. While the priest invoked the descent of Murugan, he passed a brazier of smoking incense back and forth. Gradually the devotee seemed to lose awareness of his sur-roundings, and then his eyes closed. The priest rubbed sacred white ash (*vibhuti*) on the man's chest and then took the hooks and skewers of vow fulfillment from the tray of offerings held by his assistant. The silver hooks had been sharpened and polished to a bright sheen in the days of preparation before the Thaipusam festival, and the priest quickly inserted them, just under the flesh. The man showed no sign of pain. Offerings in the form of small pots of milk were sus-pended from these hooks. This young man was also to have a *vel*, the invincible weapon of Murugan, pierced through his cheeks. The priest covered his fingers with ash and placed them inside the man's mouth, forcing the spear through the left cheek first and then the right. This required considerable force, for the spear was a half inch in diameter. All the while, the priest gently twisted the spear. When the weight of the spear was balanced, the man reached up to hold it on ei-ther side.

The final act of piercing was the hardest to watch. The man stuck out his tongue, and the priest took it in his hand, covering it with ash. He took up the last skewer, a silver replica of the vel of Murugan about eight inches long. The priest seemed to use all his strength when he pierced the devotee's tongue and forced the vel to pass through the muscle. This was the only time that the man seemed to emerge from his trance, but the insertion was completed expertly.

The Thaipusam festival, which honors the god Murugan, lasts for three days in Penang. On the first day, several hundred thousand devotees of the god come to Penang for the procession, in which the image of Murugan is taken from the center of George Town, the colonial entrepôt established by the British on Penang Island, to the Nattukottai Chettiar Murugan Temple at the edge of the city. At the end of the third day of the festival, the god is brought back to his abode in George Town in another grand procession, which lasts all night. The second day of the festival is especially auspicious for the worship of Murugan in pilgrimage tem-ples. On this day devotees come from the estates, where they work on the main-land of the Malay peninsula, to fulfill vows at the Arulmigu Bala Thandayutha-bani Hill Temple of Murugan in Penang.

We had brought our two sons, aged five and one, to watch the preparations for ritual vow fulfillment at the Mariamman Temple. For several hours the four of us wandered through the square in a state of stunned fascination. Many of the men who were to fulfill vows had prepared a special kind of kavadi that consisted of a large platform that was supported on both shoulders. This arch could also be attached to the back and chest by long skewers that penetrated the devotee's flesh or by strings that ended in small hooks embedded in the skin of his chest and back. Other devotees had large hooks embedded in their backs, by which they pulled small chariots with an image of Murugan or their chosen deity. There were also men and women who chose to have only their tongue or forehead pierced by a miniature vel. Sometimes, as the priest attempted to induce a trance, a devotee would begin to dance wildly or take a martial stance and challenge those nearby to a fight. Occasionally someone collapsed in a faint. When the trance came in these ways, sacred ash would be pressed onto the forehead of the person by a priest or a friend. In a moment or two this remedy invariably brought the person back to a state of withdrawn composure in which the hooks and skewers of vow fulfillment could be inserted.

Finally, I went inside the small temple of Mariamman, which was also crowded with worshippers waiting patiently for a priest. The air was heavy with the smell of burning incense and the fragrance of jasmine, mixed with the scent of souring milk. The murmur of the priests' prayers and the chanting of "*Vel, vel, vetri vel*" produced a hypnotic drone. When an explosion of coconuts hurled to the ground announced the arrival of pilgrims from another temple, everyone pressed even more tightly together to allow another spear-impaled devotee to make obeisance before the goddess. Then a piercing cry announced that the trance had descended on yet another worshipper, and the hair on my arms stood on end. For a moment I was afraid that I, too, might enter a trance. I left the temple.

As the sun was now beginning to beat down on the streets, we decided to take the children home so they could play in the cool compound of expatriate houses where we were staying, while we followed the devotees of Murugan on their pilgrimage to his temple located several miles away on the side of Penang Hill. All along the route to the temple, onlookers had gathered in pavilions built for the festival. Accompanied by music played over loudspeakers, the spear-impaled devotees of Murugan performed a dance. Sometimes an escort of youths circled around the entranced dancer as a drummer marked the beat. The mood was joyous, and spectators (especially Western tourists) were encouraged to join in the celebration.

Late in the afternoon we returned to check on our children. At first no one responded to our calls. Drawn by the sound of singing and clapping from the homes of Tamil servants who lived at the back of the compound, we came upon a disconcerting sight. To the chant of "Vel, vel, vetri vel," our five-year-old son was dancing in the center of a circle with a sharp pencil clenched in his teeth and protruding from both sides of his mouth. I suddenly saw how exciting and grand the ritual must have seemed to him. Although I was horrified at the idea of his skin being pierced by a six-foot lance, I realized that he did not think in terms of pain or suffering and that small Tamil boys must also dream of the day they would be in the center of such a circle of admiring faces with a spear pierced through their cheeks. Was Thaipusam a rite of transition to manhood? But then, what of the women and older men who fulfilled vows?

Reflecting on my first Thaipusam, I was reminded of Norman Cohn's study of the millenarian movements of Medieval and Reformation Europe and imagined myself stepping back into the Middle Ages when flagellants beat themselves in rituals of mass penance.[1] Was Thaipusam, like medieval penitential cults, a form of social and ethical protest by the poorest and most disadvantaged? Is that why the devotees who pulled little carts by hooks embedded in their backs and those who carried a coolie's shoulder pole with offerings seemed to represent themselves as beasts of burden? If so, why were these rituals of vow fulfillment so joyous? Why didn't people voice their protests in other (political) ways? What kind of a deity would ask such a penance of his devotees? Was this rational behavior? Why did women seem especially susceptible to outbursts of dramatic, angry dancing when they went into trance? How was the concept of vow fulfillment related to the concept of penance? What did the lance that devotees used to pierce their bodies symbolize? Was I interpreting the Thaipusam rituals through an ethnocentric lens—the Christian conception of sin and the politics of religion?

The most striking and unchristian part of the ritual was that (unlike Christian flagellants) the devotees of Murugan did not seem to experience any pain, because they were in a trance state. I wondered about the significance of the trance that devotees entered. I had witnessed trance before, both in the performances of stage hypnotists that had fascinated me as a child and in the performance of *dukun* (shaman) among the highland Pasemah of South Sumatra, with whom I had lived between 1971 and 1973. However, in these cases only a few individuals had gone into trance, and the trance had seemed rather like a performance with a discernible purpose.

In Pasemah, trance was understood to be a medium through which the ancestors communicated with their descendants. The dukun, most of whom were women past the age of menopause, sought to resolve a communal crisis or to affect a political situation by reminding people of the force of tradition that the ancestors represent, as in the case of the *pasirah*'s wife. The pasirah was a locally elected official who mediated between the Pasemah of the area where we lived and the *camat,* a Javanese official appointed by the central government. The pasirah's wife had fallen ill shortly after his election. He consulted the Western-trained doctor in Pagaralam, but his wife's illness did not respond to treatment, and she languished in bed for weeks. As is the custom in the highlands, many people came to visit her. One afternoon when I was sitting with the other women by her bedside, Nenek Dukun arrived.

Nenek Dukun was often consulted about the fevers that so frequently strike the highlanders, which she treated with massage and rituals inspired by her trance encounters with the spirits who are believed to cause such illnesses. Her position in Pasemah society was unusual in that she was a widow and lived alone rather than with any of her married children. Because she was free from household responsibilities and could move about as she pleased, she acted as a petty trader as well as a healer, bringing buttons, thread, scarves, and so forth to the homes of women who rarely went to market. Her trading activities not only supplemented her income but also increased her importance by allowing her to collect gossip and convey information.

After treating with massage the painful aching that the pasirah's wife suffered, Nenek Dukun prepared to go into a trance. She took a brazier and some incense out of her bundle and, invoking the spirits in an almost unintelligible mumble, rocked back and forth until she fell, apparently unconscious, into the arms of another woman. After a few minutes she sat up again and began to speak in a gruff, low voice. This was said to be the voice of the snake spirit that was tutelary ancestor of the clan traditionally identified with the villages that the pasirah represented. The spirit complained that the pasirah had not fulfilled a vow made during his election campaign—that he would kill a goat as an offering to the clan ancestor if he won the election. The spirit demanded its *sedekah* (ritual offering meal) at Tanjong Tebat, the spring where it resided. Later Nenek Dukun explained that the snake was holding the internal organs of the pasirah's wife in its coils and making her ill. If the pasirah fulfilled his forgotten vow, his wife would recover.

There had been rumors that the pasirah won his office in a recent election because of the financial influence of his father-in-law, who was said to have sponsored his son-in-law's candidacy as a way of increasing his own political influence. The inhabitants of Pagaralam and its surroundings wondered whether the new pasirah's loyalty to his father-in-law and the interests of his wife's family might outweigh his concern for the interests of the community he represented. I never heard that the pasirah acknowledged having made a vow, as Nenek Dukun claimed. But as Nenek Dukun traveled from house to house, telling the story of her encounter with the spirit who had caused the illness of the pasirah's wife, rumors of threatening portents—a snake that stood up in the middle of the road, another found wrapped around the handle bars of the pasirah's bicycle—spread throughout the community. It became clear that Nenek Dukun had succeeded in making the pasirah aware of his community's concern that he would not respect their traditions and represent their interests.

In time the pasirah's wife recovered from her illness. No one was sure why, and no one discounted the possibility that Nenek Dukun's ministrations had been effective. From all that I knew and could see, I was fairly certain that Nenek Dukun had not consciously deceived the community about her contact with the ancestors. I saw that she had found a role that gave her an effective voice in community affairs.

The acts of ritual vow fulfillment performed by the devotees of Murugan on Thaipusam were harder to understand. Because these rituals involved what should have been painful piercing of the body, the trance of ritual vow fulfillment was more disturbing and could not easily be seen as a performance for political ends. I sympathized with the correspondent for the *New York Times* who wrote, "Once over the shock at first sight of the hooks and spikes, I simply wonder, why? No one has compelled these people to perform this extreme act of devotion and sacrifice. Why, I ask myself, would anyone put himself through an ordeal like this?"[2]

In 1980, five years after our first Thaipusam festival, my family and I returned to Penang for a period of research, and I began to pursue my questions about the meaning of ritual vow fulfillment and the Thaipusam festival for Hindu Tamils. I began by naively asking participants, "Why do you pierce your body?" They explained that they were fulfilling a vow and usually recounted the problem that had led them to ask the help of Murugan—a serious illness, for example, or difficulty in arranging a love marriage or in conceiving a child. However, when I tried to get people to explain the symbolism in ritual vow fulfillment, asking, "But, why do you *pierce your tongue?*" or "What is the meaning of the kavadi?" they were puzzled and could not answer my questions. Most often, I was referred to someone whom they thought of as an authority in religious matters, usually a priest.

I was not alone in finding it difficult to obtain the participants' own interpretations, an emic account of meaning (see Dundes 1962b). For example, in an essay on the fire-walking festival of the Tamils of Fiji, Carolyn Henning Brown (1984) writes:

> Indians do not ordinarily provide or perform exegesis on their rituals, at least not on rituals such as this one, rituals of ancient, low caste, non-Brahmanical, orgiastic origin. The annals of Dravidian ritual practice are full of puzzled descriptions of rites but faintly understood either by their ethnographers or, apparently, by their practitioners (e.g. Whitehead 1921). The ritual specialists are notably mute when it comes to explanations of the ceremony. . . . The concern is primarily with procedure: this must be done and that must be done. The red flag is "for" Devi, the limes purify, the water cools, etc. (226–27)

This tendency to emphasize the importance of proper ritual performance—while remaining unable to articulate the meaning of the ritual—is characteristic of not only Hindu Tamils. Bourdieu has described such "embodied" (performed and enacted) understandings of the relation of human beings to a divine/natural order as *doxa,* contrasting these unarticulated understandings both with the *orthodoxy* by which specialists of high status claim authority to determine the true meaning of doctrine and ritual practices, and with the *heterodoxy* of religious movements that arise in opposition to orthodox dogma and the hierarchical institutions legitimated by that dogma.

Such understanding of one's own culture and practices as natural—the way the world is—occurs in all cultures. As the anthropologist Roy Wagner (1981) points out, people usually become aware of their own customs as distinctive only when they confront different forms of life. Indeed, he suggests that anthropologists "invent" their own culture only as they reflect on how the people they are studying live in a different world:

> In experiencing a new culture, the fieldworker . . . comprehends for the first time, through the intimacy of his own mistakes and triumphs, what anthropologists speak of when they use the word "culture." Before this he had no culture . . . since the culture in which one grows up is never really "visible"—it is taken for granted, and its assumptions are felt to be self-evident. It is . . . only through the experienced contrast that his own culture becomes "visible." In the act of inventing another culture, the anthropologist invents his own, and in fact he reinvents the notion of culture itself. (Wagner 1981, 4)

When one lives and talks with the Hindu Tamils of Penang, gradually one sees that the goddess Devi, who is associated with red and fire, is full of a hot energy called *sakti*. The color white, by contrast, is pure, cooling, and male. Thus milk is used to cool the red heat of the Devi, and the white ash vibhuti can be used to bless and cool a worshipper and to drive out possessing spirits. Yellow, the color of the clothes worn by devotees who fulfill vows to Murugan on Thaipusam, denotes that someone is in a sacred state (see also Beck 1969; and Babb 1974, 1975a). Thus I began to learn the ritual language of the Hindu Tamils of Penang.

Although the world represented in Hindu Tamil ritual is symbolically ordered, this does not mean that people agree in their understanding of ritual gestures. As I conversed with the ritual specialists who had been recommended to me and listened to others who volunteered their own understandings of ritual vow fulfillment, I discovered that there was considerable disagreement about the meanings of ritual acts performed on Thaipusam. For example, a pujari (or non-Brahmin priest) explained the symbolism of the coconuts that are hurled to the ground in front of each shrine along the pilgrimage route:

> Breaking of coconuts is actually to smash the impurities of the heart. You see the coconut has a tough husk on it. Below the husk you have a hard shell and inside the shell you have a white kernel. Our heart is something like that. Before you pray to God, you must cleanse and purify your heart. Here is a man gone into a trance. He has almost forgotten himself in love of God. The hard, outer shell of the human ego must be broken apart to reveal the inner purity of an enlightened soul.[3]

This priest, who spoke in English, emphasized that the goal of ritual vow fulfillment is enlightenment. In his interpretation of the symbolism of the coconut, he followed the popular devotional tracts (in Tamil and English) that are published in India and sold in bookstalls in Penang. One tract in English explains that the outer husk of the coconut stands for *anavam* or ego, the hard inner shell for *malam* or materialism, and the pure white inner core for *mayi* or awareness (that is, awareness of worldly illusion).

Another worshipper interpreted the coconut as a representation of the head of the ascetic god Shiva: "The three eyes of the coconut stand for the three eyes of

Shiva that symbolize enlightenment, and the growth of the tough husk at one end stands for the topknot which symbolizes his ascetic retreat from the world." And a Western-educated professional explained that the coconut was a symbol of the self, and the breaking of a coconut symbolized the sacrifice of self for god. While these interpretations differed, both associated the coconuts that were smashed with ascetic renunciation. However, most devotees I had interviewed had not mentioned enlightenment as their goal but rather said that they had made a vow to Murugan, asking him for help in their everyday worldly lives.[4] They wanted good health, success in an examination, a job, a love marriage, a son. They described the coconuts as offerings to the deities of the shrines. Or they said that the coconut offerings were meant to "drive off" (or propitiate) demons and evil spirits.

The Hindu Tamils of Penang also disagreed about the reason for the Thaipusam celebration. Some said that the festival marked the day that Murugan received the vel from his mother, the goddess, and set off to do battle with the demon Surapadma; others maintained that Thaipusam celebrated Murugan's marriage. According to a guidebook and some of the priests, Thaipusam marked a conjunction of astrological forces, which made the day an auspicious one to seek the aid of Murugan—worshipped in the form of the Thandapani Avatar, a youthful "staff-bearing" celibate ascetic (see chapter 2).[5] Not only did people provide different reasons for the festival, their accounts pointed to contradictory aspects of the festival. For example, Murugan is worshipped as an ascetic, celibate youth in the Penang Hill temple where vows are fulfilled, whereas during the Thaipusam procession, he is worshipped as a god-king and is said to be married.

In time I came to see that the different interpretations of the Thaipusam festival and of rituals performed by devotees of Murugan reflected social, economic, and political divisions within the community of Hindu Tamils.[6] The majority of Tamils in Malaysia are descendants of indentured laborers who were brought to work in the British colony during the first three decades of the twentieth century. Although many of these estate laborers moved to cities in recent decades and now work in factories or as household help, they generally hold low-paying jobs and have remained at the bottom of the social ladder. There is also a small middle class composed of Indian merchants. Many are descendants of Muslim merchants, known as Chulias, who came from Tamilnadu in the nineteenth century. This group also includes Sikhs from Punjab, and Hindu Punjabis, Gujaratis, Sindhis, Marathis, as well as Jaffna Tamils from Sri Lanka. Particularly important are the Nattukottai Chettiars, a money-lending caste who also came from Tamilnadu to Malaysia in the nineteenth century. Finally, there is a Western-educated elite of doctors, lawyers, professors, and successful entrepreneurs. Many of these are the descendants of Jaffna Tamils who came to work in the colonial civil service or as clerks on British estates. Since the 1930s, this professional elite has sponsored a movement to reform Hindu practices in Malaysia.

Viewed from the outside, the Hindu Tamils of Penang appeared to share a symbolic language and ritual tradition. However, when viewed from the inside, this shared culture could be seen as fragmented and contested (Bakhtin 1937; Clifford and Marcus, eds., 1986).[7] But lines of fracture in the Hindu community are often obscured by claims that Hinduism encompasses differences in practice and interpretation. When I asked a pujari about the different accounts of the Thaipusam festival and the different interpretations of important symbols, he was not disturbed by my question and explained that each account reflected the teller's level of understanding. In this way he also emphasized his own authority as a religious specialist.

The understanding of ritual vow fulfillment that I present in this study is rooted in a view of ritual as a kind of language, a form of symbolic action. Just as people do things with words when they promise or lie, for example, they are doing something when they perform a ritual. However, ritual is a special kind of doing, not an instrumental doing (in which magic and ritual are considered to be a kind of primitive science), but a performative doing that uses symbols to express a claim about oneself and about the world.[8] From this perspective, the meaning of a ritual does not simply inhabit the person who performs the ritual, or the person who officiates at the ritual and claims authority to interpret it; but rather, different interpretations of meaning connect participants (and observers such as anthropologists and their readers) in particular ways. The symbols employed in rituals have both cognitive and emotional content, thereby evoking the involvement of participants and interpreters in ways that may transform their sense of themselves and their relation to others. This view of ritual as a form of symbolic action makes it possible to bring together the various perspectives of psychology, anthropology, history, religion, and political science.

Murugan, the god of the Thaipusam festival, is introduced in chapter 2. By exploring the ritual traditions that have claimed Murugan as a representation of particular ideas and values, I came to see that the Thaipusam festival in Penang could be seen as two separate festivals conjoined. One was modeled on the annual festival of a god-king, who was the patron of the dominant caste or of the ruler of a territory. This festival consisted of a procession symbolically marking out the territory ruled by the king, as representative or incarnation of the god-king, and rituals confirming the legitimacy of the existing political and social order as a divinely ordained hierarchy. The second festival was the festival of Murugan, worshipped as an ascetic youth in a pilgrimage temple at the margins of the kingdom. This festival was traditionally associated with devotional worship, particularly vow fulfillment by low-caste and untouchable devotees. In this context, ritual vow fulfillment could be seen to express egalitarian values and resistance to the hierarchy of caste that the god-king represented.

The socioeconomic context of the Thaipusam celebration in Penang is explored in chapter 3, which follows the procession of Murugan on the first and final days of the festival. This journey shows how the community of Hindu Tamils in Malaysia is divided by class and caste differences and by different religious practices. Working-class Tamils, who came to colonial Malaya as indentured laborers, brought with them the religious traditions of their villages in Tamilnadu. These traditions included the worship of both an Amman mother goddess and semi-demonic deities, who were guardians of her temples and lineage deities of low status groups, along with the propitiation of demons, who (like the goddess) required blood sacrifice. These low-caste and untouchable laborers also worshipped Murugan in the form of an ascetic youth as represented in the egalitarian tradition of *bhakti,* or devotional worship. On the other hand, the Nattukottai Chettiars—a money-lending caste who became very rich in colonial Malaya—brought to Malaysia orthodox Hindu traditions, which emphasize caste distinctions and practices based on purity and pollution (such as a vegetarian diet). They worship Murugan as their lineage deity and sponsor the Thaipusam procession, in which Murugan is represented as god-king. The Malaysian Indian intellectuals and professionals, who are descendants of those who came to Malaya to work in the colonial civil service, were most influenced by Western views of Hinduism and have in the twentieth century organized a Hindu reform movement. They tend to be sympathetic to the tradition of devotional worship known as bhakti because of its egalitarian premises, but they oppose rituals of low-caste and untouchable groups that they regard as primitive. These different religious traditions, interrelated historically in a dynamic tension, provide the terms and arguments that shape participation in the Thaipusam festival by individuals and various groups in Penang today.

The Penang Thaipusam festival in its ever-changing variety is sketched in chapter 4. Because the celebration of Thaipusam is never exactly the same from one year to the next, and there is no single authority to be consulted about what belongs to the festival tradition and what is the incidental contribution of a participant, there can be no definitive account of the festival. In fact, I found nobody who could explain to me why all the events that took place fairly consistently every year were part of the celebration of Thaipusam. In my description I have emphasized continuities in the festival as celebrated from 1975 to 1985, but I also include individual stories and puzzling observations about which I can only make a few comments. Malinowski referred to this ever-changing variety as the "chaos of social reality." And Pierre Bourdieu (1977, 1990b) disparaged the anthropologist's description of pattern and totality in society as a distortion of reality as lived by participants. Nevertheless, people do learn from their culture to see the world in relatively ordered ways, imposing structure in the form of narratives and categories that allow them to assess, predict, and intend. That this order is not total, that different orders exist within any culture, and that people hold inconsistent views of the world is also clear. However, as Bourdieu points out, people are rarely confronted with the contradictions and inconsistencies in their understanding of the world and in their practices (except perhaps when an anthropologist calls these to their attention).[9]

One way of making sense of different interpretations of and changes in the

Thaipusam festival is by seeing events against the background of sociohistorical changes in Malaysia and the politics of its Hindu Tamil minority. Over the five decades following World War II, vow fulfillment to Murugan on Thaipusam has become increasingly popular, and each year the Thaipusam festival attracts more people. During the same period there has been a decline in vow fulfillment to the Amman goddesses of estate temples. This suggests that the moral order and socioeconomic patterns associated with the Amman goddess and the closed world of the estate have begun to disappear and/or are being challenged by Tamil laborers. In chapter 5, I explore this hypothesis by reviewing studies of Hindu religious life on Malaysian estates to see how economic and political changes have affected the world of the plantation and the lives of estate laborers. These studies and my interviews with Tamils in Penang about the histories of their temples suggest that groups within the Tamil working class have turned to religious activities that are not restricted by the state, in an attempt to maintain temples as institutions of collective self-rule. In the context of restrictions on genuine participation in political institutions, ritual vow fulfillment on Thaipusam gives expression to their vision of a more egalitarian moral order. Conflict over the celebration of Thaipusam—ostensibly centering on the question of which practices embody authentic tradition—reflects tensions between different classes. At the same time, the politics of Thaipusam show how, in the competition for social, economic, and political advantages, class identity may be submerged in a collective ethnic (or national) identity. In this context, the syncretistic symbols of Tamil Hinduism have been used in the celebration of Thaipusam to promote contradictory interests.

Malaysia's Hindu Tamils distinguish different forms of trance, which are treated quite differently. The possession trance of women and low status men is generally thought to be caused by demonic beings and is treated with rituals of exorcism, which intimidate and coerce the malicious spirit into leaving his victim (and the victims into an accommodation with society). By contrast, the priest who is thought to be possessed by the Amman goddess or a warrior deity becomes a spokesman for the deity. His trance is empowering. The social framing of trance in accord with hierarchies of power is explored in chapter 6. I. M. Lewis, who has formulated an ecology of trance showing how the relation of a group to its environment and internal structures of power shape the ways in which trance is understood and used, describes possession trance as "essentially a philosophy of power" but "tinged with a kind of Nietzschian desperation" (1989, 183). Here he echoes Sartre, who writes in the preface to Frantz Fanon's *The Wretched of the Earth* (1963) of episodes of mass possession in colonial Africa:

> In certain districts they make use of that last resort—possession by spirits. Formerly this was a religious experience in all its simplicity, a certain communion of the faithful with sacred things, now they make of it a weapon against humiliation and despair; Mumbo-jumbo and all the idols of the tribe come down among them, rule over their violence and waste it in trances until it is exhausted. (16–17)

Such episodes of mass possession tend to emerge in times of social unrest and political and economic change. They often function as a release mechanism that
serves to maintain the social order, such as carnivals and other rites of reversal,
which allow the oppressed to express their protest against the "humiliation and
despair" of their everyday lives. For the limited period of the festival, the poor
and powerless are allowed to play the role of powerful beings.

Against the anthropological and sociological view of trance as shaped by external pressures and cultural constraints is a contrasting perspective that emerges
from psychological studies of trance. In the discipline of psychology, ego psychologists, object relations theorists, and researchers on multiple personality disorders show how unacknowledged or unrecognized parts of the personality are
expressed through trance. Some of these undeveloped self-fragments are repressed as (morally) unacceptable, but others may be acceptable to the self but
not acceptable to society. For example, the trance of ritual vow fulfillment may
be seen to give low status Tamils the opportunity to disavow socially ascribed,
stigmatized parts of their identity and to represent themselves as individuals who
have been recognized as morally worthy by the god Murugan. From this perspective, the divine trance of devotees on Thaipusam should not be seen as a fu-
tile gesture of illusion. Rather, one could argue that it contains the seeds of a
widespread, egalitarian social movement.

To interpret the meanings of individual acts of vow fulfillment, I turn to
Tamil folklore (as expressed in proverbs, folktales, legends, myths, and especially the tales of Murugan and the Thaipusam festival), which provides a reser-
voir of cultural narratives that give meaning to the symbolic enactments of ritual
vow fulfillment. Clifford Geertz's famous essay on the Balinese cockfight (1973,
412–53) provides the model for this analysis of cultural forms as stories that people tell about themselves. My method of interpretation has something in common
with psychoanalytic interpretation. Just as Freud's patients did not understand the
meaning of their symptoms, the devotees of Murugan usually cannot explain the
meaning of their ritual acts. Indeed, they have no conscious memory of the
thoughts or feelings that accompany the experience of divine possession on Thaipusam. Their amnesia, which is taken as evidence for the "fact" that trance involves possession by a supernatural being (so that the devotees feel no pain while
the hooks, skewers, and vels of vow fulfillment are inserted in their bodies), pre-
cludes awareness of one's thoughts while in the trance state. Psychoanalytic interpretation is based on the premise that symptoms and dreams are a form of (unacknowledged) action and have meaning—even if the actor is not aware of the
meaning, indeed does not consciously accept the symptom or dream as meaningful. Although dreams are private, rituals are public, and symptoms are both public and private, all are taken to communicate meaning in a symbolic form that can
be interpreted through cultural and personal associations. Following Ricoeur
(1970), religious narratives are not interpreted reductively in terms of archaic
childhood origins but rather are seen to provide culturally approved resolutions

for psychic conflict (see also Obeyesekere 1990). From this perspective, ritual involves a dialectical process between culture and psyche, so that meaning is both imparted by culture and selectively appropriated from culture to become subjective reality for the person who uses a cultural symbol.

The themes of the Tamil legends, myths, and stories that provide associations to rituals of vow fulfillment performed on Thaipusam are explored in chapter 7. These narratives contain cultural paradigms—Shiva, the omnipotent, uninvolved ascetic; Amman (or Kali), the devouring and dangerous mother; Sita, devoted wife of Rama; Murugan, who was not only a conquering warrior and triumphant ascetic but also a divine lover and a savior; Valli, the lowly tribal maid beloved of Murugan; and Idumban, the demon-devotee who is conquered by Murugan—that can be appropriated by individuals to organize their experience of self. These tales of divine ascetics, deities, and demons provide a culturally sensitive framework for psychoanalytic interpretation, as opposed to using the paradigms of Freudian and Jungian theory developed to help people in Western societies understand their experience of self. The cultural paradigms of myth and legend not only provide models for the imaginative construction of individual identities; they also can be associated with unconscious parts of the self and with self-images that are not acknowledged by others. The symbolic enactments of ritual vow fulfillment allow for the expression of such multiple, ambivalent meanings, held in tension so that the mask of civility and accommodation that people must wear in their ordinary social interactions is not disrupted.

The occasional participation of members of the Australian forces stationed in Penang, Chinese Malaysians, and a European or American tourist in ritual vow fulfillment on Thaipusam suggests that the stories of Murugan also have relevance to people from other cultures and reflect transcultural human dilemmas. The need for moral redemption, the desire for submission to a powerful divine being, longing for union with a beloved person, jealousy of a rival, the triumph of conquest, and the desire to rebel and overthrow those who have power—themes represented in the narratives associated with vow fulfillment—tap strong and ambivalent emotions in all human beings, because we all begin life dependent on the love of powerful others. The psychoanalytic strategy also provides a way to understand how the rituals of vow fulfillment appeal to people who do not share Tamil culture and its construction of experience.

In chapter 8, I argue that the symbolic actions formalized in ritual allow for the development of the moral capacities of human beings and culturally constructed ethical systems. My thesis grows from this study of Thaipusam, which is grounded in an attempt to provide what Wittgenstein calls a "perspicuous presentation" of the event. This requires that Thaipusam be presented against the background of its social and political context and that one know something about (what might be called) the grammar of ritual form and the semantics of Tamil Hindu traditions. This background shows the place of the festival in the lives of its participants, its significance, or what Wittgenstein more poetically called "the inner nature of the practice." From such a presentation we can see that the spirit of ritual vow fulfillment on Thaipusam is moral redemption. We see also that moral redemption is framed in a variety of ways by religious narratives about the god Murugan and other deities, so that individual psychological needs are fulfilled (in fantasy) and vow fulfillment has particular meanings to each individual participant. Moral redemption is manifest by the successful fulfillment of one's vow and by *arul*, the trance that is experienced as a divine blessing and empowerment by Murugan. The egalitarian implications of these two themes—empowerment and moral redemption—give the festival its political significance, such that it comes to be a vehicle of protest against elites and their claims to privilege and power.

Wittgenstein suggests that when one seeks to understand a ritual, the paradigm of explanation is misleading because we must look for the meaning of symbolic actions, not their causes. In a critique of Freud, Wittgenstein also objects that the paradigm of explanation leads to an essentialism that is reductionist. There are many sorts of rituals, and one must look for the spirit of a *particular* ritual and see how people are using the ritual in a *particular* context. To illustrate once again how a perspicuous presentation produces understanding (which is always contingent upon the way subsequent events and information bear out one's understanding), I tell the story of Sheilah's vow fulfillment to the Amman goddess. Sheilah's story illustrates how a person can draw upon the tradition of ritual vow fulfillment to express personal interests and feelings (including unconscious conflicts) in a context of political and social constraints and interests. We see how Sheilah's actions are framed by conscious intentions, by unreflective decisions, and by unconscious ideas and feelings.

In the final part of chapter 8, the implications of Wittgenstein's suggestive *Remarks on Frazer's Golden Bough* (first published in English in 1971) are elaborated in a discussion of works on rituals by three other contemporary philosophers—Susanne Langer's *Philosophy in a New Key: A Study in the Symbolism of Reason, Rite, and Art* (1942); Herbert Fingarette's *Confucius: The Secular as Sacred* (1972); and Richard Wolheim's "The Sheep and the Ceremony" (1979, reprinted in *The Mind and Its Depths,* 1993)—to show how, in rituals like vow fulfillment on Thaipusam, people invoke representations of good and ethical relations, thereby reproducing (and potentially reshaping) society in terms of shared moral values.

In the final chapter, the tradition of anthropological theory about ritual is contrasted to the view of ritual developed in the previous chapter. Anthropologists have built on the foundational work of Durkheim, *The Elementary Forms of the Religious Life* (1915), which describes ritual as a cognitive system that (1) orders society and people's experience,[10] (2) creates social integration through *collective representations* that are symbolized,[11] and (3) has deep emotional roots,[12] a perspective that Clifford Geertz has summed up in his classic formulation of ritual as a symbol system that provides a "model for and of the world" (1973, 93–94, 123).[13]

In this tradition, the work of Victor Turner (1967, 1969, 1974) has been especially significant. Turner (1969) applied Van Gennep's analysis of rituals of transition as a process consisting of three stages—separation, transition (or a liminal stage), and reincorporation—to rituals such as festivals and pilgrimages, more commonly found in post-tribal societies. He observed that such rituals also involved the suspension of the normal social order so that hierarchical distinctions were replaced by equality and symbolic poverty, creating an ethos of *communitas*. Thus the symbols employed in ritual did not, as Durkheim suggested, simply represent the timeless values and structured order of a society. Some rituals masked social differences (especially hierarchical ones), temporarily creating social solidarity, and they provided a moment of social drama in which factional conflicts might be enacted, possibly leading to social change (Turner 1974). In this sense, ritual traditions may be said to constitute an unreflective politics or a pre-political social order.

Within this tradition, two distinctive approaches to ritual have developed. One, which emphasizes what ritual does to people, is exemplified in the work of Michel Foucault (1980). The second, which emphasizes what people do with ritual, is exemplified in the work of Pierre Bourdieu (1977, 1990b). The first underscores the ways in which the behavior of people is shaped by culture, language, and hierarchies of power (or structure). The second stresses the conception of human beings as agents who act upon the world and try to reshape it to reflect their values and interests (or agency). This chapter explores how Clifford Geertz (1973, 1983) and Stanley Tambiah (1985, 1990) have sought to resolve this tension between structure and agency by formulating theories that keep in view both the felt experience of human agency in imagining, intending, choosing, innovating, resisting, and initiating, and an awareness of the ways in which human action is shaped by forces beyond our unreflective awareness. Their work draws on the philosophical writings discussed in chapter 8, along with work by other philosophers who write in the Wittgensteinian tradition, but neither of these theorists pays sufficient attention to the role of ritual in constructing the moral dimension of a human life and shared conceptions of a just social order. Chapter 9 concludes that two counterbalanced perspectives are necessary in the study of ritual. One perspective emphasizes the moral capacities of human beings and looks at ritual as a medium through which people constitute themselves as moral beings and collectively reproduce a social order based on shared values. The second is a hermeneutics of suspicion, which looks for the ways rituals and concepts implicate people in relations of power. I conclude that anthropological theories that show how ritual is used to construct forms of power, but fail to reflect the power of ritual in configuring a moral order, breed cynicism and thereby contribute to the erosion of conceptions of moral autonomy and agency.

2

## MURUGAN AS METAPHOR

The Thaipusam festival can be likened to a tapestry woven of traditional patterns. Both those who commission the work and those who produce it make a contribution, drawing on a rich symbolic heritage to express desired themes. To interpret their contributions, we must begin by understanding the significance of the images and ritual forms in their heritage. The many forms in which the divine is represented and worshipped in Hinduism have evolved over more than two thousand years as the result of the imagination and activity of many people with different conceptions of the divine and with diverse worldly interests and purposes as well. In this chapter I explore the complex iconography of Murugan, who is worshipped both as god-king, ruler of a divinely ordered society, and as a young god who has challenged the older gods and overturned their orthodoxy; both as an ascetic renouncer of the world and as a sensual lover; and finally, as a transcendent deity. I have organized the material thematically and historically, tracing a kind of etymology of Murugan as a symbol, showing how the iconography of Murugan is related to political and religious institutions, particularly the festival of the god-king and the pilgrimage temple tradition.

In Hinduism the divine is understood to be manifest in the world, and it can be represented and worshipped in a natural object or an icon. The physical form in which the divine is represented (*murthi*) allows the worshipper to focus his attention and evokes an emotional response. Thus, the form of a particular deity makes a metaphorical statement about the nature of the divine and the relation of humankind to the sacred.

## Velan: Bringer of Trance

In the centuries before the present era, at the beginning of the historical record for southern India among the Dravidian tribes who inhabited the mountainous areas of Tamilnadu, a shaman presided over sacrifices of cocks and goats to Murugan (Zvelebil 1981, 7). The shaman (who was said to be possessed by Murugan) was called *velan* for the vel, a spear with a leaf-shaped head that identified him with the god. Like the shaman, Murugan may be addressed as "velan" (Clothey 1978, 27–33). The jungle-dwelling peacock, Murugan's mount or vehicle (*vahana*), is another reminder of Murugan's association with jungle peoples.

As a tribal deity, Murugan was associated with the hunt and war, but he was also known as a divine lover. His name is said to be derived from *muruga*, meaning "tenderness, youth, beauty" (Hart 1975b, 22). He was pictured as a handsome youth who possessed the young maids of the tribe (Clothey 1978, 25–33). A poem dating from the first centuries of the current era describes the dance of a shaman called to treat a girl, who is said to be possessed by Murugan:

> Women who utter ancient truths, skilled at lying,
> spread out rice in a winnowing fan to discover the truth
> and say, "It is the presence of Murukaṉ, hard to bear."
> Mother believes them,
> and in a house so well made it could be a picture,
> she prays:
> "May my daughter's loveliness, as lovely as a doll's, return."
> The sweet instruments are played together,
> the floor is prepared,
> a large pandal [pavilion] is decorated with ornaments for the dance,
> they put on katampu [red flowers] and white pieces of palmyra leaves,
> the sweet drone sounds behind a compelling beat,
> they cry out the great name of the god
> throwing up their hands,
> and the priest makes the large floor resplendent
> with his frenzied dancing,
> moving like a puppet
> manipulated by a skillful puppeteer.
> *Akam* (in Hart 1975b, 28–29)

*Shilappadikaram,* a poem written in the fifth century by a Jain prince, also refers to Murugan's possession of young maids (Shulman 1980, 5). The poignancy and irony of this girl's lovesick lament speak directly to us across the enormous gulf of time and culture:

> Good girls with rich bracelets!
> My mother makes me laugh.
> She thinks I am possessed
> by the handsome god Murugan.
> She called an exorcist, not noticing
> what all the village talks about.
> My illness sprang from love alone,
> and from a prince, and a cool hill
> where pepper grows.
>
> Good girls with bright bangles!
> I had a good laugh when the exorcist
> said he could heal the curious malady
> a mountain prince has caused.
> This man is hopelessly obtuse.
> And if the god who clove
> the sacred heron rock
> obeys an exorcist like him,
> he must be rather dull himself.
>
> Good girls with heavy bracelets!
> I laughed aloud when the exorcist
> tried words to cure my malady—
> gift of a prince and of a fragrant hill.
> This man has lost his wits.
> And if the son of Shiva,
> who sits beneath a holy tree,
> obeys him and appears before us,
> he is not too clever himself.
>
> Graceful girls, preciously adorned!
> Really one has to laugh
> when an exorcist attempts
> to cure the lovely malady
> caused by embraces of a mountain prince.
> He seems to be a bit naive.
> And if the god who's garlanded
> in rice shoots and in winter blooms
> appears before us, he's as foolish
> as the exorcist who tries to cure me thus.
> (Adigal 1965, 150–51)

Trance dancing in Murugan's honor is described in another early poem:

> They put on *nīlam* [eye liner]
> and the fragrant green leaves of margosa,
> bring me to the house of Murukan
> fearful in his preeminence,
> bowing as sweet instruments play
> behind a swelling drone . . .
> and they sing of his katampu tree and of his elephant
> and, shaking, take palmyra leaves
> and katampu garlands
> and dance all night.
> *Akam* (in Hart 1975b, 29).

There are also records of this ecstatic dancing in the trading cities that grew up at the center of small Dravidian kingdoms. In the ancient city of Kaveripatti-nam, where a great temple festival in honor of Murugan was held annually, women danced the *kuravai*, a ring dance, and the *veriyattam*, which is described as "a weird dance marked by the expression of frenzy" (Clothey 1969, 309). This ancient tradition of trance dancing is still associated with the worship of Muru-gan during the Thaipusam festival, and the metaphor of Murugan as a divine lover who possesses his worshippers continues to have a strong appeal.

## MURUGAN AS GOD-KING

### From Warrior Deity to God-King

During the Cankam or Sangam era (from c. 100 B.C.E. to c. 200 C.E.)—named after a form of oral poetry composed by illiterate bards—Tamil warrior chiefs established the first Dravidian kingdoms. The Cankam poet who sought the patronage of one of these kings would sing of the king's valor in war and of the prosperity he brought to his kingdom, comparing him to the war god Muru-gan (Clothey 1978, 34–35; Hart 1975b, 13–20, 86–93; Zvelebil 1981, 7; Stein 1984, 4–9). In the following poem, a Chola chieftain is praised for his fearsome prowess in war, which, like the wrath of Murugan, destroys all enemies.

> O fearsome Chief! Your wrath is like that of the God Murukan's [*sic*]; the san-dal paste of your body is dry; your sword smells of flesh; you gain victories fighting unaided; your boundless armies appear to fill all available space. They advance breaking up the enemies' front with swift horses useful in war, and shields of the color of clouds spread across. They plunder the grain-producing fields, and lead their elephants to immerse themselves in the guarded drinking-water tanks. Using the timber of the houses as tinder, they set fire to them; the glow of the burning fires in the country-side resembles the red-dishness of the radiant sun in the evening sky. Even your elephants fought well in accordance with your plan of waging a terrible war; they helped to devastate the guarded

> great country, rich in agricultural tracts . . . where there is no jungle other than
> that of sugar-cane. (*Purananuru* 16; in Stein 1984, 5–6)

As the Tamil war chiefs consolidated their kingdoms, they sought new ways to legitimate their rule. They brought Brahmin priests from northern India to their southern Indian courts. These priests introduced royal sacrifices and the tradition of the Vedas. Following the Shaka, Kushana, and Gupta dynasties of northern India, the Dravidian monarchs became patrons of the cult of the warrior deity Skanda, whose image they used on royal seals and coinage (Clothey 1978, 48–49), and the warrior god Murugan came to be identified with the warrior deity Skanda, as a god-king who was responsible for the order of the kingdom and the universe (see Hart 1978). As god-king, Murugan acquired the insignia of Tamil kingship: banner, umbrella, war-drum, horse, elephant, chariot, garlands, crown, and capital city (Clothey 1978, 35; Hart 1975b, 13–20).

Known as Somaskanda, Murugan now acquired a legendary history. The myths relating to Skanda, collected in the *Skanda Purana* (seventh century), are known in a Tamil version called the *Kanta Purana*. The climactic event of this work is the battle between Murugan and the demon (Tamil *cur*; Sanskrit *asura*) Surapadma and his two brothers. Murugan is given his invincible weapon—the vel (spear or lance)—by his mother, the goddess Parvati. He first defeats the demon Taraka and then goes to Tiruchendur, located on the seashore in Tamilnadu, where he confronts Surapadma and his remaining brother, Sinkamukan. Murugan and his adversary take various forms in their fight, until finally Surapadma becomes a gigantic mango tree rooted in the ocean. Murugan splits the tree with his vel. One half of the tree takes the form of a peacock and becomes the vehicle of the god. The other part becomes a rooster and is displayed on Murugan's pennant (Zvelebil 1981, 33–35). After his victory over the demon, Murugan is given Deviani (or Devasena, meaning "army of the gods"), the daughter of Indra, in marriage. These events are celebrated on Skanda Sasti in October–November at the temple of Tiruchendur, one of the six sites sacred to Murugan in Tamilnadu (Clothey 1978, 122).

Murugan's marriage to the daughter of Indra can be seen as a symbolic representation of his incorporation into the Vedic pantheon of northern India. His defeat of the demons who make war against the high (Sanskritic) gods and who threaten to bring chaos to the world makes him a symbol for the political order that the king brings to the world of men. As god-king, Murugan (like the Dravidian warrior kings) was thought to be distinguished by *irai* (eminence or that which makes one excel). *Iraivativam* (from *irai*, the divine, and *vativam*, shape or form), meaning the manifestation of the sacred in a concrete form, referred both to the iconographic representation of a deity and to a king (Clothey 1978, 12).

The Tamil word for temple, *koil* (*ko*, king, and *il*, house), means literally the house of the king (Hart 1975b, 13). Like a living king, the image of Murugan is perceived to be a magically charged object that is invested with divine power. Brahmin priests, who possess the requisite purity of mind and body and know the proper rituals, are responsible for maintaining the god's image and temple in an auspicious and pure condition so that they will be suitable vessels for sacred power. They care for the deity, waking, bathing, dressing, feeding, and entertaining him.[1] Murugan is also married like a king and tours his capital city in a triumphal procession, which is the model for the Thaipusam procession.

Jain merchant communities flourished in the rich Dravidian kingdoms of the sixth and seventh centuries. Stein (1984) suggests that it was Jain philosophers who first developed the idea of ethical kingship that came to be associated with the god-king. In the ethical purview of Jain thought, irai came to denote the ethical quality that distinguishes a ruler who embodies the moral order, and it was thought that a kingdom with a king who possessed this quality would prosper (15; see also Hart 1975b, 13). Natural or political disasters were taken as signs that the king no longer possessed this divine excellence and power. *Shilappadikaram,* the fifth-century work of a southern Indian Jain prince, tells of the destruction of the kingdom of Madurai because the king failed to act justly.

Just as a king is held responsible for the prosperity of his subjects, as a god-king Murugan is expected to provide worldly security and prosperity to his worshippers. This worldly emphasis appears to characterize much of the vow fulfillment to Murugan on Thaipusam, for most worshippers say they have sought his help in resolving the problems of existence in the secular, everyday world.

## Competition for Honors and Loyalty

Stein (1984) has pointed out that the ties binding southern Indian village communities into a kingdom were fragile. Only the subcaste lineage group (*kulam*) was united by a shared identity. The social relations of caste hierarchy provided links between dominant castes and their service castes,[2] but each lineage or caste subunit was primarily concerned with competition for high status within the hierarchy of caste, and members of dominant lineages did not necessarily feel personal loyalty to the monarch. The problem for the ruler was to cultivate loyalty to the kingdom and the king. Stein suggests that the Hindu kings of the Vijayanagar period (1336–1646 C.E.) gave their patronage to the Dasara *(Dasarah)* festival (also known as Navaratri or Mahanavami), during which the Ramayana is enacted, because the epic gave expression to the themes of legitimacy and loyalty to one's sovereign. The god-king Rama is portrayed as destroyer of the demon Ravana, who represents the forces of evil that threaten the kingdom, and Hanuman and Lakshmana are portrayed as noble exemplars of loyalty and devotion to the sovereign. According to Stein, medieval kings used the occasion of the festival to present honors to important lineages (which were taken as signs of their high status in the caste hierarchy) in return for expressions of loyalty to the royal line. Stein describes this ritualistic "prestation" (*dana*) as a means by which the king cultivated the loyalty of powerful caste lineages (302–26).[3] Geertz (1980), writing about the Hindu kingdoms of Bali, has called this form of political legitimacy, "ritualistic authority."

Kings no longer rule Tamil communities or serve as the major patrons of religious performances. But the Thaipusam celebration continues to have political significance as a setting in which social groups vie for status and honor and as a festival that attracts the participation of virtually all segments of the Hindu Tamil community. Wealthy members of the Tamil Hindu community in Penang act as sponsors to voluntary associations, which build pavilions *(thaneer pandal)* where guests who come to see the procession of the god-king may sit in the shade and be offered a glass of water. There is much competition in the elaborate decoration of these pavilions. Thus the Thaipusam festival involves relations that tie high status members of the community to lower status groups and provides an opportunity to compete for honors. Important sponsors are honored by being presented with garlands of flowers or silk scarves by the priests who attend the chariot of the god-king. And political leaders attend the festival to show their commitment to the values and interests that Hindu Tamils share.

## Marriage of the God-King and Goddess

In almost every village in southern India there is a temple dedicated to the goddess, who is believed to control the coming of rain, the fertility of animals, and the prosperity of human beings in the territory she protects. The goddess is everywhere addressed as Amman, mother, but she is also worshipped under distinctive names as the goddess of a certain village or as the goddess who brings a particular disease, such as Mariamman who brings smallpox (Bean 1975). These goddesses—known as village goddesses *(gramma devata)*—are associated with the land and with life (Moffatt 1979, 124–26, 270–89).[4]

The divine energy of the goddess, called *shakti* (power, in Malaysia *sakti*), is conceived to be a kind of heat, the animating force in all living beings. It is represented in the blood, which gives and sustains life, and in fire, which both warms and destroys. However, in the full intensity of drought, fire, or the fever of disease, and the bloodshed that accompanies war, the *shakti* of the goddess becomes dangerous to life. The searing heat of drought and the attack of fever is regarded as the goddess's punishment for her children's sins and their failure to worship her. Thus, the village Amman goddess, like a mother, is perceived to be the source of all that is needed and desired, and at the same time she is feared as a violent and hostile deity who embodies the destructive forces of nature—drought, famine, disease, and warfare. A great deal of the ritual of goddess worship in the village is intended to appease the goddess and bring her powers under control. The traditional way to appease the Amman goddess was to offer her blood (animal) sacrifice (Moffatt 1979). Another way to control her was through her marriage to a Brahmanic deity, who stands for the political and social order of caste hierarchy.

The iconography of the goddess shows how she is transformed by marriage. As Durga, slayer of Mahishasura, the great buffalo demon, or as Kali, who wears a necklace of skulls, or as the village Amman goddesses, she is understood to be unmarried and dangerous. She holds a sword, her lips drip blood, and her victim lies beneath her feet. As wife and mother, the goddess is shown as auspicious, adorned with jewelry. She may be shown with her husband and children or surrounded by signs of her fertility. She is identified with Parvati, the wife of Shiva, or with Devi, the great goddess, and receives only "pure" offerings of flowers or vegetarian foods (Moffatt 1979, 281–87; see also Babb 1975b, Wadley 1975, and Beck 1981).

Stein (1984) suggests that the medieval kings of southern India transformed the annual festival of the goddess into a festival that celebrated her marriage to the god-king, who was patron or lineage deity of the king, thereby bringing the village tradition of goddess worship that ensured the prosperity of the land into conjunction with the Sanskritic rituals that legitimated the sovereignty of the king. Responsibility for the fertility and prosperity of the realm and responsibility for maintaining social order (the hierarchy of caste) were conjoined and symbolically vested in the earthly representative of the goddess and god-king, the king of the realm (or the dominant lineage), as patron of their temple. The most famous of these festivals is celebrated on Chittirai in Madurai, where the god-king Sundareshvara (the Beautiful Lord, a form of Shiva) is married to Minakshi(–amman), the goddess with the fish-shaped eyes.

According to the legendary history of the Minakshi Temple, Indra, king of the gods, had murdered a Brahmin (who was actually a demon in disguise). For this sin, Indra wandered about in suffering, until one day he came upon a tank, where he bathed. Finding that his sin had been washed away, he built a temple at the site. Sometime after this, the god Sundareshvara appeared to the Pandyan monarch in a dream and directed him to build his capital city at the site of this temple. The Pandyan king is thus seen to be guided by the god-king, who can redeem sins and reestablish social order when it has been disrupted (in this case by the murder of a Brahmin).

Over the twelve days of the Chittirai festival, the legend relating the birth and career of Minakshi is enacted. This legend tells how once the Pandyan king and queen performed a sacrifice to obtain a son. Out of the sacrificial fire came a three-year-old girl with three breasts. The king was told that this girl should be raised as a prince and trained in the arts of war and that her third breast would disappear when she met her future husband. On the eighth day of the festival, Minakshi is crowned Queen of Madurai, and on the following day her conquest of the world (symbolized as a battle with the lords of the eight directions) is enacted. This is followed by her meeting with Sundareshvara. The goddess and the god engage in a battle, from which Sundareshvara emerges victorious. The marriage of Minakshi is celebrated on the tenth day, and the festival culminates on the twelfth day, with a reenactment of the establishment of the temple and the founding of the city of Madurai and with acknowledgment of the Pandyan monarch as patron of the temple and legitimate ruler of the kingdom. In a great procession, three chariots tour the city of Madurai: one bears the image of the god-king Sundareshvara, a second bears that of Minakshi as consort of the god, and the third bears the image of the unmarried goddess, who is addressed as Shakti (power).

As Hudson (1977) has shown, Tirumala Nayak—the Telegu-speaking ruler who broke away from the Vijayanagar Empire and reestablished independence of the former Pandyan kingdom in Madurai—instituted changes in the festival celebrating the marriage of Minakshi. He moved the festival to the full moon day in the month of Chittirai (April–May), in order to bring into a single framework the festival of the Minakshi Temple and the festival of Alagar (Azhagar or Aragar), an incarnation of Vishnu. The lord Alagar is associated with the Kallars, a tribal group newly integrated into the caste-structured culture of the kingdom of Madurai in the period of Nayak rule.

The festival of Alagar, which begins several days after the beginning of the festival in Madurai, lasts for nine days. It begins with the worship of Karupanaswami, the lineage deity of the Kallars and guardian of Lord Alagar's temple. Alagar is dressed like a Kallar, thus honoring the martial Kallars as guardians of the frontier of the kingdom. Alagar then begins his journey to Madurai to attend the wedding of Minakshi, who is said to be his sister. This kinship tie, which makes Shiva and Vishnu brothers-in-law, joins Shaiva and Vaishnava sects in a relation of equality and mutual respect appropriate to caste equals who intermarry (Hudson 1977, 116). However, tensions between these communities—one primarily urban and high caste, the other rural and low caste—are also evident in the Chittirai festival, for Alagar's procession arrives in Madurai too late to attend the wedding. He is said to be angry that the ceremony was performed without him, and his procession does not enter the city (giving symbolic expression to the resentment of Vaishnava groups in a realm ruled by a Shaiva king?). The devotees of the Lord Alagar gather at the edge of Madurai to fulfill vows that typically involve blood sacrifice and body piercing. In the evening the procession moves to a Muslim village, where the god is said to have a Muslim consort with whom he spends the night. In this way the Muslim minority is also drawn into the relations of reciprocity and respect to which the festival gives symbolic expression.

In the Chittirai festival, political relations are symbolically represented in a religious idiom. The festival encompasses worship of a god-king conducted by Brahmin priests according to rites prescribed in Sanskrit texts; worship of the goddess as Shakti, the primeval energy that animates all life; and the fulfillment of vows by low-caste and untouchable worshippers of Lord Alagar.[5] The major groups that composed the kingdom—rural and urban, high and low caste, Shaiva and Vaishnava—all participate in the Chittirai festival celebrating the sovereignty of the ruler, but as Hudson (1977) concludes, the festival could be said to "symbolize a tension ridden unity," for the metaphorical representation of the relationship of various groups in the kingdom to each other is not without contradiction (see also Banninga 1913).[6]

The Thaipusam festival similarly conjoins the procession of the god-king with ritual vow fulfillment by low status worshippers and brings together groups that otherwise do not share ritual observances. The thematic resonance between Thaipusam and the Chittirai festival in Madurai is evidently not lost on worshippers in Penang, for some claim that the procession of Murugan goes to the Nattukottai Chettiar temple where his marriage is to be celebrated. In Penang, the account of Murugan's marriage is proffered with a twist (as will be seen in chapter 4) that can only be taken as an ironic commentary on the Chettiars of Penang as patrons of the festival of the god-king.

## BHAKTI DEVOTIONALISM

On Thaipusam, Murugan is worshipped not only as god-king and warrior, but also in several forms associated with the tradition of devotional worship known as bhakti. These include Somaskanda, the divine son of Shiva, and Bala Murugan, the child form of the deity; Brahmashasta, the youthful Murugan as teacher of Brahma; Thandapani, the ascetic youth who rejects his high-caste heritage; Subrahmanya, an immanent deity who has the power of the transcendent Brahma and who as personal savior can redeem his followers from sin and worldly cravings; and Murugan, the divine lover who brings possession, ecstasy, and trance to his devotees. In these images the youth of Murugan is emphasized, and he is represented as supplanting the older gods of the Brahmanic pantheon.

### Kumara: Divine Son

On Thaipusam, devotees sing this hymn to Arumugam (Murugan with Six Faces), praising him as the "Beautiful Lord" and invoking him as savior:

> With vel, peacock, and rooster you appear.
> All my bad deeds disappear.
> Please come on your beautiful peacock,
> Lord Kumara, whom I adore, please come.
>
> How could I praise your beauty
> I can only say that you are the son of Iswari.
> You absolve me from my evil deeds.
> Kanda-Kumara protect me.
>
> Lord Arumugam of the six faces, come and grace me.
> Beautiful Murugan of Perambu, come and grace me.
> Come on your beautiful peacock,
> Lord Kumara, whom I adore, please come.[7]

The *Kumarasambhava,* composed by Kalidasa in the fifth century, recounts the birth of Skanda and explains why the god is sometimes portrayed as having six heads and twelve arms: The gods were faring badly in their war with the asuras (or demons). They turned to Brahma for help, and he assured them that a son of Shiva would defeat the asuras. The gods sent Parvati to Shiva, who was meditating in the Himalayas, but Parvati was unable to arouse Shiva from his meditations. Kama, the god of love, tried to help by shooting the ascetic deity with his arrow, but Shiva, angry at being disturbed in his meditation, destroyed Kama with his third eye. So Parvati decided she also would become an ascetic. Finally Shiva agreed to marry her, but no child was born. The gods then sent Agni (fire god) disguised as a dove. The dove carried Shiva's seed until he could bear its heat no longer. The seed dropped into the Ganga, the celestial river, which carried it to Mount Sveta. This mountain turned to gold, and Skanda was born. To satisfy the six Krittika maidens who nursed him, Skanda took six forms. When Parvati embraced the child as her own, the six infants became one child with six heads (Clothey 1969, 240–41). The forms of Murugan that represent the deity with six faces and six arms—Arumugam, the All-Seeing (known as Karttikeya in northern India), and Sanmukha, who rides a peacock—are sometimes said to symbolize the god's multifaceted and syncretistic nature (Clothey 1978, 173–77).

In the *Kumarasambhava,* Skanda defeats the rebellious demons that challenge the rule of the high gods enthroned in the Himalayas of northern India (who symbolically represent the social order of caste associated with Brahmin orthodoxy). The earliest Tamil version of the birth of Murugan, which is found in the *Paripatal* (fifth or sixth century),[8] complicates the narrative by introducing the theme of generational rivalry in which the son appears as a threat to the rule of the high gods. Indra, king of the gods, asks the wives of the seven *rishis* (Hindu sages) to bear the semen of Shiva, but they refuse for fear of losing their chastity. Indra then gives the semen to the Krittika maidens. They deliver six children on a lotus. Indra attempts to slay the children with his weapon, the *vajra* (thunderbolt), but they fuse into one child with six heads and twelve arms. Murugan then fights with Indra, who finally makes peace with the child (Zvelebil 1981, 8).

This conflict may be understood to reflect tension between the Vedic deities of northern India and the indigenous deities of southern India and resistance to their incorporation into a Vedic pantheon.[9] It also introduces the theme of oedipal rivalry between a son and a father figure,[10] and conflict between younger and older gods. This conflict is elaborated in the Tamil *Kanta Purana* (said to have been composed by Pacciyappacivacariyar in the fourteenth century), which includes incidents emphasizing the son's superiority to the Brahmanic deities. For example, the child-god Kumara asks Brahma the meaning of the sacred syllable *om,* but Brahma is unable to explain it to him. Then the young god explains to Brahma the true significance of *om.* As teacher of Brahma, he is given the title *Brahmashasta.* This event is said to have taken place at Swamimalai, one of the six sites sacred to Murugan in Tamilnadu (Clothey 1969, 82). Such narratives identify Murugan as the initiator of a new order, the stream of devotional worship that arose in southern India in the seventh century. In bhakti the devotee has direct access to knowledge of the divine, attained through personal devotion to the god. He has no need for the Brahmin priest as intermediary.

The story of how the youthful Murugan became teacher of the high gods of the Brahmanic pantheon is very popular in Penang because it implies that Brahmin ritual specialists do not even know the meaning of their own mantras.[11] This depreciation of Brahmins was also the theme of several anecdotes related to me, some of which commented disparagingly on the Brahmin claim to purity (see chapter 3).

### Subrahmanya: Personal Savior

The *Tirumurukarruppatai* or "A Guide to the Lord Murugan" from the collection known as *Pattupattu* or "Ten Odes," generally thought to have been composed before the seventh century (Basham 1954, 330),[12] is one of the earliest texts to give expression to the devotee's emotional involvement with a merciful god who offers personal salvation (Zvelebil 1981, 24). In this poem, a pilgrim's guide to the chief shrines of Murugan in Tamilnadu, the meeting between the devotee and his lord is described as a moment of deep emotional intensity:

> When you see his face, praise him with joy,
> worship him with joined palms, bow before him,
> so that his feet touch your head.
> . . .
> Holy and mighty will be his form,
> rising to heaven, but his sterner face
> will be hidden, and he will show you
> the form of a young man, fragrant and beautiful;
> and his words will be loving and gracious—
> "Don't be afraid—I knew you were coming."
> *Tirumurukarruppatai*, 285–90 (in Basham 1954, 330)

The *bhakta* (devotee) poets of the seventh century, who wrote hymns to Shiva and Vishnu, addressed them as deities who appeared to them in visions and were experienced personally in ecstatic communion. Many of these poet devotees were not Brahmins. Among the sixty-three *nayanmars (nayanars)* or poet devotees of Shiva there were also a woman, the untouchable *pariah* Nandan; a Pallava general, Tirunavukkarasu (or Appar); a Vellala (landowning agriculturist) Jain monk who converted to Shaivism; Gnanasambhandar (Nanasambhandar), a Brahmin who converted the Pandyan monarch from Jainism; and Sundaramurti, a poor Brahmin, who became advisor to the Chera ruler.

The egalitarianism of bhakti (devotional worship) presented a radical challenge to Brahmanic orthodoxy. In the theology of bhakti, all worshippers are believed able to approach the deity directly. The emphasis on devotion and emotional involvement with god eliminated the ritual role of Brahmin priests as intermediaries between lower castes and the gods, and Brahmin scholars were confronted with the challenge of reconciling their conception of a deity such as Brahma, who was all-powerful but remote and uninvolved in the concerns of humankind, with the bhakti conception of immanent deities who were intimately involved with their worshippers. For example, *kalpa,* a "day of Brahma," was 4,320 million earthly years long. In the eighth century, the theological foundations of a monistic and ritualistic Hinduism were established on the basis of the philosophy of ritualism (known as Mimamsa, or "Inquiry") developed by Kumarila, and the monistic theology of Vedanta developed by Sankara. During the Chola period (from the eleventh to the fourteenth centuries), the theology of Shaiva Siddhanta—contained in fourteen Shaivite texts in Tamil called the *Siddhanta Shastras*—fused the bhakti theme of devotion to an immanent deity with worship of a transcendent deity.

In the theology of Shaiva Siddhanta, the contradiction between a transcendent and an immanent deity is resolved by dividing reality into three parts: *pati* (god), *pacu* (soul), and *paca* (worldly bonds). Pati is transcendent. Pacu, like pati, is formless and all-pervasive, but it never stands alone; pacu is immanent, a manifestation of the divine in concrete form. Pati and pacu both possess *icca* (emotion), *jnana* (intellect), and *kriya* (will), but pacu also is tainted by paca. With the help of divine energy (shakti), the soul may be liberated from paca and led to pati (following Clothey 1978, 92–94). Shakti, the divine energy of a deity (often identified with his female consort), furnishes the transcendent deity Shiva with form(s)—that is, makes him concrete and immanent.

In Shaiva Siddhanta, Murugan is the immanent lord who stands for Shiva, the transcendent deity, and as his son manifests the energy of Shiva in a concrete form. He destroys the bonds of paca and leads his devotees to pati, enlightenment or the understanding of god. When Murugan is addressed as Subrahmanya (a title that refers to him as "having the quality of Brahma, the transcendent deity") or represented in the form of the *guru murthi* (as a teacher), the theology of Shaiva Siddhanta is evoked. As Subrahmanya, the guru murthi, Murugan is pictured as an ascetic *brahmachari* (one who leads a celibate and austere life as a student of the Vedas), who has conquered passion and attachment to the world. This is the form of the image in the pilgrimage temple in Penang, and, on Thaipusam in Penang, Murugan is most frequently addressed as Subrahmanya.

### Murugan as Divine Lover

The most popular devotional hymns of the Thaipusam celebration are addressed to Murugan as a divine lover:

> Like a child unto the barren womb,
> Like a mine of new-found treasure,
> Like a floor of diamonds,
> So be my songs.

> Like the wilful embrace of love's soft bosom.
> Like a string of the purest gems

Like a garden of fragrant blossoms
Like the River that descends from Heaven
Even so be my songs.

Like the daughter of the Ocean,
Like eyes unto poets,
Like a stream full to the brim easy to drink of,
Like the taste of the nectar of thy beauty,
So be my wondrous songs of love,
By thy grace, O Lord.
Arunakiri (in Clothey 1978, 112).

This theme is brought to its fullest form in the story of Murugan's wooing of the dark-skinned tribal maiden Valli, which appears in the Tamil *Kanta Purana*.[13] Valli is introduced as a daughter of Indra by way of an elaborate history of previous incarnations, a device often used to bring non-Vedic deities into the Sanskritic pantheon. The story continues: Valli was found as a baby in the jungle under a yam vine (*valli*) by a hunter chieftain at a place known as Vallimalai. She was brought up by the hunter and his wife as their daughter. Like all tribal girls, Valli spent many hours watching over the millet fields and chasing away the birds. She also dreamed of her future lover, for she had been told by a fortune-teller that she would be married to Murugan. Hearing of the beauty of Valli, Murugan went to see for himself. He appeared before her as a handsome young hunter and wooed her without success, for she did not recognize him. When the girl's father and brothers returned to the field, Murugan took the form of a *venkai* tree, but the men decided to cut the tree down. Then Murugan took the form of an ascetic and asked the hunter's permission for Valli to remain with him as his handmaiden. Even as an ascetic, however, Murugan could not resist making amorous advances, which Valli again rejected. Then Murugan remembered that he had neglected to ask the aid of his brother, Vinayagar (the elephant-headed god, known as Ganesha in northern India), who must be invoked at the beginning of any enterprise. At Murugan's request, Vinayagar appeared as a wild elephant and frightened Valli, who ran to the old ascetic for protection. Then she yielded and agreed to marry him, at which point Murugan revealed himself to her in the form of a handsome youth (Clothey 1978, 83–84; Shulman 1980, 275–78; Zvelebil 1981, 40–43).

As a vine in the jungle clings to the *venkai* tree (Murugan), Valli (the yam vine) clings to her lord. Similarly, the devotee of Murugan is united with god through *icca shakti* (the power of desire). As in the bhakti tradition that centers on worship of Krishna, in worship of Murugan the raptures of erotic love and sexual union are employed as a metaphor for the ecstasy of the devotee's union with the deity. The relationship of *kalavu*, the spontaneous love without marriage that exists between Valli and Murugan, suggests as a metaphor that love of god, like the emotional abandon of erotic love, is overwhelming. This relationship is more highly valued than the marriage sanctified by ritual that binds Murugan to his high status wife Deviani (Beck 1975, 107–10).

Murugan is also worshipped in the form of a child, as is Krishna. Pictures of the infant Krishna are sold in Penang as pictures of Murugan, the identity of the deities easily suggested by their adornment of peacock feathers. Here the love of the devotee for god is metaphorically compared to a mother's love for her child. Like erotic love, love for a child is spontaneous and natural. There is no need for rules of purity or ritual. In fact, stories of Krishna and Murugan often show outrageous breaches of purity.

## Temptation, Sin, and Redemption Through Love

Arunakirinatar (1370–1450) was a Murugan *bhakta* of the Vijayanagar period,[14] who wrote songs that are still sung by Murugan's devotees today:

> I was ensnared and smitten with love
> of maids whose tresses are fragrant night,
> I was attached to mountain-like breasts
> of women arousing lust,
> fed by desirous lips
> of females skilled in Madana's tricks!
>
> But you have never forgotten
> your friendship,
> you have not left me alone
> enmeshed in desire,
> you have endured my sins
> and you gave your grace
> to live in the shade of your sacred feet
> and grasp your eternal bliss!
>
> O Guha,[15] master of Shiva,
> lover of Valli, your bride!
> You dwell in Tiruverakam
> on Kaviri's northern shores
> with full-grown shady groves,
> sweet child of Umai, Ganesha's brother,
> great hero, destroyer of demoniac pride!
> Arunakiri, *Tiruppukal,* 200 (in Zvelebil 1973b, 241)

The legend of Arunakiri (the short form of Arunakirinatar) teaches that the blessing of Murugan is granted freely to the most unworthy sinner: Arunakiri was born in Tiruvannamalai, where he was known in his youth as a drunkard, brawler, and seducer of women. Only his sister, who prayed to Murugan for him, had any hope for his salvation. Finally, however, Arunakiri himself became disgusted with his life and decided to commit suicide. He climbed to the top of the tower of the Tiruvannamalai Temple and threw himself down. However, an old ascetic appeared at the bottom of the tower and caught the youth in his arms. This ascetic proved to be the god Murugan himself, appearing in answer to the prayers of Arunakiri's sister. Murugan touched the chest of the youth with his vel, casting out the threefold craving for earth, gold, and women. Then he touched his lance to Arunakiri's tongue and said, *"Ni patu!"* (Sing!). But Arunakiri was unable to sing. So Murugan sang the first verse of a hymn, after which Arunakiri was able to continue (Clothey 1978, 87; Zvelebil 1981, 156).[16]

In Arunakiri's hymns, Murugan is described in terms of the theology of Shaiva Siddhanta: He is the immanent lord manifest in the world and at the same time the transcendent deity, a metaphysical abstraction who is formless. He represents both being and nonbeing:

> Murukan, birthless, deathless Lord,
> Who abducted the daughter of the deer,
> You took all other meaning from me
> When You said: 'Be still; think not.'
>
> Not knowing, despite His grace,
> Murukan of the lance is the supreme Guru,
> Is not knowing Being is neither formed nor formless,
> Existent nor non-existent, darkness nor light.
> Arunakiri, *Kantaranuputi,* 12, 13 (in Clothey 1978, 112)

He is the *guru murthi* who teaches the devotee and leads him to enlightenment, bringing salvation:

> Formed and formless, being and non-being,
> Flower and its fragrance, jewel and its luster,
> Embryo and its life, goal of existence and its way,
> Come, You, as the Guru, and bestow Your grace.
> Arunakiri, *Kantaranuputi,* 51 (in Clothey 1978, 111)

The theme of salvation through devotion also appears in other works associated with Murugan, most notably in the Tamil film *Kantan Karunai,* which was extremely popular in Penang in the 1970s. The folk drama *Nondi Natakam* tells the story of a lame man who regained the use of his foot and arm because of his devotion to Murugan (Chettiar 1973, 177). In these popular stories, pilgrimage to a shrine of Murugan is understood to provide both enlightenment *(mukti)* and material reward *(bhukti),* thus resolving the tension between Murugan worshipped as ascetic renouncer and as god-king.

### *Thandapani: The Ascetic Youth of the Palani Temple*

The Thaipusam celebration in Malaysia is modeled on the pilgrimage tradition of the Palani Temple in Tamilnadu. The legendary history of this temple tells how one day the sage Narada brought a golden mango to Shiva and Parvati, who were sitting with their children, Vinayagar and Murugan. The two brothers began to quarrel over the mango. Finally they were told that whoever circled the world first would be given the mango. Immediately Murugan set off on his peacock. But Vinayagar, famed for his cleverness, looked at his vehicle, the rat, and sat down to think. Then he rose, mounted the rat, circled around his parents (or mother, as in many tellings recorded in Penang), and demanded the mango. Astonished, his parents asked him to explain. He replied that his parents (mother) were all the world to him. This answer pleased his parents, and Vinayagar was given the mango. When Murugan returned and saw his brother enjoying the mango, he was enraged. He took off the sacred thread that distinguishes the pure "twice-born" castes of high status from the Shudras and untouchables, thus renouncing his high-caste status. He then went to southern India, where, dressed in a simple loin-cloth, he took up the life of an ascetic. When Shiva went looking for his son, he found Murugan meditating on the top of a hill. When he realized that his son would not return home, Shiva recognized his son as his true representative and said to him, *"Param ni"* (You are the fruit). Because of this utterance the place came to be called Palani.

This story is frequently told in India, and by high-caste groups in Penang, to illustrate the cleverness of Vinayagar (who is worshipped by students hoping to get good grades in school). However, the story is interpreted differently in the tradition of bhakti devotionalism, as revealing the superiority of meditation (Murugan's ascetic practices) over ritual purity (the thread of the twice-born castes) and Brahmanic forms of worship. In Penang, Tamils tell this story when explaining why the priests of the temples of Murugan are not Brahmins.[17] In Penang, lower-class Tamil worshippers who tell the tale portray Murugan as a less favored son who leaves home, descending to earth to live in Tamilnadu, suggesting the appeal of Murugan to the Tamils of Malaysia whose forefathers also left their homes in India because of being less favored (born to poverty) to make a new life in another land.

The anti-Brahmin sentiments associated with bhakti devotionalism are often given expression in the legendary histories *(sthalapurana)* of pilgrimage temples. For example, the legendary history of the Murugan Temple at Tiruvannamalai includes the story of Venrimalaikkavirayar, who was a Brahmin but who could not master any of the Brahmin rituals. He was put to work in the temple kitchen, where he meditated on Murugan as he worked. One day, lost in worshipful thought, he forgot to prepare the food offering for Murugan. The Brahmin priests beat him and expelled him from the temple. Venrimalaikkavirayar went to the edge of the sea, to throw himself into the waves, calling out to Murugan, "Lord, I have failed in your service." But the waves washed him back up onto the beach. Then Murugan appeared before him in the form of Sanmukha with six faces and twelve arms and blessed him, telling him that he was to be the author of the *purana* of the temple of Tiruvannamalai (Shulman 1980, 34–37).

Murugan's special relationship to his low-caste devotees is illustrated by another legend in the *Palani Sthalapurana,* which explains why pilgrims to the Palani Temple carry a kavadi. According to this story, the sage Agastya was given two hills, named for the god Shiva and his consort Shakti, to take to southern India. The asura (demon) Idumban was ordered by the sage to take the hills to Tamilnadu. When the demon stopped to rest and set down the hills, which were suspended from the pole across his shoulder, he found himself confronted by a boy, dressed in a loincloth and holding the staff of an ascetic, who claimed the hills were his. Not recognizing the boy as Murugan, Idumban challenged him to fight. When Idumban was killed in the ensuing battle, the demon's wife and the sage Agastya came to plead for him. Murugan brought the demon back to life and made him guardian of the Palani Temple, consecrating him as the model of the devotee who would come to worship Murugan bearing the shoulder pole, or kavadi, of a coolie (Tampy 1961; Somalay 1975, 13; Clothey 1978, 119).[18]

This legend rests on the association of the demonic asuras and rakshasas of Hindu mythology with low-caste and untouchable groups. This allows the many Hindu legends about rebellious asuras and the warrior deities who defeat them to be interpreted as legitimating the social and political order of caste (see Dumont 1959b). Idumban, like many of these demonic beings, is transformed after his defeat into a devotee of the high god (on the "demon devotee," see Shulman 1980, 317–46). Thus the *Palani Sthalapurana* cuts both ways. On one hand, the temple legend shows Murugan as rejecting the hierarchy of caste (represented by the thread of the pure, twice-born castes) and as patron of untouchables and those from the lower castes who become his devotees. On the other hand, Murugan is represented as subduing the demonic asura associated with the service castes (the coolies, from Tamil *kuli*). The legend thus represents as legitimate the subordination of these groups, who are given their proper task as guardians of the temples and devotees of the god, to whom they bring kavadi offerings. This is a paradox that will reappear in the Thaipusam festival.

The following description of a man "in the grip of Murugan" on a pilgrimage to the temple of Tiruparankunram in Tamilnadu comes from the Reverend C. G. Diehl (author of an important study of Hindu ritual):

> He was carrying a Kavati with an earthen pot attached to it. In the pot was a snake, which he was going to let loose on the Tiruparankunram hill near by, a place famous for its temple to Subramanyan. . . . He was also dragging a small temple car with hooks fastened in the muscles of his back. His skin was pierced with scores of needles, his eyes were protruding and his whole appearance out of the ordinary[,] as was his strength and capacity of enduring pain. In his normal state the man, I was informed, was a worker in the Mathurai cotton mills and a member of the local tradeunion. (1956, 223)

The working-class devotees who fulfill vows to Murugan in the manner of Idumban with the kavadi shoulder pole—and through other symbolic gestures that represent them as beasts of burden (as when they pull a cart with an image of the god by means of ropes, like a bullock, but with hooks embedded in the skin of their backs)—appear to have internalized their abject status. In the theology of bhakti, these ritual acts are interpreted as a symbolic expression of devotion, demonstrating the pain the devotee is willing to undergo to break the bonds of worldly desire and the humble submission with which he receives the god.

### Murugan as a Political Symbol

Temples associated with bhakti were usually located in remote places in the jungle or at the tops of hills, sites far removed from the power structure of caste hierarchy.[19] However, as pilgrimage temples became important sites for popular devotional worship, they developed into centers of trade. Religious schools and facilities for pilgrims were built with funds endowed to the temple. Markets grew up next to the temples, and particularly well-endowed temples sometimes came to manage the agricultural development of villages in the area around them (see Stein 1984, 282–301).[20] Such temples became institutions of political importance, and rulers sought to secure the loyalty of a temple's priests and followers, often by further endowments. Through the intermediation of the king and high-caste patrons, Brahmin priests sometimes gained control of pilgrimage temples and restricted access to those of high caste. In such cases, low-caste and untouchable devotees could worship the deity only on the occasion of the temple festival, when the deity was taken out of the temple in a chariot procession.

During the colonial period, disputes over temple entry erupted.[21] As a result of agitation under the leadership of the Nadars (a caste of low rank that had become wealthy and powerful), the Madras legislature passed the Temple Entry Act in 1939.[22] From this period the association of Murugan with low status and untouchable groups was used in political agitation and organization. For example, Tiruvi Kalyana Sundaranar, who started the first labor union in India in the 1920s and 1930s, was a devotee of Murugan who wrote a tract entitled *Muruku Allatu Aluku* (Murugan, or beauty; see Clothey 1978, 114). Murugan was also invoked by Tamil nationalists. For example, the poet C. Subrahmanya Bharathi (1882–1921), who was active in the anti-Brahmin movement and an agitator against British rule, invoked Murugan as a warrior god who could free Tamilnadu and India from the yoke of foreign powers (Irschick 1969, 285–88). And the poet, mystic, and humanist Ramalingam Swami sought to establish a "universal religion" based on worship of Murugan (Clothey 1978, 114–16).

When the Dravida Munetra Kazhagam (DMK)—the political party that grew out of the anti-Brahmin movement of the early twentieth century—came to power in Tamilnadu in 1967, there was a resurgence in the popularity of Murugan in Tamilnadu. The number of visitors to the six pilgrimage sites sacred to Murugan increased enormously (in part due to improvements in transportation), and all six temples were enlarged and renovated with increased endowments. Under DMK rule, non-Brahmins were appointed executive officers in temples.

Other reforms also were adopted to reduce the influence of Brahmin priests, such as having the *arcanas* (hymns of praise) sung in Tamil rather than in Sanskrit (Clothey 1978, 115–16; Fuller 1984, 129).[23] Speaking at Palani in 1971, the chief minister of the DMK referred to Murugan as the "god of the DMK," drawing on this anti-Brahmin tradition and Murugan as a symbol of Tamil nationalism (Clothey 1978, 116).

In an attempt to win the support of working-class voters and to bolster their claim to represent all Tamils, politicians in Malaysia also appeal to Murugan (see chapter 3). Temple entry disputes have been important in the politics of the Hindu Tamil community of Malaysia as well. And in Penang, conflict over how the Thaipusam festival should be celebrated reflects the strain between the egalitarian sentiments of lower-class Tamils and the hierarchical claims of high-caste Chettiars and upper-class professionals. However, this egalitarian tendency and the potential political significance of the cult of Murugan are attenuated by the emphasis on spirituality and otherworldliness that urges devotees to turn away from the temptations of this world.

## CONTRADICTION AND CONFLICT

In the long history and rich iconography of Murugan as a symbol of divinity, we find deep tensions between different representations of the god—divine lover and celibate ascetic, renouncer and god-king, immanent and transcendent deity. For the most part Hindus gloss over these differences as unimportant distractions. For example, an English language booklet published by the Palani Murugan Temple in Tamilnadu maintains that there is no contradiction between worshipping Murugan as an ascetic who rejects the world and as a king who rules it:

> Muruga[n], in His aspect of Lord Thandayuthabani, stands for RENUNCIA-
> TION. Eschewing all worldly possessions, the only apparel He has chosen to re-
> tain is a brief cloth called *kaupeenam* or loin cloth. But His devotees are not tired
> of offering Him costly garments and enriching His wardrobe with luxurious
> royal clothes[,] which are used to adorn Him when the devotees desire to see the
> Lord in the vesture of a King. So His State is Kingly and thousands at His bid-
> ding are ready to enrich the great Renouncer with gifts of every kind. (Somalay
> 1975, 13)

Likewise, most worshippers in Penang claim that Murugan's many forms are simply a sign of the god's omnipresence.[24]

The nature of divinity is complex and mysterious, and human understanding and representation of the divine are bound to be contradictory and inadequate. Presumably, nothing binds the divine to principles of logical consistency as recognized by humans. All religious traditions encompass a variety of ways of understanding and responding to the nature of the divine, as Geertz (1973) has pointed out:

Traditional religions consist of a multitude of very concretely defined and only loosely ordered sacred entities, an untidy collection of fussy ritual acts and vivid animistic images which are able to involve themselves in an independent, segmental and immediate manner with almost any sort of actual event. Such systems meet the perennial concerns of religion, what Weber called "the problems of meaning"—evil, suffering, frustration, bafflement, and so on—piecemeal. They attack them opportunistically as they arise in each particular instance—each death, each crop failure, each untoward natural or social occurrence—employing one or another weapon chosen, on grounds of symbolic appropriateness, from their cultural arsenal of myth and magic. (172)

Yet, anthropologists do look for pattern and logic when they analyze the sacred symbols of a culture. In an often quoted passage, Geertz also makes this point: "It is a cluster of sacred symbols, woven into some sort of ordered whole, which makes up a religious system. For those who are committed to it, such a religious system seems to mediate genuine knowledge, knowledge of the essential conditions in terms of which life must, of necessity, be lived" (129).

One popular way that Penang's Hindus understand the paradoxes represented by the imagery and history of Murugan is to interpret contradictions in terms of different paths to salvation (also see Beck 1975, 107–10; Clothey 1978, 85, 123; Shulman 1980, 281; Zvelebil 1981, 28, 40–53). My Tamil teacher, among others, urged this solution on me. He explained how these different paths to the divine are reflected in the iconography associated with Murugan, particularly the popular representation of Murugan as guru murthi, in which Murugan is shown standing with his lance in his hand—his high-caste wife, Deviani, the daughter of Indra, on his right and his beloved Valli, the tribal maiden, on his left.

Deviani, the virtuous wife who possesses chastity, stands for the worshipper who seeks god through observing dharma (one's duty as determined by caste), according to my teacher. The relation of the god to such a worshipper is symbolized by Murugan's marriage to Deviani, which was arranged according to caste prescriptions and carried out according to the correct ritual. This is the path of *kriya shakti* (the power of deed), ritual correctly performed by a Brahmin priest. Valli, the dark-skinned tribal maid, stands for the path of bhakti. Valli's relationship to Murugan is not sanctified by ritual. Her love of Murugan represents the power of devoted love or passion *(icca shakti)* and is characterized by abandonment of the self. Murugan's lance stands for the power of knowledge, *jnana shakti* (or the way of enlightenment), which is the path of ascetic renunciation. With his lance Murugan vanquished the demons that symbolize desire and fear, the passions to be overcome by the devotee who seeks enlightenment. My teacher said that he followed the path of knowledge.

However, such a tolerant interpretation of the contradictions represented in the iconography of Murugan does not obliterate real tensions that exist. For example, another worshipper (who presumably followed the path of *kriya shakti*) claimed that Deviani represented "spirituality," whereas Valli stood for "worldly desire." In the remainder of this chapter, I explore the tensions reflected in the contradictions between Murugan worshipped as a god-king associated with the tradition of Brahmin orthodoxy and caste hierarchy and Murugan worshipped as a celibate ascetic or divine lover in the tradition of bhakti devotionalism.

In popular Hinduism, knowledge about how the world is ordered and the place of human beings in that order is not explicated as a doctrine; rather it is a kind of implicit knowledge embodied in ritual practices, such as *puja* (worship) and proscriptions on dining with others, diet, and dress, which shape people's relation to others and their self-understanding. The conceptions connected with these practices, such as purity and pollution, shakti (divine power), dharma (duty, justice), and karma (action, rite, deed, fate),[25] construct conceptions of a good life and of how the social world should be ordered. The contradictory imagery of Murugan and disputes over ritual practice capture an ethical debate among Hindu Tamils.

## The Divine Hierarchy: The Order of Purity and Pollution

Louis Dumont argues in *Homo Hierarchus: The Caste System and Its Implications* (1966) that the social order of caste is based on principles of purity and impurity (pollution). For Dumont, "the caste system is above all a system of ideas and values, a formal, comprehensible, rational system, a system in the intellectual sense of the term" (35). From a Brahminical perspective, pollution is inherent in the human condition because we are beings with bodies that decay and produce polluted substances (Stevenson 1954). Furthermore, pollution is identified with evil. This understanding of the relation of purity to virtue, and pollution to evil, is not unique to Hinduism. Ricoeur (1992) points out that "the most archaic symbolism from which we can start is that of evil conceived as defilement or stain, that is, as a spot which contaminates from the outside" (225).

In Western cultures also, people assert that cleanliness is next to godliness. In many cultures the association of purity with virtue is taught in early childhood, when children learn to distinguish clean from dirty and to feel disgust for their own bodily products, particularly excrement. What the caste system adds to this association is the idea that pollution is contagious. Elaborate rules circumscribe the temporary pollution of birth, death, and menstruation, and those who are polluted by occupation are shunned and avoided. Furthermore, the pollution of those who are born untouchable is not due simply to contagion from their occupation or ritual duties (such as tending the funeral pyre); it is inherent, like the inherent purity of the Brahmin.

Dumont suggests that caste must be seen as a state of mind. The logic of equating purity and pollution with moral qualities (a kind of moral materialism) requires the containment of contamination through social hierarchy. Human beings (and spirits) contaminated by pollution represent a dangerous threat to good and order and must be controlled. Only the pure have virtue sufficient to maintain order in the world and "the execution of impure tasks by some is necessary to the maintenance of purity for others" (Dumont 1966, 55). The hierarchy of caste, according to Dumont, is ethically justified by the concept of dharma, which is usually translated as duty (but may also mean justice) and refers to the reciprocal obligations that those of superior and inferior status owe each other. Ideally, the hierarchy of caste, organized by the distinctive duty of each group, provides security for all. Those of high caste receive respect and privilege but are bound by duty (and the supposedly innate virtue of high-caste people) to provide for those of lower status. And lower castes should consider it equally their sacred duty to wait on the upper castes. Observing one's dharma is virtuous and ensures that the community as a whole will be secure and prosperous.[26] A person who does not fulfill his dharma acts without respect for the hierarchy that protects virtue and without consideration for the caste ties that bind individuals to each other. Such a person is thought to be like the selfish, power-hungry, greedy, malicious, polluted demons who must be defeated by the goddess or a warrior god.

The logic of a hierarchy based on purity and pollution is represented in a divine hierarchy. This hierarchical ordering of the gods, analyzed by Babb (1975b) and Wadley (1975), does not come directly from the statements of Hindus themselves. Rather it is an interpretation, constructed by anthropologists, of statements that worshippers make about the gods and about the rituals appropriate to particular deities. Put another way, the logic that ties purity to power is implicit in the practice of orthodox Hinduism, as observed by anthropologists, but these principles are not enunciated as dogma by the upper castes who benefit from the claims legitimized by these beliefs.

In the divine hierarchy, the most pure and highest form of divinity is unembodied essence, *kadavul* or *iraivan* (the atman). Deity in this form is abstract and cannot be worshipped. Next are the high, pure gods who maintain the world order: Brahma, Shiva, and Vishnu (with their consorts), the Brahmanic deities of the sacred texts. In Tamil Hinduism, these gods are considered to be "invited deities" (*kumpitu*, or *kumpatu devam* or *kuppitu devankal*) because they appear only if invited to be present in an image that has been properly purified and sacralized by Brahmin priests (Pfaffenberger 1982, 115). They are given only vegetarian offerings. Although the purest deities do not intervene directly on behalf of human beings, they ultimately maintain the divine order that keeps the malevolent forces under control at the bottom of the hierarchy.

At the next level of the hierarchy of the gods are Murugan (Skanda) and Ganesh (Vinayagar). These deities are also benevolent and receive only vegetarian offerings. Compared to the highest deities—Shiva and Vishnu—they are more accessible to their worshippers (and do not always require the intermediation of Brahmin priests), but their powers are more limited. As a "self-manifesting" or "self-born" deity *(tantonri devankal)*, Murugan is involved in the world. Like a Kshatriya king, the warrior-god Murugan is contaminated by the pollution of blood. As a pilgrimage deity, his worship is restricted to a fairly well-defined geographical area (associated with a pilgrimage temple). Similarly, Ganesh, who is known as a "Remover of Obstacles" and as a patron of scholars and thieves, has relatively specific powers.

Below the benevolent deities are the unmarried goddesses and the village Amman goddesses, who are unpredictable and bring the afflictions that they also cure. These deities are alternately pure and impure, beneficent and maleficent. In some contexts they receive vegetarian offerings, but in others they require blood sacrifice (Pfaffenberger 1982, 115). As "self-manifesting" deities, they are intimately involved in the lives of their worshippers and often possess their bodies, bringing illness or other disasters to their lives. These deities are worshipped primarily by the landowning castes (in Tamilnadu, generally Shudras) and their dependent service castes, all of whom are engaged in agriculture and are, from a Brahmanical view, subordinate to the Brahmin and Kshatriya castes.

Next come the guardian deities, the conquered demons, who require blood offerings. These polluted deities are malevolent beings, but when they act as guardians of a temple, their power is brought under the control of the god or goddess, and they protect the humans who worship there.[27] They are served by non-Brahmin priests (see Moffatt 1979, 231–34). At the bottom of the hierarchy are the totally malevolent demons who demand blood sacrifice, as well as the spirits of humans who committed suicide, died violently, or died in childbirth. These impure and dangerous spirits attack and possess unwary humans and must be exorcised.

The highest gods are parallel to the Brahmins, who abjure violence and theoretically stand at the top of the social hierarchy because of their purity. Warrior deities (such as Murugan and Durga, the goddess who vanquishes the buffalo-demon Mahishasura) doing battle with rebellious demons that threaten the world with chaos are symbolically equivalent to the Kshatriya warrior caste. A Kshatriya may rule as a king, but he ranks below a Brahmin because he must absorb pollution in fulfilling his duty as a warrior. At the bottom of the hierarchy are untouchables and tribal peoples, who are like the unruly demons that cause suffering and bring evil into the world.[28] They represent a threat to a prosperous and properly ordered, harmonious society and must be controlled by those who are pure and virtuous.[29]

Puja (literally, "worship") has been interpreted by Babb (1975b) as a ritual in which the structure of the social world as an ethical hierarchy based on the contrast between purity and pollution is made apparent and validated (54–57). In puja, a deity is honored through various gestures of respect, each with its own meanings, but the one essential element is a food offering that is subsequently eaten by the worshippers as prasad. Babb observes that normally one who receives food from another is considered subordinate, so in the Hindu view, an asymmetrical exchange in which the deity is the recipient of food would negate the superior status of the god. Therefore the equilibrium of exchange must be reversed by the distribution of prasad to the worshippers. The food offering is thought to be consumed by the deity, and the food that is distributed to worshippers as prasad is, therefore, the *jutha*, or leavings. The jutha, which is contaminated with saliva, is polluting. However, a person may intentionally take on such pollution as an acknowledgment of inferior position and as a demonstration of deference and respect. Edward Harper (1964) has referred to this as "respect pollution." A wife gives food to her husband and then eats from his leaf, thus consuming his jutha and acknowledging her inferiority. Another traditional instance of respect pollution among Hindus is the gesture of touching the feet of a deity or superior.

The principle of "holism" (as Dumont puts it) and the ties of duty or dharma that link the hierarchically ranked castes are symbolically represented when puja is performed in the communal setting of Amman worship in a village. All worshippers, high and low alike, participate in the commensality of taking prasad. Like the Eucharist, puja (in this context) is a communal meal and therefore a ritual expression of group identity: those who eat together share a common flesh. However, hierarchical caste distinctions are expressed in the patterning and order of the distribution of prasad and the exclusion of untouchables from eating at the festival (see chapter 5).

The principles that justify caste discrimination are learned, not as a logical system but from images, narratives, and ritual practices such as the elaborate rules that circumscribe the "temporary pollution" of birth, death, and menstruation, hygienic practices, and rituals of purification. As an ideology, the logic of purity and pollution formulates an ethical system in which moral and physical categories are conflated and ethical judgment is embodied in physical sensations of repugnance and disgust toward those associated with pollution. For this reason, it is difficult for individuals or groups to challenge the hierarchy of caste as ethically unjustified.

## Resistance to Caste Hierarchy and Its Ethical Principles

Many anthropologists have criticized Dumont's description of caste hierarchy as a system based on moral principles for presenting a Brahmin view of society.[30] Berreman (1979) argues, "Any social hierarchy . . . is perpetuated by elites and is struggled against, as circumstances permit, by those they oppress" (155). From his fieldwork he gives examples of untouchable groups that have struggled to free themselves from a traditionally stigmatized occupation, but these examples come from a westernized urban environment and point to political, economic, and social changes that introduce new ideas and enhance the possibility of social mobility.[31] Berreman also describes a man who becomes a religious hermit, a case that shows that for an *individual* to reject his caste identity in a society still ruled by tradition is a kind of social death, involving the loss of social identity and all social relationships (164–76).

In his ethnography of an untouchable community in Tamilnadu, Moffatt

(1979) follows Dumont in showing how the lowest, untouchable castes, who might be expected to reject the social and religious institutions based on caste hierarchy that so disadvantage them, replicate the hierarchical ordering of the higher castes in their own social relations, seeking always to establish distance and distinctiveness relative to castes that may be stigmatized as being still lower because of the pollution inherent in their lifestyle and occupation (also see McGilvray 1983). The efforts that such low status groups make to establish the relative purity of their lineage (through the adoption of Brahmin customs, such as a vegetarian diet, for example) can be interpreted—given an understanding of the relation of purity to virtue in Hindu ritual practice—as not simply an attempt to raise the status of their lineage but as a moral endeavor.

However, Moffatt (1979) also finds in ritual worship of the village goddess a tension between hierarchy and equality:

> In their relations of worship to these goddesses, all worshipers are on the one hand equal: they all express their equal subordination to the goddess by accepting her *prasadam,* and they all receive the goddess's equal protection over the territory they inhabit. Some worshipers are, on the other hand, more equal than others. In ritual practices to these territorial [deities], members of the higher castes take precedence over members of the lower castes, and higher-caste persons play specialized ritual roles of a higher nature than do lower-caste persons. (246–47)

Pfaffenberger's studies of Hindu Tamils of the Jaffna district of Sri Lanka (1977, 1980, 1982) have captured the egalitarian tendencies of the Amman tradition in action. In the Jaffna district, the Vellalars (a Shudra caste) are the major landowners and dominant caste.[32] To strengthen their claim to high-caste status (with the purity and virtue necessary to take responsibility for the fertility of the land), the Vellalars have become builders and maintainers of *agamic* temples in which Brahmanic ritual is practiced. They have also instituted reforms in village goddess temples, which raise the status of the Amman goddess (whom they claim as their caste-deity), ritually treating her as an invited deity. This means that fire-walking has been banned and the goddess no longer receives blood sacrifice. However, when the goddess is worshipped as a pure deity, she does not possess her devotees and intervene on their behalf. Consequently, low-caste devotees no longer fulfill vows at goddess temples controlled by the Vellalars. They have turned to Murugan, who can be worshipped as a "self-manifesting" deity in the pilgrimage temple at Kataragama (Pfaffenberger 1980, 215–16). According to Pfaffenberger, in the Vellalars' view:

> the propensity of the god Murukan to reveal himself to Veddah hunters, women, and Karaiyar fishermen, who are polluted or otherwise low status persons, demonstrates just how antinomian the primordial propensities of the god can be. Murukan, in his wilderness appearance at any rate, cannot serve as the foundations for social order; indeed, he is oblivious to it and destroys it. (1982, 121)

Worshipped as an "invited" deity, Murugan (or the goddess) can be taken as symbolically affirming the order of caste hierarchy. However, worshipped as a "self-manifesting" deity who possesses devotees and redeems the lowliest sinner, Murugan (and to a lesser extent the goddess) represents a more egalitarian vision and a threat to the society of caste hierarchy.

### Ritual Vow Fulfillment to Murugan as a "Chosen God"

The collective ritual patterns for worship of the god-king and the village Amman goddess contrast with worship of a "chosen deity" *(ista devam)* who grants *individual* salvation.[33] As Dumont (1967) has pointed out, the ascetic practices of bhakti devotionalism are modeled on the behavior of the religious hermit, the *sanyasi*, who chooses to live in isolation outside the social order, renouncing the world of relationships and thereby escaping being defined by caste. In bhakti, Dumont writes, "the divine is no longer a multiplicity of gods as in ordinary religion, it is a unique and personal God, the Lord, Ishvara [Shiva], with whom the devotee may identify himself, in whom he may participate" (1966, 282). Reflecting on bhakti poetry, A. K. Ramanujan (1989) writes, "every pigeonhole of caste, ritual, gender, appropriate clothing and custom, stage of life, the whole system of homo hierarchicus ('everything in its place') is the target of its irony" (54). The devotee who identifies with the divine stands in contrast to "homo hierarchicus," the person of caste, the self-in-relation whose identity is ordered by relationships of deference and duty: high caste/low caste, father/son, older brother/younger brother, husband/wife.

In bhakti the concept of purity—the bodily lack of pollution in persons of high caste—is reinterpreted (Dumont 1966, 282–84). Pollution is replaced by an internal state of sinfulness. George Hart (1979b) writes:

> Bhakti is inextricably entangled with the notion of sin that the *bhakta* [devotee] has, for that is the source of his fear before God, his desire to reach Him, and of his desire to attain a sinless state through devotion. So prominent is this consciousness of sin among the Tamil bhakti poets that one can scarcely read more than one or two of their poems without coming across some reference to the debased state of the poet. As Appar says, "My clan is evil, my qualities are evil, my intentions are evil. I am big only in sin." (11)

Sin, in the theology of bhakti devotionalism, is not simply the result of sinful acts; it is a state of mind of sensuous attachment to the world. Only an unqualified love of the god combined with an undistracted focus of thought on the deity—spiritual purity—will bring absolution. The extreme devotion required by bhakti turns the devotee's attention to inner experience. Dumont says that bhakti thus encourages the development of an individual identity, reflected in a personal relation with a deity.

The focus on the inner life of the devotee, according to Dumont, means that the challenge to the ideology of caste hierarchy that bhakti implies is not directed outward against society but, rather, becomes a personal renunciation of the world and worldly pleasures. Bhakti brings the potential ascetic back into the world by internalizing renunciation of the world (1966, 282–83). In his study of the Hindu Tamils of Singapore, Babb (1974) appears to follow Dumont when he suggests that Thaipusam provides the occasion for a symbolic affirmation of both individuality and social interdependence. He describes vow fulfillment—which involves personal goals—as ritual in a "singular mode," which "imparts religious reality to the autonomy of the individual." Indeed, he calls vow fulfillment an act of "ritual self-creation." However, puja performed as a collective act of worship emphasizes a person's membership in a group, and the individual as significant in relationship to others. Babb concludes that among the Hindu Tamils of Singapore the experience of the self is "allowed a delimited zone of operation, but in the end social identities prevail" (1975a, 21).

The emphasis on collective membership in a group and the "inner turn" of bhakti do not, however, necessarily cancel out the political significance of the greater individual and collective autonomy constructed by bhakti theology and ritual practices. In a study of the Hindu Tamils of Fiji, Carolyn Henning Brown (1984) has shown that they became able to assert their political interests more effectively, in part because of their experience of empowerment through ritual vow fulfillment and the experience of collective organization in temple-based communities:

> Partly through symbolic expressions of South Indian power, such as in the fire-walking puja, and partly through the powerful sociopolitical organization of the Sangam, which played a dominant role in the formation of the sugar cane unions and the rise of the first political party in Fiji, South Indians have lost much of the inferiority which gave rise to the Sangam in the first place. Their story, in the community of Indian ethnic groups, has been a success story. (241)

Similarly, in the context of Malaysian politics, the impressive sight of over a thousand working-class devotees pierced by Murugan's lance constitutes an emphatic rejection of the ideology of caste and the claims of high-caste and better-educated Hindus to legitimate power and privilege. The working-class devotees of Murugan, political leaders of the Tamil community, and Malaysians who view the festival are reminded that Murugan's power, manifest in his devotees, derives from egalitarian values that challenge hierarchies of power.

45

3

# THE HINDU TAMILS OF PENANG

## Gurus, Brahmins, and Pujaris

The most famous and dramatic ritual of the year in the tradition of southern Indian Hinduism is the procession of the goddess and/or the god-king. In villages throughout southern India, the Amman goddess is taken on a tour of the territory she protects during her annual festival. The goddess and god-king tour their capital city during the Chittirai festival in Madurai and the great chariot festival in Puri. The sacred geography of these processions, sanctified by tradition, reflects the heritage of caste and the social and political relations that divide the community of worshippers into stratified groups with different interests. In this chapter we shall follow the route of the Thaipusam procession in Penang, which also reveals a legacy of caste and class stratification that divides the community of Hindu Tamils in Malaysia.

### The Nattukottai Chettiars: Patrons of Murugan's Procession

The Thaipusam procession begins at a freshly painted shop-house (138 Penang Street) in the heart of old George Town, near the harbor. Here are stored the silver image of Murugan that is taken in procession *(utsava murthi)* and Murugan's silver-plated chariot *(ratam)*. This building, the image, and the chariot are owned by the Nattukottai Chettiars, who worship Murugan as their lineage deity and who sponsor the Thaipusam procession. The Chettiars were early arrivals in Malaysia. They are said to have settled in Malacca before the coming of the Portuguese in 1511 (Hatley 1969, 459). The subgroup of Chettiars known as Nattukottai Chettiars are a money-lending caste originating from the Ramnad district of Tamilnadu, south of the city of Madras (Thurston 1909, 5:249–71). In the nineteenth century they became wealthy, lending large sums to Malay nobility and peasantry. Through default of loans, they became owners of valuable urban properties in Penang (Arasaratnam 1979, 36).

The Nattukottai Chettiars like to tell a story about Murugan's chariot, which was brought from India on special order in 1890. They say that two chariots had been ordered, one by the Chettiars of Penang and the other by the Chettiars of Singapore (or Kuala Lumpur, according to some). Quite naturally, the larger and more prosperous Chettiar community of Singapore ordered a larger and more lavish chariot. However, when the chariots were shipped to colonial Malaya, someone made a mistake, and the more expensive chariot was sent to Penang. The Penang Chettiars claimed the error revealed the will of Murugan and the special favor he felt for them, and they refused to exchange chariots. Told by a Nattukottai Chettiar, this story evokes the special tie of the Penang Chettiars with Murugan. Others in Penang tell the tale in a way that emphasizes the cleverness of Chettiar moneylenders and their readiness to take advantage of any situation. According to a newspaper report in 1980, the value of the chariot and the bejeweled image of Murugan amounted to between five and eight million Malaysian ringgits, or (at the then prevailing exchange rate) between two and a half and four million U.S. dollars. On Thaipusam, this figure is frequently cited as an indication of the enormous wealth of the Nattukottai Chettiars of Penang.

In the early hours of the morning, the procession of Murugan wends its way through the neighborhood of small shops where Indian merchants live and sell their wares—spices, grains, bright-colored saris, brass and steel cooking vessels, religious books and articles for worship imported from India. Penang's Malaysian Indian community (35,690 in 1970) includes merchants from all over India. There are Gujaratis, Sindhis, Marathis, Punjabi Hindus, and Sikhs (5% of Malaysian Indians), along with Malayalees from Kerala (5.7%) and Tamils. Approximately 70 percent of Malaysian Indians are Hindu, but there are also Indian Muslims (Nagata 1979, 34). The Thaipusam procession will pass along Chulia Street (named for Tamil Muslims, known as Chulias, who settled in Penang in the first half of the eighteenth century). The procession also passes by Prangin Road Ghaut, which bears an Anglo-Indian name for the flight of stairs that leads to a riverside landing where Indian merchants unloaded their goods. This was also the place that Indian *dhobis* (launderers) washed clothes.

About mid-morning, the procession of the Lord Murugan arrives at Dato Keramat Road, a main thoroughfare that leads to the edge of the city. This street is lined with industrial concerns such as the Eastern Smelting Company and the shops of Chinese merchants. Murugan's chariot halts here, in front of the Shiva Temple built by the Nattukottai Chettiars, who are devout Shaiva Hindus. This temple and the Nattukottai Chettiar Murugan Temple are the two largest Hindu temples in Penang. The Shiva Temple is the only temple where Brahmin priests preside, performing orthodox (agamic) rituals. Five Brahmin families live here. They are a kind of service caste for the Nattukottai Chettiars, sign of the Chettiars' status as high-caste Hindus who are patrons of the temple of a Brahmanic deity worshipped according to orthodox rituals prescribed in the texts.[1] Other Tamils (especially upwardly mobile, white-collar workers) who do not approve of the ritual practices in temples belonging to low-caste communities also come to worship in the Shiva Temple. But they sometimes complain that they are treated in a demeaning manner by the Brahmin priests. For example, one worshipper complained that the priest drops the sacred ash vibhuti into the worshippers' hands instead of placing it on the forehead, as if he were trying to avoid the pollution of bodily contact. (Non-Brahmin pujaris place the ash on the forehead of an adult. Both Brahmin priests and non-Brahmin pujaris will place ash on the forehead of a child.)

Just behind the Shiva Temple are spacious old homes that housed the Nattukottai Chettiars of Penang before they moved on to more fashionable suburbs. The procession waits here for an hour or so, while the priests and the members of the Nattukottai Chettiar Murugan Temple committee who have accompanied Murugan's chariot rest from the morning's labors.

### Kampong Java Baru: Murugan's Lowliest Devotees

After leaving the Shiva Temple, Murugan's chariot stops in front of the Meenachiamman Temple, which is located a short distance away. This is the temple of an Amman goddess who is worshipped as the lineage deity of a goldsmith caste of relatively high status. Farther along Dato Keramat Road, the procession passes by Kampong Java Baru. In this neighborhood live Tamil laborers from the docks and quarries, along with former untouchables, who are now employed as garbage collectors by the Sanitation Department of George Town. The temple for this community is the Sri Raja Mariamman Temple. This temple was founded by the reformer Swami Ramadasar, a Malaysian Tamil who worked to eradicate caste and to educate and uplift the poorest Tamils. Swami Ramadasar had traveled to India, where he was influenced by anti-caste movements of the Tamil Renaissance. In 1937 he returned to colonial Malaya and settled in Kampong Java Baru, where he fought against practices that distinguished between castes, such as restrictions on who could draw water from a particular tap. He urged people to give their children "good" names—that is, names that were not identified with caste. He also established a school for the children of Kampong Java and organized a campaign against the drinking of cheap toddy (sold in shops licensed by the government). Under his leadership, the Tamils of Kampong Java Baru built the Sri Raja Mariamman Temple, which was consecrated in 1938. The design of this temple is unusual; unlike most village temples it has no entry gate or walled courtyard. Rather, the temple consists of a spacious hall open to all, and the image of the goddess is not secluded in a chamber that only her priests are allowed to enter. Thus, the architecture of the temple expresses the idea that the goddess is available to all her worshippers and does not distinguish among them on the basis of caste.

The Sri Raja Mariamman Temple illustrates how a community-based temple can become an important institution of collective self-rule and a locus of political conflict. When the colonial government wanted to incorporate the River Road Tamil School into the national educational system after World War II, a faction of the Kampong Java community objected to the loss of control over their school. This faction was associated with the trade unions, which the government viewed as communist organizations. This conflict was resolved when Swami Ramadasar finally opted for placing the school under the authority of the Malaysian government.[2] In 1960 the Sri Raja Mariamman Temple was renovated with funds from a rural development program. Further construction in 1977 was funded by the Malaysian Indian Congress (MIC), which sought to win the electoral support of working-class voters (see chapter 5).

Many of those who will fulfill their vows to Murugan begin their pilgrimage from the Sri Raja Mariamman Temple on Thaipusam Day. However, the procession of Murugan sponsored by the Chettiars does not enter Kampong Java Baru or visit its temple.[3]

### The Sri Muthu Mariamman Temple

Past the road to Kampong Java Baru at the junction of Dato Keramat Road and Lorong Kulit, the chariot of Murugan stops again. This lane leads to the square where the municipal bus company parks its buses when they are not in service. Here, crammed into a corner of the square, stands the Sri Muthu Mariamman Temple, said to be the oldest Hindu temple in Penang. On Thaipusam Day, over six hundred devotees who are fulfilling vows to Murugan will come to this temple to pay obeisance to the goddess.

According to the secretary of the temple committee, the Sri Muthu Mariamman Temple was built by convicts and indentured laborers who were brought to Penang Island to construct the first colonial settlement. The first worshippers at the temple were manual laborers who came from the untouchable castes of Pallans (agricultural laborers), Dhobis (launderers), and Chakklians (leather workers). However, in the 1920s, control of the temple was wrested from these groups, and the *Dhobis* built a new temple for the goddess in a nearby coconut grove where they lived.[4]

Today most of those who worship at the Sri Muthu Mariamman Temple are upwardly mobile, white-collar clerical workers and professionals. Many are the descendants of immigrants from Sri Lanka, who are known in Malaysia as Jaffna Tamils. The president of the committee of management for the temple, a Jaffna Tamil, began worshipping there in 1924. In 1936 he was elected a member of the temple committee. He reports that in the 1960s when temple renovations were being planned, conflict broke out in the community that worshipped at the temple. Some people objected to the special honors and privileges that were to be accorded to wealthy donors (Jaffna Tamils), who were paying for the renovation of the temple. There was also a division among worshippers over who was to be employed as priest for the temple. The Jaffna Tamils wanted a Brahmin priest, who would be able to perform the rituals in an orthodox manner. They were opposed by others (mostly descendants of immigrants from Tamilnadu) with strong anti-Brahmin sentiments, who preferred a pujari and rituals conducted in Tamil rather than Sanskrit. Eventually a compromise was reached: the new priest is a non-Brahmin pujari who has studied and traveled on pilgrimages in India. The reforms that he has instituted—invoking the goddess with Sanskrit mantras and conducting the prayers at the intervals specified in texts—make the ritual observances more orthodox. This pujari insists that the new form of ritual observances does not discriminate among worshippers on the basis of caste. He maintains that "casteism" is long gone in Malaysia, but to prove his point he notes which members of the temple management committee are of low-caste background.

There are many tales that attest to the power of Mariamman, who is worshipped at the Sri Muthu Mariamman Temple in Lorong Kulit. It is said that the colonial government wanted to tear down the temple in 1940 so that municipal buildings could be built on the site. A holy man named Muniandi was possessed by the goddess and cursed the white man who was responsible for the order to tear down the temple. Before anything further could be done, the Japanese invasion drove the British out of Malaysia. When the municipal authority again claimed the site of the temple in the 1970s, the temple committee applied for title to the land. This dispute continues to simmer unresolved, but worshippers point out that the municipal building next to the temple is subsiding into the ground, indicating the sakti (power) of Mariamman.

### The New Suburbs of George Town: The English-Educated Elite

Late in the afternoon, the procession of Murugan passes by the General Hospital and the colonial-era Sports Club, where Tamil waiters still serve drinks to a Malaysian elite. At the edge of George Town is a suburban development that houses the professional upper class of Penang. Formerly, in front of the houses of prominent members of the Hindu Tamil community who lived on the road that the procession passed down, pavilions (thaneer pandal) were set up for those who attended the festival. The power for the lights that decorated the pavilions and the loudspeakers that broadcast devotional music, along with water and other necessities, came from the homes of prosperous professionals from the Tamil community. Due to the complaints of their non-Indian neighbors, the Thaipusam procession now passes relatively quietly and quickly through this neighborhood along Western Road.

During the period of colonial rule, many English-educated Tamils gave up the traditional practices of Hinduism—such as temple worship and observance of restrictions associated with the pollution of birth and death and inter-caste dining. However, very few converted to Christianity.[5] Over the course of the twentieth century, the Tamil cultural renaissance in India and the rise of Indian nationalism (encouraged by the Japanese during World War II) contributed to a revival of interest in a reformed and modernized Hinduism. This reformed Hinduism drew on the tradition of bhakti devotionalism and worship of a personal or chosen deity *(ishta deva)*. The egalitarian (anti-caste) implications of bhakti tradition appealed to these English-educated Hindus, who were acutely sensitive to British criticism of the institution of caste. In Penang, some claim that caste is not a genuine part of Hinduism but a corrupt practice introduced in ancient times.

The Tamil professionals of Penang generally do not go to a temple to worship. Rather they meet in their homes for weekly prayer meetings and meditation sessions with a guru. The teachings are delivered in English, although Tamil and Sanskrit may be used for chants and hymns. One such study group in Penang is called the Shiva Family. It is associated with a reform movement known as the Temple of Fine Arts, which is led by Swami Santhananda.[6] The Divine Life Society, founded by Swami Shivananda Saraswati, a medical doctor in colonial Malaya who went to India during the anti-Brahmin campaigns of the early twentieth century, has been another important vehicle for the reform of Hinduism through education.

After the departure of the British from Malaya in 1957, Tamils who had worked for the colonial civil service or as professionals, found themselves members of an ethnic and religious minority in an Islamic nation (Arasaratnam 1979, 213–17).[7] Muslim Indians could identify with the Malay majority, but Hindu Tamils tended to be identified with working-class Tamils and their religious observances. Many were embarrassed by the image of popular Hinduism, particularly ritual practices they felt to be primitive, such as animal sacrifice and rituals of vow fulfillment that involved piercing the body. This led them to renew their efforts to reform Hindu practices through education. On occasions such as the Thaipusam festival, the reformers set up booths to distribute the literature of the Divine Life Society and other groups. They also write and distribute tracts, in English and in Tamil, that explain Hindu practices to others, namely, tourists and the less well-educated devotees of Murugan.

The reformers object to what they consider the carnivalesque aspects of Thaipusam—film music played on loudspeakers in the thaneer pandal, flamboyantly decorated kavadis, and trance dancing. They urge devotees to carry "simple *kavadis*" and teach that ritual practices involve an inner spirituality (Karthigesu n.d., 7). In an essay entitled "The Image of God," Prof. R. Karthigesu writes:

> When we go to temple it is not enough that we see the image of God that has
> been adorned beautifully. The good devotee, while worshipping the image,
> closes his eyes[.] We wonder why he does that, instead of filling his eyes with
> this splendorous image? It is not enough that you see God with your external
> eyes. Close your eyes to see him inwardly, within your mind. (1980)

In the souvenir program for Thaipusam published by the Tamil Youth Bell Club
(1985) is an essay by Professor K. Loganathan of Universiti Sains Malaysia entitled "Why Thaipusam?" Professor Loganathan describes vow fulfillment as a
form of penance. (He does not refer to the popular understanding that Murugan
has answered the prayers of his devotees and they are now fulfilling their part of
the bargain.)

> The organized and elaborate manner in which this penance is offered may sur-
> prise the ignorant but it should be remembered that all over the world and in all
> religions the idea of penance and sacrifice has a central place though it takes a
> variety of different forms. Fasting, abstinence from sexual gratifications, giving
> away wealth and such other things that are dear to oneself, forgetting one's own
> problems and helping others, controlling the inner passions through meditations
> and so forth are all aspects of penance. It is torturing the animating psyche
> through the *denial* of its clamourings, which sometimes takes grotesque forms.
> (Longanathan 1980)

According to Professor Loganathan, the goal of vow fulfillment is enlightenment,
following the theology of Shaiva Siddhanta:

> According to Shaiva Siddhanta, a scientific theory of human behaviour that also
> accommodates the religious dimensions of human behaviour, the self is birthless
> and deathless—it is *anati*. Initially it is engulfed in complete "Darkness"—a
> state of existence where there is no consciousness whatsoever. . . . With this
> rudiment of consciousness, the psyches struggle to liberate themselves uncon-
> sciously at the lower levels, consciously at higher levels from this Darkness that
> surrounds them in and out. This struggle is the *meaning* of life, the primary sig-
> nificance of life. The end of this struggle is a state of existence without any
> Darkness whatsoever within the soul—a fully *illuminated* existence, an exis-
> tence fully in the divine presence of Shiva-Sakti, the creative Power full of love
> and grace.

The reformers emphasize the scientific validity of Hindu teachings and practices.
One anonymous essay (in Tamil and English), entitled "Why I Am a Hindu" and
distributed by the Penang Hindu Youth Organization, explains:

> The doctrine of Karma is a perfectly scientific law. The law of evolution, the
> theory of heredity and demonstrated proofs of being able to recollect his or her
> past life amply support that there is a certain element of pre-determination in
> one's present life on the physical and mental planes. . . .

> Logic and faith complement each other in Hinduism. Reasoning and scientific appraisals help to avoid errors and pitfalls, and faith resulting from an investigative and rational approach remains indelible and permanent. The combination of reason and faith corresponds to the philosophy and religion of Hinduism. (Ganesh Printing Works Sendiri Berhad, Penang)

Yet, even the reformers tell stories of miracles associated with devotion to Murugan and the fulfillment of vows. For example, a devotee who participated in the celebration of Thaipusam in Kuala Lumpur told researchers:

> Ten years ago, I became very antagonistic to the practice of Thaipusam. I felt it was primitive and agitated against it. With others I tried to have it banned. This lasted over a period of years. Then about five years ago, my mother developed cancer of the esophagus. It was removed and a gastric fistula constructed. She responded badly to the operation and suffered a cardiac arrest. The doctors said she would die. I was afraid and promised to carry *kavadi* if only she stayed alive until my brother had time to return from India to see her. She did survive about six weeks until he returned. Two days afterwards she died. (Simons, Ervin, and Prince 1988, 259)

The reform movement has played an important role in reshaping the Thaipusam festival. The Arulmigu Bala Thandayuthabani Temple of Murugan on Penang Hill and the Sri Arul Maha Mariamman Temple in George Town are managed by committees appointed by the Hindu Endowments Board of the Malaysian government, which has responsibility to oversee the finances and management of temples not owned by a caste lineage.[8] Reformers have been appointed to these committees where they have instituted new rules, supervised temple renovations, and urged reform. Funds raised from fees and donations collected during the Thaipusam festival have been used for construction at both the Penang Hill Murugan Temple and the Sri Arul Maha Mariamman Temple. At the Penang Hill Temple the improvements, which include a pond where the birth of Murugan is depicted, were consecrated in January 1985. Six plaster infants, each supported by a lotus blossom, float on the pond. This image evokes the devotees' love of the infant god, rather than emphasizing the power of Murugan manifest in ritual vow fulfillment and the ecstatic trance of divine blessing, arul.

### The Shrine of Muniswara (Munishwara)

The Sri Muniswara Kuil (this is the spelling painted on the lintel over the images) sits under a large, old pipal tree at the intersection of Western Road, Gottlieb Road, and Waterfall Road. Penang Hill rises on one side of Waterfall Road, and the walled compound of the Nattukottai Chettiar Murugan Temple stands on the other. This is where the city ends and countryside begins.

According to a plaque found during recent renovations, the shrine of

Muniswara (consecrated in 1857) was built by Tamil laborers, who worked in a nearby quarry when the area was still considered a wild and dangerous place at the edge of the settled order of village life. As such, it was an appropriate place to worship a deity such as Muniandi, one of the semi-demonic warrior deities that guard a Tamil village. Over the last decade, the shrine has been renovated by Muniandi's worshippers, who have built a roof over the images and covered the floor in tile. They now address their deity as Muniswara (Munishwara), a title that identifies him with Shiva *(Ishwara)* and suggests he is a form of the highest deity, rather than a village deity subservient to the Amman goddess or a low-caste lineage deity. However, the iconography of Muniswara's image remains a reminder of his origins as a semi-demonic deity of low-caste folk. Muniswara is portrayed as a squat, fierce deity with bulging eyes. He is dressed as a warrior with bristling mustache and turban, and he carries a sword and a club. In his right hand is Shiva's trident (an association to the high god); his left hand rests on the head of an erect cobra that is coiled around a pot (imagery that associates him with the village goddess).

The pujari of this shrine is Arumugam, a vigorous and charismatic man of fifty known for his spiritual power and his ability to treat demonic possession. He is employed as a gardener in the Penang Botanical Gardens at the end of Waterfall Road and lives in the small Tamil settlement just behind Muniswara's shrine. Many young men come regularly to the services conducted by Arumugam at 7:30 P.M. on Tuesday and Friday evenings. They perform service *(thavam)* to Muniswara by cleaning the shrine and preparing offerings. After the ritual worship of Muniswara, Arumugam attends to those who come to the shrine for an exorcism (see chapter 6). At the end of the evening, he calls the young men, one by one, to receive the blessing of Muniswara, who has possessed Arumugam. Some of them fall into trance as the pujari places the sacred ash on their forehead. Most of these youths have recently finished their schooling and are now looking for jobs. They hope that Muniswara will help them.

### The Nattukottai Chettiar Murugan Temple

Between the shrine of Muniswara and the Nattukottai Chettiar Murugan Temple, Waterfall Road takes on the appearance of a fairground. During the Thaipusam festival, it is lined with stalls displaying bangles, brightly polished brass and chromed cookware, religious pictures, Indian sweets, audio cassettes of devotional and popular music, peacock feathers, and much else. People gather here to await the arrival of Murugan's chariot. The Nattukottai Chettiar Murugan Temple, where the Chettiars worship Murugan as their lineage deity, is also full of people on this night, although the temple is rarely visited by other Hindu Tamils except on Thaipusam. Most of those who crowd into the temple even on this night come from Penang's Chinese community. They share with the Tamils a belief in the existence of a great variety of powerful spirits and expect that

Hindu deities will respond to their prayers as do the Chinese deities. The Tamil concept of *kulam*—the endogamous clan group that forms a subcaste or lineage, such as the Nattukottai Chettiars—is familiar to Penang Chinese, who have clan *(kongsi)* temples. The presence of Chinese worshippers is also a demonstration of the special ties that have grown up between the Chettiars and the Chinese merchants of Penang.

### The Sri Arulmigu Maha Mariamman Temple

On the third night of the Thaipusam festival, Murugan returns to the center of George Town by a different route. The procession goes down Gottlieb Road to the beach, which is lined by the mansions of very rich, mainly Chinese, residents of Penang. Passing by the fields of the Sports Club, where the colonial elite played polo, and by the great Banyan tree planted to celebrate Queen Victoria's Jubilee, the procession turns into Burma Road, which is lined with Chinese department stores. It is past midnight when the procession arrives in the area of old George Town near the harbor. Here Murugan's chariot wends its way through the cramped and narrow streets of the old business district in order to pass by shrines built for lineage deities of Tamil laborers and dockworkers.

Murugan's chariot arrives at the Sri Arulmigu Maha Mariamman Temple[9] on Queen Street just before dawn. In 1933 this was the first Hindu temple in Malaysia to open its doors to all, regardless of caste. This reform was initiated by the Tamil employees of the municipality of George Town and by the dockworkers of Penang, who were the most militant and best-organized group of Tamil laborers.[10] Together they had organized to protest the exclusion of untouchable worshippers from the temple. The campaign was also supported by the English-educated reformers. An elaborate rededication (Kumba Abhisheka) marking the centenary of the temple announced the opening of the temple to all. According to the secretary of the temple management committee, this was the origin of the celebration of Chitraparvam (Chitraparvanam, or Chitrapaurnami) in Penang. On the full moon day of the month of Chittirai, a procession of Murugan, worshipped in the form of Subrahmanya (Subramaniam), goes from the Sri Maha Mariamman Temple on Queen Street to the Arulmigu Bala Thandayuthabani Temple on Penang Hill, and devotees fulfill vows to Murugan.[11]

During the 1970s, a movement to promote the celebration of Chitraparvam as an alternative to vow fulfillment on Thaipusam was organized by the Hindu Mahajana Sangam and the Mukkulathar Sangam. The Hindu Mahajana Sangam (which has ties to the politically conservative Jan Sangh party of India) is supported by dockworkers from the Penang waterfront. The Mukkulathar Sangam is an association formed by three low-caste lineages that had been excluded from the Dravidian Association, composed of middle-level castes. The members of these organizations particularly objected to the prominent role of the Nattukottai

Chettiars in the Thaipusam festival, because in their eyes the Chettiars stood for orthodox Hinduism and caste hierarchy.

In 1980 only 350 worshippers were present for the celebration of Chitra-parvam, and twenty-plus devotees fulfilled vows by carrying a kavadi. Ironically, the efforts of the Hindu Mahajana Sangam and the Mukkulathar Sangam to pro-mote the celebration of Chitraparvam as an occasion for vow fulfillment have foundered in part because, although these organizations are explicitly opposed to caste, they are associations of low-caste peoples. In Penang, as in southern India, "Temple festivals attract little public interest when they exclude locally recog-nized big-men from receiving and bestowing honors" (Mines and Gourishankar 1990, 772).[12] Educated Tamils in Penang oppose the festival on the grounds that it divides the community. They argue that the prestige of the Malaysian Indian community is enhanced most by a single grand festival.

## CASTE AND CLASS

The route of Murugan's procession reflects both the common heritage that binds Malaysian Hindu Tamils together and the differences that divide them. Al-though almost all Hindu Tamils of Penang and the surrounding areas participate in the Thaipusam festival (indeed, it is the only festival that brings together Hin-dus from different classes), some object to the festival and refuse to participate, like those who fulfill their vows on Chitraparvam. Others dismissively refer to the first day of the festival as "Chetty Pusam," suggesting their hostility to the Chettiars' role in the festival.

As Arasaratnam (1979) has pointed out, the religious orthodoxy of the Chet-tiars (who practice caste endogamy, strict intra-caste dining, vegetarian diet, and prohibition of widow remarriage) has isolated them from the larger community of Hindu Tamils who generally oppose caste (92–96). As sponsors of Murugan's procession, the Nattukottai Chettiars take the role of a dominant caste (or king of a medieval kingdom), by implication claiming not only high-caste status and the respect due to a ruling lineage but also the right to confer honors on others of lower status. However, despite their considerable economic resources, the Nat-tukottai Chettiars have not been able to establish themselves in the role of a "dominant caste" because other Tamils are not economically dependent on them.[13] A major impediment was the Malay Reservation Act of 1933, which pro-vided that Malay lands were not to be transferred, charged, leased, or otherwise disposed of to any non-Malay.[14] The act was directed at the Chettiars, and they protested it, arguing that existing loans should be safeguarded. But no organized group of Indians in Malaysia supported the Chettiars in their protest. In 1935 the Money-lenders Ordinance, also directed against the Chettiars, gave courts the power to review loans that were challenged as harsh and unconscionable. Again the Chettiars were not supported by any segment of the Malaysian Indian com-munity when they objected. More recently, in 1970, resentment of the Nattukottai Chettiars and suspicion that they might be profiting from their role as patrons of Murugan's procession on Thaipusam led to the formation of the Action Committee of the Hindu Worshippers of Penang, which charged the committee that managed the Murugan Temple on Waterfall Road with malpractice and misappropriation of funds.[15] The charges were investigated by the Hindu Endowment Board, which concluded that there had been no graft (*Straits Echo* and *Times of Malaya,* February 2, 1970).

Over twenty years ago R. K. Jain (1970) concluded his study of the Tamil plantation labor force in Malaysia with a comment on the class divisions that prevented Tamils in Malaysia from acting effectively in pursuit of shared interests:

> The central fact . . . is that there were few unifying forces that might have welded the Indian ethnic category into a structural block. Alliances were formed on the basis of narrower criteria than that of race. There is also evidence that the upper class of Indian merchants and traders had ties with Malays and Chinese that cut across ethnic boundaries. . . . Tamil laborers on estates were thus effectively cut off from other sections of the Indian ethnic category. (428)

Today the 1.4 million Malaysians of Indian descent (8% of the population of Malaysia in 1990) are still deeply divided by class and ethnic differences and the vestiges of caste prejudice.[16] About 85 percent of Malaysian Indians are originally from the state of Tamilnadu in southeastern India, and most of these (80%) are Shaiva Hindus (Arasaratnam 1979, 162). However, even this relatively homogeneous group can scarcely claim to be a community. One can distinguish three broad classes: a small English-educated class of professionals; a merchant middle class, including the Chettiars (roughly 15%); and working-class laborers (80%). To some extent this mirrors the traditional hierarchical social structure of Tamilnadu (Maloney 1975, 169), which consists of a tripartite division among Brahmins (3%); non-Brahmins, primarily Shudras (approximately 60%); and untouchables and tribal groups known as Adi-Dravidian peoples (35%).[17]

Tamil laborers are the descendants of immigrants from Tamilnadu, most of whom came to the colony after 1884 when legislation in the Federated Malay States provided for the import of Indian laborers needed to work as tappers on rubber plantations. They settled in the west Malaysian states of Penang, Selangor, Perak, and Negri Sembilan (see Hatley 1969; Jain 1970, xv; Wiebe and Mariappen 1978, 6–7; Arasaratnam 1979, 10–48, 196–97). Generally these laborers came from *kuliyal* (unemployed landless laborers) and *adimai* (dependent agricultural laborers) groups. There are no reliable statistics on what proportion were from untouchable, as opposed to "clean caste," groups. Estimates range from more than one-third (a figure derived from a 1931 census) to 60 or 70 percent from Adi-Dravidian (untouchable) groups (Arasaratnam 1979, 26). These plantation laborers and their descendants are entirely dependent on wage labor, because (unlike poor Malay families) they do not own any land.

For the descendants of those who came to colonial Malaya to work on plantations and in quarries and construction, on the docks, and as household servants, there has been little upward mobility. In 1984 over 70 percent of Malaysian Indian households still made their living as laborers on rubber, oil palm, and tea plantations. Furthermore, according to government statistics, the incidence of poverty on estates had increased from 35 percent in 1980 to more than 50 percent by the end of 1983 (*FEER,* July 26, 1984). In 1987, 50 percent of estate housing had no electricity or piped water. Estate schools were poorly staffed and recorded high dropout rates.[18] And fifteen thousand Tamil estate households nationwide were classified as living below the poverty line (*FEER,* February 15, 1990). In 1990 a strike declared by the National Union of Plantation Workers (NUPW) sought to establish a minimum monthly wage of 190 Malay dollars for plantation workers (for twenty-four workdays per month). The official poverty level for a family of five is 350 Malay dollars per month. The Industrial Court supported Union demands, but the strike was declared illegal. (It was said to pose a threat to the nation's economy.)[19]

In the decades between 1970 and 1990, Tamil estate workers began to leave the plantations to obtain employment in pioneer industries, which were being developed as part of the New Economic Policy. A 1980 survey of the Rubber Research Institute reported that 70 percent of youths growing up on estates wanted to migrate to towns. The reasons given were higher wages and better job security, as well as the opportunity to live outside the estate (Aznam 1990, 19). The young men expected to find jobs building roads and driving trucks; the young women expected to work as domestics. However, it appears that jobs in pioneer industries have not provided significantly higher wages for Tamil laborers, who are often poorly educated, nor have such jobs meant greater economic security. Between 1970 and 1975, unemployment among Malaysian Indians rose from 11 to 12.2 percent, while unemployment among *bumiputra* (ethnic Malays) declined from 8.1 to 7.2 percent during the same period, making Indians the worst off among the three ethnic groups (Malay, Chinese, and Indian). In the first decade of the New Economic Policy (1970–1980), the absolute and relative share of national wealth controlled by Malaysian Indians fell (*FEER,* July 26, 1984). In the 1980s a reverse migration back to the estates was observed.

The merchants, traders, and moneylenders who compose a small middle class number from 15 to 20 percent of Malaysian Indians. Given the overall poverty of Malaysian Tamils, they are relatively prosperous. However, they control an insignificant proportion of the economy, owning only 1 percent of Malaysia's capital.

At the top of the pyramid in Malaysia is a class of professionals—descendants of Tamil and Malayalee immigrants (some with degrees from Indian universities) and Jaffna Tamils from Ceylon, who came to work in the British civil service or as clerks on colonial estates (Jain 1970, 211). Despite their different backgrounds, these English-educated white-collar Indians were unified as a class by their identification with British culture and interests. After Malaysian Independence, these clerks and civil servants became doctors, lawyers, and teachers, and today they are an important component of the professional classes of Malaysia, constituting almost 30 percent of the lawyers and 36 percent of the doctors in peninsular Malaysia.

The Tamils of Penang do not identify themselves in terms of class, as I have sketched above, nor do they identify themselves by caste. Caste in the form that prevailed in rural Tamilnadu and Sri Lanka—institutionalized as hereditary rights to customary ritual functions and as rigid deference rules imposed by high groups—never existed in Malaysia (for example, see McGilvray 1983). However, as R. K. Jain (1970) has shown, there is a sense in which the caste system of southern India was replicated on the plantation in colonial Malaya. The new categories (European bosses, the *kirani* clerical staff of the plantation, the *kangani* contractors who recruited the laborers from India, and the laborers) were, like castes, organized in a rigid hierarchical order based on occupation. Each group was also "ethnically" distinct: bosses were white; the kirani were generally Jaffna Tamils or Malayalees or university graduates from Tamilnadu; and the kangani were recruited from different caste groups than the laborers (Arasaratnam 1979, 79). Specific status symbols—housing, styles of dress, modes of conveyance, and elaborate rules of deference and demeanor—also distinguished the "castes," and there was no inter-caste mobility. Furthermore, like a village in Tamilnadu, the plantation tended to be a closed world. Jain has described it as a "total institution." The kangani, kirani, and European managers conducted all their major social activities within the limits of the estate (or, in the case of the Europeans, in the planters' clubs). Estate laborers were not generally free to move from estate to estate (in which case little in their situation changed), nor were they equipped to find other kinds of employment. Whether a person was born on an estate or came as an immigrant, he found it difficult to extricate himself from the social relations that organized the estate world (Jain 1970, 295–97).

However, there were also important differences between "caste" in Malaysia and caste in a Tamil village. On Malaysian plantations, the housing built for laborers (called the "estate lines") consisted of two lines of buildings, one for "clean" Shudra castes and the other for "untouchable" castes. No further distinctions were made. More important, caste endogamy proved impossible to maintain. At first, few women immigrated to Malaya, and the high mortality rate led to a high rate of remarriage. Most marriages in Malaysia took the form of unformalized or secondary marriages. Furthermore, no system for the registration of marriages existed until 1924 (Jain 1970, 275). Only the Nattukottai Chettiars—who sent their children back to India to make a suitable match—claim a purity of caste lineage.

Virtually all Tamils today say that "caste is disappearing from the Malaysian scene." When asked what they mean by this, young people say that they do not know the caste of their grandparents and that nowadays education and a job are more important than caste in arranging a marriage.[20] Nevertheless, there is evidence that caste continues to shape the social interaction and consciousness of Malaysian Hindus. In privacy, the Tamils of Penang note personal names that signify an individual's caste. Occupation continues to be an important caste marker: the trishaw drivers are said to be Pallans (a caste of agricultural laborers); employees of the Municipal Department of Sanitation are said to be Paraiyans (drummers), Vattians (gravediggers), or Chakklians (sweepers), all of which are untouchable groups. The Tamil language also marks caste differences. For example, among those of high-caste background, the word *satam* is used for rice and *am* for house, whereas those of lower-caste background use *chor* for rice and *veedu* for house. High castes will switch to a low-caste vocabulary when bargaining in the market, and educated Tamils from low-caste backgrounds may use an upper-caste vocabulary when speaking Tamil with those who are not their friends and neighbors. However, in any prolonged interaction it is difficult to hide one's caste background. Pronunciation and vocabulary will also tell whether a person's family comes from Jaffna or Kerala, as opposed to Tamilnadu.

Ritual practices are another marker of caste and class difference. Those of low-caste background generally worship the Amman goddess and/or one of the warrior deities. Thus, Pallans are said to worship Maduraiviran, and Chakklians to worship Muniandi, Mariamman, and Maduraiviran. By contrast, the educated elite from upper-caste backgrounds worship high "invited" deities, like Shiva. They also function like a caste in the exclusivity of their weekly prayer and meditation sessions. The Nattukottai Chettiars worship exclusively in their own temples. The way in which worship is conducted by different classes varies as well— from lectures given by a guru when the Shiva Family meets, to orthodox rituals performed by a Brahmin priest in the Shiva Temple, and the appeasement of the Amman goddess and warrior deities by non-Brahmin pujaris.

Middle-level caste lineages form associations such as the Nadar Sangham and the Dravidian Association, which exclude lower or formerly untouchable groups. These associations provide their members with a degree of economic security and help in arranging marriages, providing for burials, settling disputes, and so on, just as kin-based caste groups *(jati)* once did. There is even a Brahmin Association of Malaysia with a membership of about three hundred families. (These Brahmins are professionals, not priests.)

One consequence of these associations is the suspicion that higher status groups actually want to retain caste. Working-class Tamils often criticize their political leaders on the grounds of their attitude toward caste. Politicians who are believed to be of low-caste background are accused of distancing themselves from their origins by adopting high-caste status markers; those thought to be of high-caste background are thought to be secretly supporting caste.

Almost all Malaysian Tamils are bilingual—speaking both Tamil and Bahasa, the national language of Malaysia—and many are trilingual, speaking English as well, but class differences that rest on occupation are also marked by different degrees of fluency in Tamil, English, and Bahasa Malaysia. Tamil is the first language of the working class, who also learn some Bahasa in school. Those who work for English-speaking employers also speak some English, and others may speak a dialect of Chinese (especially if they have worked on the docks). However, working-class Tamils are not literate in the other languages they speak, and they are generally not successful in passing the examinations in Bahasa Malaysia that are required for higher education and white-collar employment in the civil service. Consequently, they are restricted to jobs that require manual labor and little education. English is usually the first language for Tamils from the professional class, who attend the best schools and also do well in Bahasa Malaysia. Whereas most speak some Tamil, few are literate in Tamil.[21] Middle-class Indians are often trilingual as well, speaking the language of their ethnic group (Bengali, Punjabi, Gujarati, and so on) along with Bahasa and some English.

These differences in language and the religious conceptions they frame make it difficult to bridge the widely varied religious understandings that are found among Hindu Tamils in Penang. Whereas the Western-educated professional elite tends to view devotion as a matter of inner spirituality, and to ground theology in the authority of science, the Chettiars stress ritual orthodoxy (and caste purity). And Murugan's working-class devotees from low-caste backgrounds, who are possessed by their god as they dance in ecstasy, ground their belief in religious experience rather than in theology.

# 4

## THAIPUSAM IN PENANG

Before dawn on the first day of the Thaipusam festival, a crowd gathers at the shop-house where the chariot and the image of Murugan are stored until the annual festival of the Nattukottai Chettiar Murugan Temple. This shop-house is distinguished from its neighbors by stucco images of Murugan, Murugan's brother Vinayagar (the elephant-headed god known as Ganesh in northern India), and Murugan's disciple Idumban. The doorway of the shop is flanked by freshly cut banana trees. Auspicious garlands of plaited palm fronds (tied into an odd number of knots, usually five or seven) hang across the front of the building and drop from ropes suspended over the street. Two matched bullocks bedecked with richly embroidered red cloths stand waiting to be yoked to the chariot. Inside, the chariot of carved teak plated with silver has been polished to a brilliant shine and decorated with glittering ornaments and dangling red tassels.

Around 5:00 A.M. the chief priest of the Nattukottai Chettiar Temple, who is a *pandaram* (a non-Brahmin priest), begins to perform the puja (worship) to Murugan.[1] The puja follows orthodox Shaiva praxis, rituals in which the god is treated as king, including anointing the image *(abhishekam)*, dressing the image *(vastram)*, and showing the lights to the image *(aratanai)*. At about 6:00 A.M. Murugan's escort begins to emerge from the shop-house. There are about twenty men and one or two young boys, who all carry kavadis, wooden arches that are borne on the shoulder of the devotee. Two small brass pots of milk are attached to each arch as an offering to Murugan, and the kavadis are decorated with palm fronds, peacock feathers, and pictures of the deity. The Chettiar kavadi carriers wear a white cloth *(veshti)* wrapped around their waist, which is traditionally required for attendance at a temple. A red or saffron-colored silk sash is tied around each man's waist as a sign that he has taken a vow. These kavadi carriers also wear beautiful silk turbans and necklaces of prayer beads covered with gold *(rudraksha mala)*, which are the distinctive dress of the Chettiar caste on ceremonial occasions. However, the kavadi carriers walk barefoot as a sign that they are making a pilgrimage. Next come musicians, who play the *nadaswara* (a reed instrument similar to a clarinet) and small drums called *melam*. Murugan's entourage also includes two fan bearers and an attendant who twirls his fly whisks.

The members of the Nattukottai Chettiar Murugan Temple committee who have the honor of bearing the litter of Murugan bring the image to the doorway. Murugan holds his lance or vel in his right hand, and his left hand is open, with the palm facing out and the fingers pointing to the earth in a gesture symbolizing the granting of boons and generosity *(varada mudra)*. The image is enveloped in jewelry and garlands. One of the committee members leads the crowd in singing devotional hymns *(katiyam)*. These tell the story of Murugan setting forth to do battle with the demon Surapadma. The audience responds with *"arogara"* (praise Him) after each verse.

When asked what Thaipusam celebrates, the Chettiars relate the story of Murugan's conquest of the demon Surapadma. They tell how the demon was terrorizing the people so that they went to Parvati to plead for her assistance. She agreed to help, but Murugan was then living as an ascetic. So the people made a procession bearing offerings to the place where Murugan was meditating at Palani. Moved by their devotion, Murugan agreed to help them. On Thaipusam Day he was given his weapon, the vel, by the goddess. Then he set forth to do battle (see Arasaratnam 1966, 14).

After the singing of hymns, the members of the temple committee place the image of Murugan on a swing in the chariot.[2] Once the image is secured, the chariot is loaded with the necessary ritual supplies. These include brass pots for donations of money, buckets of holy ash, several cases of camphor incense, and scarves *(pattu)*, which are to be presented to certain honored worshippers. Then the pandaram, carrying a bell and oil lamps used in worship, mounts the chariot along with several members of the temple committee who have been awarded the privilege of attending Murugan during the chariot procession.[3]

Before the bullocks can move, worshippers press forward with trays of offerings lifted over their heads. Most of those who come to worship Murugan on the first day of the festival are not Chettiars. They come from the surrounding rubber plantations with their families or from the suburbs where they work in the factories and in the homes of the affluent.

In the press of worshippers around the chariot, the first trance of the morning occurs: one gaunt man, his hands clasped in homage, suddenly falls backward. His neighbors hold his limp body until someone finds some vibhuti, which is pressed to the forehead of the man. After a moment or two, he regains consciousness.

It is almost two hours before the bullocks finally lurch forward, but they move only a few feet as more worshippers fill the street. Another half hour passes before the chariot finally emerges from Penang Street preceded by the escort bearing the regalia of kingship, Murugan's banner emblazoned with the sun, his royal umbrellas, and his pennants, including the saffron pennant that signifies all will be fed at the festival of the temple. This escort is, however, made up of the poorest beggars of Penang, who are given alms for their service. To a Western eye they are, perhaps, an incongruous honor guard, but their presence bespeaks the generosity of the god.[4]

Behind the chariot trails a throng of women who reach out to Murugan. If they cannot get close enough to touch the chariot, they rest their hands on the shoulders of others who are closer. They thus form human chains, yet each woman seems alone, totally immersed in her own devotion. Some close their eyes; others have a glazed expression.

> Acchi
>
> Among these women is Acchi, who works as a servant in the house of a friend.
>
> She has come with her sister and two adult daughters. Acchi says that she will follow the chariot of Murugan "until her legs hurt." She has not asked Murugan for a particular boon, but only wishes to show her devotion. Acchi says that one can feel sakti (energy) that flows from the image of the god through the chain of devotees that follow his chariot.
>
> Ordinarily Acchi worships at the Mariamman Temple on Queen Street or at the Kaliamman Temple in Glugor near where she lives, but as often as once a month she makes the journey to the Murugan Temple on Penang Hill to worship there. Acchi chooses to come to the first day of the Thaipusam festival because she does not entirely approve of the trance dancing of ritual vow fulfillment. She says it is not serious enough. Her daughters disagree and avow that they love the trance dancing and the excitement of ritual vow fulfillment.

In a clear space in front of the procession, the Chettiar kavadi carriers have formed a circle to perform the kavadi dance *(kavadi attam)* to the music of the nadaswara and melam. Most of the dancers circle in a swaying, stamping walk, but two move into the center and begin to dance more quickly, dipping and twirling with their kavadis. The bells around their ankles jangle at each step. As the tempo of the music increases, the dancers close their eyes or stare unseeingly, and their dancing becomes wilder and wilder. They appear to enter a trance. Changes in the mood and tempo of the music—signaled by the leader of the group of dancers—cue and control the trance. In the ring that circles the central dancers, another kavadi carrier begins to sway back and forth. As if overcome by emotion, he trembles, and silent tears stream down his cheeks. A man steps out from the crowd of onlookers and holds the dancer in his arms, wiping the perspiration from his face, and straightening his *veshti*.

The progress of Murugan's chariot is very slow; innumerable stops are made so that well over ten thousand people—not only Hindu Tamils but many Malaysian Chinese as well—can make offerings to the god. The journey of seven miles takes over fourteen hours. Some of Murugan's worshippers prostrate themselves in the path of the chariot. Most begin by making a small cash donation, which is collected by temple committee members who push a small cart just in front of the chariot. Others bring coconuts as an offering. These are broken at the cart, and a portion of each is kept as the share of the temple. The worshippers then place chips of camphor incense in the remaining piece of coconut. The incense is set aflame and put on a tray with other traditional offerings—a banana, betel leaves, flowers, camphor, saffron, *kunkumam* (red powder), and a scarf or garland of flowers arranged on a banana leaf. From each family one person presses into the surging throng of devotees around the chariot to hand the offering to the priest or one of the attendants on the chariot. Each offering is passed in front of the deity; then some vibhuti is placed on the tray, which is returned to the worshipper.

The worshippers touch the sacred ash to their foreheads. Some also place the ash on their tongues and throats. Again, worshippers cannot explain the significance of this gesture, but a pujari explains:

> The sacred ash is smeared on the forehead to remind one of death. We come from earth and we return to earth. Finally we all turn to ash. It reminds the human being that death is there; it cannot be avoided. If you remember that one day death will claim you, you will remember God. Without this reminder of death, men will think they are all powerful, that they are gods themselves and they will commit all sorts of crimes. The sacred ash reminds one of the final day so that he will be a good person.

Later each family will consume the offerings of fruit and coconut, called prasad, which are believed to incorporate the blessing of the deity.

Many of those who have come to see Murugan bring their children and babes-in-arms who are handed up to the chariot to be garlanded and receive the blessing of Murugan. Each child clutches a small donation in one fist.

At about noon the procession arrives at the Shiva Temple on Dato Keramat Road. Here the priests and temple committee members dismount from the chariot to rest, bathe, and eat. The kavadi carriers enter the temple and there fall into an exhausted sleep. Their wives or mothers join them and sit quietly fanning away the flies as they sleep for an hour while the procession pauses.

A devotional group singing the *kavadi cintu*, songs of the bhakti poets, joins Murugan's procession. Many of their hymns celebrate Murugan's love for Valli, the dark-skinned tribal maiden (Chettiar 1973, 163). Devotional music that evokes Murugan as divine lover is also broadcast over loudspeakers from the temporary pavilions (thaneer pandal) that have been built along the procession route.

To build a thaneer pandal is also an act of worship. A thaneer pandal (literally, "watershed") is a light structure of wood or bamboo roofed with palm leaves, as is built to shelter the guests for a wedding celebration. Before beginning construction, a post is placed at one corner of the structure and adorned with mango leaves, grasses, and red cloth. A puja is then performed to purify the site and prepare it as a sacred space where devotees who are possessed by Murugan and guests of the festival may be served.

The building of a thaneer pandal may be organized by members of a temple committee, a neighborhood association, a student activity group, or employees of a major concern—such as the Tamil Students' Association of Penang Free School, the Sri Maha Muniswara Temple of Weld Quay, the Noordin Street Flats Tenants' Association, and the Tamil Employees' Association of the Eastern Smelting Company. Volunteers form the organizing committee, arrange for a site where an electrical hookup and water can be obtained, and provide the labor to erect and decorate the structure. Funds for the thaneer pandal may be solicited from a sponsor, such as one of the multinational electronics firms or major hotels that have large numbers of Tamil employees, or from a wealthy Tamil lawyer, doctor, or businessman. These associations may persist for years and establish important ties between working-class Tamils and their political leaders. For example, one of the most elaborate thaneer pandals in 1985 is jointly sponsored by the Tamil Telikom employees and a prominent Tamil lawyer, M. Ramanathan, who has been appointed to the committee that manages the Arulmigu Bala Thandayuthabani Temple and supervises the Thaipusam festival in Penang.

M. Ramanathan

M. Ramanathan's family, which came originally from the Jaffna district of Sri Lanka, has resided in Malaysia for several generations. M. Ramanathan and his cousin who is chairman of the committee that supervises the Thaipusam festival, are both community leaders. M. Ramanathan says that his goal is to bring greater harmony to the Tamil community of Penang, and especially to lessen tension between the "Chettys" and others.

M. Ramanathan has himself fulfilled a vow to Murugan on Thaipusam. He promised to carry a kavadi if his wife conceived a child. In 1980 he proudly held his two-year-old son in his arms and said that he would be carrying a kavadi for the second time. The previous year he had fasted and followed a regime of prayer and meditation for one month before Thaipusam. On the day of Murugan's procession he had a small vel inserted in the skin of his brow and carried a kavadi, walking behind the chariot. Recalling the experience, he thought he must have been in a trance. When M. Ramanathan fulfilled his vow for the second time, he fasted for three days and simply walked behind the chariot (without being pierced or carrying a kavadi). He found that he was exhausted by this and thought that his spiritual preparations had been inadequate so he had not gone into trance. M. Ramanathan chose to fulfill his vow on the first day of the festival because he felt that Thaipusam Day had become too much like a carnival because of the kavadi dancing. He explained that he had visited the Palani Temple in Tamilnadu, the model for the Penang Hill temple, and he thought that the mood of devotees at Palani was more "serious" and "devout" than the atmosphere in Penang on Thaipusam.

Over the last ten years, at each Thaipusam festival there have been more thaneer pandals, and greater expenditure on their decorations. The competition among the voluntary associations and their sponsors appears to be part of a long tradition in which a god-king distributes symbols of high status through his priests during his festival.[5] Volunteers who were decorating a rather simple thaneer pandal with brightly colored garlands, strings of folded palm leaves, and multicolored electric lights remarked resentfully about "those rich people who could put up a two-story shed and play the doll."

The most elaborate thaneer pandals are built with a second story where one or two men may stand while they manipulate ropes causing a small doll to swing back and forth, passing over the crowd below. Sometimes these dolls appear with wings and are referred to as angels, or *gandharvas* or *apsarasas*, the celestial musicians and dancers who entertain the gods. No one I asked could explain their significance in greater detail; they were said to "play" for "the entertainment of Murugan."[6] In this game the doll is made to swing from the thaneer pandal to the place where the chariot has stopped. Before the chariot can proceed, one of the attendants must catch the doll and take the flower garland offering from it. The person who plays the doll tries to make it swing just within reach of the attendants on the chariot, but moving too quickly to be grasped. Sometimes an attendant on the chariot, while appearing to ignore the play of the doll, makes an expert snatch at an unexpected moment, and the crowd cheers. Then the attendant places a scarf *(pattu)* around the neck of the doll and sets it free.

The decorations of the thaneer pandal emphasize different aspects of the worship of Murugan by means of the symbols chosen and the way in which the deity is represented. For example, most thaneer pandals display a hand-painted mural or plaster image of Murugan, but occasionally the deity honored is Vinayagar, the elephant-headed brother of Murugan, who is favored by higher-caste worshippers. Most frequently, Murugan is portrayed as a jewel-bedecked child or a bare-chested youth in the garb of an ascetic who carries the scepter of a king. These images conflate worship of Murugan as infant deity with worship of Murugan as ascetic youth and as god-king. Another favored representation of Murugan is as an infant, seated on the lap of Parvati, his mother, in a family scene that includes his father, Shiva, with Vinayagar by his side.

The lotus also appears prominently in the decoration of the thaneer pandal. Sometimes Murugan is shown standing on an open lotus, or the lotus blossom may be painted on the ground in the manner of the traditional rice flower designs *(kolam)* that are drawn in front of the threshold of houses and temples in southern Indian villages. At one thaneer pandal, lotus blossoms float in an artificial pond; at another, they provide the base for a fountain. Another group has constructed a lotus that opens mechanically at the approach of Murugan's chariot and releases live pigeons and the doll, which swings above the procession, sprinkling the crowd below with flower blossoms. The image of the lotus appears frequently in literature of bhakti devotionalism. A pujari explains:

> If you look at the lotus flower when it is closed, it looks like the heart itself and is also the size of the normal heart. In all the pictures of the gods, the god is sitting on the lotus because the lotus is the heart and God is supposed to reside in everyone's heart. The heart is the temple of God.

In Hinduism the lotus, which grows from the mud but rises to the top of the pond to bloom, is also commonly understood to be a symbol of purity.[7] However, this interpretation was never suggested to me, which is puzzling because purity is a theme of considerable importance to Malaysian Tamils who are descended from the untouchable castes of India.

Throughout the day, the chariot procession grows more elaborate. Troops of dancers, organized by voluntary associations, take turns performing the *kolattam*, a traditional folk dance resembling stylized combat.[8] The dancers form two circles, one inside the other, so that each dancer faces a partner. The dancers in the inner and outer circles move in opposite directions. They mark the rhythms of the dance with the stamp of their feet, emphasized by the jangle of bells worn around their ankles, and the clack of their sticks, which are hit together or on those of a partner in patterns signaled by the troop leader. The dancers may also jump over and between the sticks of other dancers, which are hit on the ground and against each other in complex rhythms executed at a very fast tempo. The dance requires that each dancer precisely regulate his or her movements in accord with those of the whole group in an ever-changing pattern, and this suggests the importance of coordination and cooperation as a value of communal life among the Tamils.

Adding to the general tumultuousness of the kolattam, the blare of music from the thaneer pandal, and the music of the nadaswara and melam, each time the chariot begins to move forward, hundreds of coconuts are hurled to the ground in a rippling explosion that drowns all else. These coconuts—piled at the edge of the street in huge mounds by worshippers, including Chinese merchants who own nearby shops—are another kind of offering to Murugan. While the coconut water sprays up from the street, the police hold back the onlookers.[9] Tamil worshippers rarely pick up the broken pieces of coconut, though they may offer one to a tourist. When consumed, the coconut offering is considered to be prasad, which incorporates the blessing of Murugan.

Leaders of the Nattukottai Chettiar community and a priest *(pujari)* from the Chettiar Murugan Temple accept offerings brought to Murugan on the first day of the Thaipusam Festival in Penang. According to a newspaper report in 1980, the value of the chariot that carries the bejeweled image of Murugan amounted to over three million US dollars.

A woman is lost in prayer as she prepares to fulfill her vow to Murugan. This is the way many devotees enter the trance of divine grace *(arul)*.

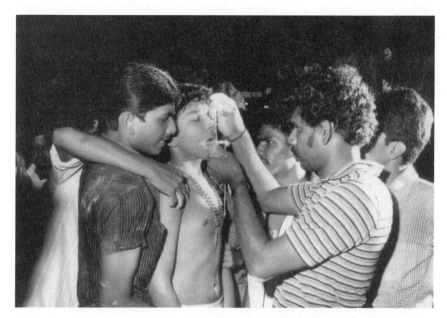

The devotee seems to lose awareness of his surroundings and his eyes close. Two men support him as his tongue is pierced with a silver replica of the lance *(vel)* of Murugan.

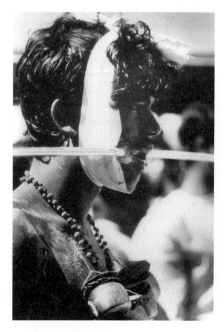

Like the demons Idumban and Sura-padma, the devotees who fulfill vows to Murugan on Thaipusam are pierced with the lance of Murugan. The demons who embody sexual desire and aggression are symbolically equated with the part of the self that feels unacceptable lust, greed, and anger, and which must be mastered in order for the self to be made worthy of god's grace. Photograph by R. J. Seward

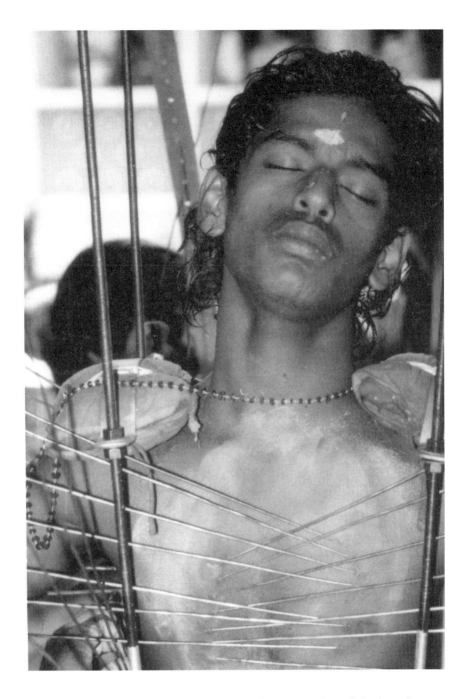

In the 1970s, long skewers inserted through the outer arches of the *kavadis* were embedded in the skin over the ribs of the devotee.

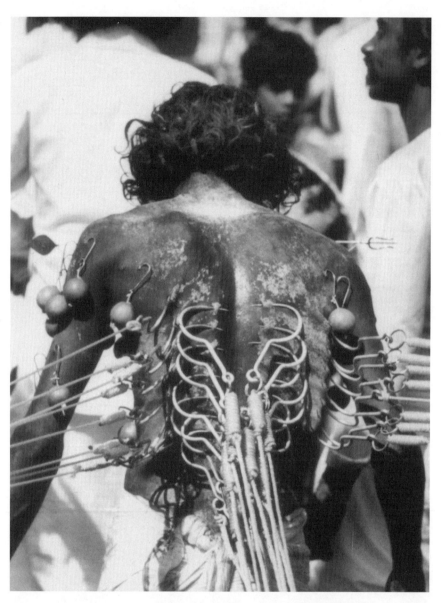

Some devotees fulfill vows to Murugan in the manner of Idumban with the shoulder pole of a coolie *(kuli)* and through symbolic gestures that represent them as beasts of burden—as when they pull a cart with an image of the god by means of ropes and hooks embedded in the skin of their backs. In the theology of *bhakti*, these ritual acts are interpreted as symbolic expressions of devotion, demonstrating the pain the devotee is willing to undergo to break the bonds of worldly desire and the humble submission with which he serves the god. Photograph by R. J. Seward

The most dramatic form of vow fulfillment combines the chariot pulled by hooks embedded in the back, limes and milk pots hung from the chest, and a six-foot *vel* that pierces the cheeks and may have pots of milk suspended from it.

This devotee caries a *kavadi* decorated with peacock feathers and, like Murugan's peacock vehicle, can be identified with the conquered demon Surapadma.

The mood of ritual vow fulfillment is festive. Drummers play while devotees perform the *kavadi* dance, modeled on the courtship dance of the male peacock. Onlookers worship Murugan by bringing water to wash the feet of those who fulfill vows, for the vow takers have purified their bodies by fasting and meditation and become like the statue of the god that has been sanctified so that the god can enter into it.

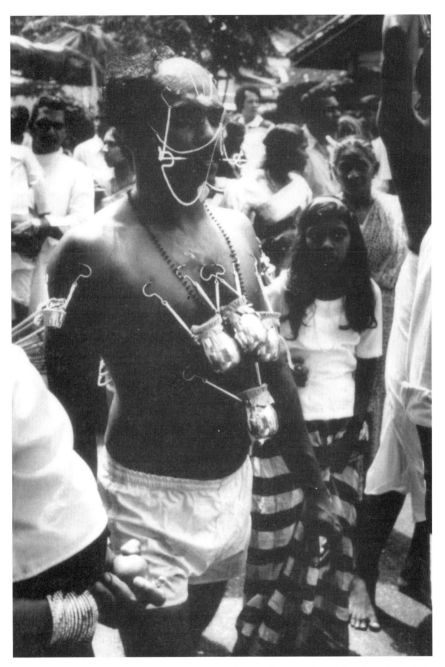

Some male devotees carry a milk offering in small pots of milk hooked into their chests. Here we find an identification with the devoted mother who expresses her love of the infant god by nourishing him and receives in turn the god's love.

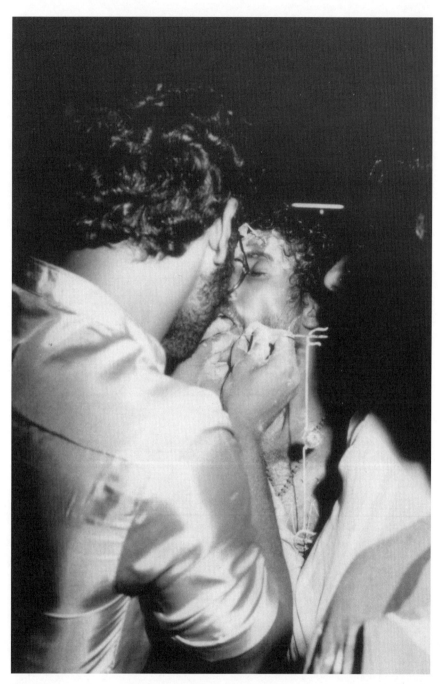

The priest presses caustic ash (*vibhuti*) to the wounds as he removes the hooks and skewers of vow fulfillment.

The kavadi dancers are not alone in their propensity for trance on the first day of the festival. Here and there in the crowd an individual, usually a woman, falls into a swoon at the sight of the gleaming spire of the silver chariot. One woman, apparently responding to the explosion of the coconuts, issues a startling shriek and bolts heedlessly toward the chariot through the crush of onlookers until she is finally restrained by bystanders, who quiet her trance by placing vibhuti on her forehead. Occasionally these episodes of trance become epidemic, and as onlookers are affected, one after another, a thrill of excitement and tension moves through the crowd.

### Chandrakumar

Near Kampong Java Baru, a large pile of coconuts to be offered to Murugan is attended by Chandra, a handsome young man of twenty-five, who is employed by the Sanitation Department of George Town. He stands holding a tray with lighted camphor, awaiting the chariot of Murugan and conversing in Cantonese with two Chinese girls, neighborhood friends. In response to my question, he shifts to Bahasa and then to English, languages he has picked up from Malay- and English-speaking bosses.

Chandra worships at the Raja Mariamman Temple in Kampong Java Baru. He has also built a shrine to Muniandi in his yard. It consists of a trident under a small roof. This trident identifies Muniandi as a form of Shiva. On Thaipusam Day, Chandra will fulfill a vow to Murugan by having a large spear pierced through his cheek and by bringing offerings of milk in small brass pots hanging from hooks that pierce his chest. This is the third time he has undertaken ritual vow fulfillment for the health and well-being of his young family. He also assists in the piercing of other devotees who come to the Mariamman Temple in Kampong Java Baru, where he is recognized as someone with spiritual power.

When asked to explain the origin of the Thaipusam festival, Chandra tells the story of the founding of the Palani Temple in which Murugan is enraged at what he sees to be the favoritism shown by his parents to his brother Vinayagar, so that he takes off the sacred thread that distinguishes the pure twice-born castes and becomes an ascetic. As Chandra relates this story, one hears the appeal of the narrative for those of low and untouchable caste descent.

Chandra continues by telling another story to explain the origin of the Thaipusam procession. He explains that Thaipusam was the day proposed for the marriage of Murugan, and the god is taken in procession to the temple on Waterfall Road for the marriage ceremony.[10] However, at a crucial moment in the marriage ritual, the Chettiar priest sneezes, and consequently (since bodily secretions such as saliva and mucus are extremely polluting) the auspicious quality of the occasion is destroyed. Thus it happens each year, and the marriage must be postponed until the following year.[11] This story continues the theme of Chandra's first story, expressing hostility toward the Chettiars for their claim to high status based on caste "purity."

At sunset, as the procession of Murugan nears the Nattukottai Chettiar Murugan Temple on Waterfall Road, the strings of multicolored lights that bedeck the thaneer pandal and the stalls of the vendors are lit, and the anticipation of the crowd grows. There has been constant activity in the temple all day long, as Chettiars arrive with food to be prepared for distribution to the crowds. On one side of the temple, Chettiar men sit in two long rows peeling pumpkins. Nearby, the women cut up mounds of vegetables and grate coconuts. In the courtyard behind the temple, cooks build fires underneath gigantic caldrons to cook the curry and rice. Assistants haul water, wash banana leaves, and grind spices.

Subramania

One of the young men assisting the cooks by stirring the curry cooking in the giant pots takes a break to speak with me. He has been working for several days, hauling wood and water in preparation for this day when the temple will distribute food packets to worshippers. To explain why the priests in the Nattukottai Chettiar Murugan Temple are not Brahmins, like the priests of the Shiva Temple, he tells the story of Murugan's quarrel with his brother Ganesa over the mango, emphasizing that in his anger over his brother's unfair victory, the youthful Murugan stripped off the thread that marked him as a member of the twice-born high castes. Thus, Subramania explains, the priests of Murugan do not wear the thread of the twice-born castes. He goes on to talk about the anti-Brahmin movement in India and says he believes that Indira Gandhi had intended to put an end to caste distinction, but due to opposition from high-caste political groups, she had been unable to achieve her goal. He laments her assassination and worries that caste will never be eradicated.

At dusk, the young men of the Nattukottai Chettiar lineage come to distribute the leaf-wrapped packets of food to the crowds awaiting the arrival of the chariot. As night falls, the crescendo of smashing coconuts announces the approach of the procession of Murugan. A dance troop leads the way up Waterfall Road and enters the temple, making a clockwise circumambulation of the temple *(pradakshina)* while performing the kolattam. Then come the men who have carried kavadis. Most of them appear to be in a state of physical exhaustion, but their faces are suffused with emotion. Some seem lost to their surroundings. A few cry out as they enter the temple, as if struggling to express some inexpressible feeling. The young boys are encouraged by older male relatives. The kavadi carriers also perform a pradakshina, their pace accelerating as they rush around the central shrine, then run back to a clear space outside the temple wall, where a vel has been implanted and many coconuts have been broken in offering. Then they dash back again around the central chamber in which the permanent image of Murugan is situated. When the last passage around the temple is complete, many of these devotees collapse. A few have to be carried to a protected area, where they are gently laid on mats to recover. Again, friends and relatives fan them, loosen their garments, wipe their faces gently, and bring them water. After a while the devotees sit up and begin to converse. Together with their family and friends, they eat the food that has been prepared in the temple kitchen.

It is almost 9:00 P.M. by the time the bullocks draw Murugan's chariot to a halt outside the temple. The processional image of Murugan is lifted out of the chariot and placed on a litter, which is carried by the men of the temple committee in a pradakshina around the central image of the temple. The crowd falls back to let the image of Murugan pass. There is an ebb and flow of movement in the temple as women reach out their arms to the image as it passes. From the shoulders of their parents, small children solemnly regard the pradakshina of Murugan. It seems that if the litter bearers paused for a moment, they would be engulfed by worshippers seeking contact with the deity. But the bearers do not stop until the image is taken into the central chamber of the temple (*garbha grha*, said to be a womb and also a tomb), where the image will remain for two nights. No one but the priests of the temple may enter this sanctum sanctorum.

## THAIPUSAM DAY: RITUAL VOW FULFILLMENT

Thaipusam falls during the first month of the Tamil year, the month of Thai, on the day closest to the full moon when the asterism (sign or constellation) of Pusam is in the ascendant. The presiding deity of Pusam is the planet Jupiter (Grihaspati, Brihaspati), which is considered to be a beneficent influence and is associated with Murugan when worshipped as an ascetic youth, a form known as Thandayuthabani (or Dhandayuthapani). In this form, Murugan is represented as a youth with shaven head who wears only a loincloth and carries the staff *(thanda, danda)* of an ascetic.

The Arulmigu Bala Thandayuthabani Hill Temple is located on the side of Penang Hill, just past the Nattukottai Chettiar Murugan Temple. This hillside temple—like the Sri Subramania Swamy Temple at the Batu Caves in Kuala Lumpur (consecrated in 1891)—is said to have been built by quarry workers (Soepadmo and Ho Thian Hua 1971). It is modeled on the pilgrimage temple of Palani in Tamilnadu and named after the form of Murugan represented in the central image there.[12] *Bala* refers to a child, and *Thandayuthabani* means "one who holds a staff," referring to Murugan as a youthful ascetic. *Arulmigu* means "of abundant grace or blessing" (from *migu*, noble or abundant, and *arul*, grace or blessing). A trance that is experienced as ecstatic contact with divine presence is also called *arul*. Thus *arulmigu* could also be translated as "bringer of trance." In the hill temple Murugan is depicted as a jewel-bedecked child in a loincloth. He holds the staff of an ascetic.[13]

The simple program for the events of Thaipusam Day, published by the Committee of Management for the Arulmigu Bala Thandayuthabani Hill Temple, states that an Abhisheka (the ceremony of anointing the deity) will be performed at 4:00 A.M., followed at 8:00 A.M. by the procession of the *utsava murthi* (movable image). This procession consists of a circumambulation of the temple.[14] The important event of the day, the spectacular and moving fulfillment of personal vows, is also noted: "Kavadis will be offered from 4:00 A.M. until 10:00 P.M."

Those who fulfill vows involving the piercing of the skin with hooks or the vel of Murugan must begin their preparations weeks before the festival. The spiritual preparation for vow fulfillment is described in the most ancient Indian texts on ascetic practices (Bhagat 1976, 59). In Penang these preparations include fasting, total abstinence from sexual activity, silence, sleeping on bare ground, and wearing only a minimum of clothing. These practices are meant to purify the body and the mind of the devotee. For up to forty days before the festival, each devotee observes the particular prohibitions he or she has decided upon. If devotees do not succeed in fulfilling a vow for any reason (even illness, for example), they will be thought to have failed in the spiritual preparation that must precede vow fulfillment.

Vow fulfillment can be very expensive. In 1980 the forty-seven hooks and four silver skewers purchased by one worshipper cost roughly one hundred twenty Malaysian ringgit (seventy-five U.S. dollars), almost a month's wages for a laborer. Even the simplest offering, a milk offering *(pal kavadi)*, can cost five ringgit a bottle, and the silver skewers used to pierce the skin of the forehead and the tongue cost about fifteen ringgit each. Each devotee also must purchase offerings of coconuts, flowers, incense, and a length of pure white cloth that is dyed a saffron color.

For days before Thaipusam, one can find devotees sitting quietly in small groups in temples, polishing and sharpening the hooks and skewers to be used in vow fulfillment. Some devotees construct an elaborate form of kavadi, a kind of altar built on a large square platform that is supported by shoulder pads and a belt around the waist. An image or picture of Murugan is placed on the platform and the arches that frame it are decorated with crepe paper, ornaments, and flowers. Others build small chariots *(ratam)*, which they will pull over the pilgrimage route by great hooks embedded in the skin of their backs.

The night before vow fulfillment, devotees usually sleep on the ground in the courtyard of a temple. The day begins before dawn with a ritual bath. Then the devotees put on the saffron-colored garb that distinguishes one who is fulfilling a vow.[15] They do not eat, for on this day the devotees will fast until they have fulfilled their vow. While it is still early, those who are to fulfill vows are joined by family and friends, who wear their finest apparel to the festival. At shrines and temples throughout Penang, crowds begin to form and the air is filled with swirls of incense, the murmur of invocations, the throb of drums, the cadence of chants, and the explosion of coconuts broken in offering.

Those who have made vows arrange an offering of milk, coconut, limes, incense, and sacred ash in front of their kavadi. Then the pujari comes to put them into trance. Family and friends begin to chant *"Vel, vel, vetri vel"* (Lance, lance, victorious lance), while the devotee stands in an attitude of prayer. The priest passes the incense in front of his face, invoking the presence of Murugan. Usually the trance comes on imperceptibly, but occasionally its onset is sudden: the body of the devotee appears to go rigid, his eyes roll back, and he slumps in a faint or begins a violent dance.

Once the devotee is in a state of quietly contained trance, the priest begins to insert the hooks and skewers that symbolize the vel of Murugan. The devotee's skin is covered with the caustic sacred ash. There is no blood flow, though great force may be required to thrust the spear through a devotee's cheeks. Devotees never cry out in pain, although their faces may be contorted and occasionally they faint. If that happens, sacred ash is applied to recall the person to a state of waking trance so that the preparations may be completed.

Bystanders also go into spontaneous trances. When a person becomes threatening or begins to dance wildly, the trance is interpreted as possession by the Amman goddess or one of the lesser but fierce and warlike deities such as Muniandi, Maduraiviran, or Aiyanar. Someone will apply sacred ash to the dancer's forehead, which usually quiets him or her. If the person in trance does not respond, further attempts will be made to apply the ash, or a pujari may gesture everyone to leave the dancer alone until he thinks that the trance can be quieted.

Devotees offer kavadis in fulfillment of a vow and to give thanks for favors obtained from Murugan, but also to secure his protection and aid in the future. In 1985, Mohan, a Public Utilities Board electrician in his twenties, promised to carry a kavadi for three years when he recovered from an illness after praying for the help of Murugan. Palanisamy, a young man in his twenties, carried a kavadi for the first time, because on Thaipusam of the previous year he had asked Murugan to help him find a way to marry the woman he loved. During the past year his parents had given up their opposition to his marriage and now accepted his choice of bride. A gardener at an elementary school, Muniandi, and his young son both carried kavadis to fulfill a vow made when Muniandi's wife had a difficult pregnancy with the boy. Narayanaswami, also a gardener, made his vow when he was diagnosed as having heart disease. He is forty-three years old and plans to carry a kavadi for three years, including hooks and a small vel through his forehead. A composed ten-year-old boy, who has his cheeks pierced with a two-foot-long vel, is fulfilling a vow his mother made when he was very ill. A father of ten at age forty-four, K. Veloo, who was carrying a kavadi for the twenty-sixth consecutive year, said he offered his kavadi "for the good health and happiness of his family." His friend had vowed to carry a kavadi yearly for the rest of his life when he was cured of stomach pains that Western doctors had been unable to treat.

### Ramasami

Ramasami is called the "Birdman of Penang," because his self-chosen vow was to be suspended by hooks embedded in the skin of his back from a wooden frame mounted on a cart that was pulled by his sons. I met Ramasami, a laborer in his sixties, at a shrine of Maduraiviran, a warrior deity who is worshipped by low-caste lineages of agricultural laborers. Ramasami explained that during World War II he had injured his leg and suffered so much that doctors had wanted to amputate the leg. Ramasami promised Murugan that he would be hung from hooks if his leg were saved, and he was cured. Ramasami fulfilled his vow, each year for five years; then he decided he would continue to do so for the rest of his life, vowing, "Formerly I suffered with this leg for nothing; now I will suffer one day a year for you."

Hook-swinging was a traditional practice of lower castes in South India, associated with the festival of the village goddess (Ramasami did not know this).[16] When prohibited by the British government—along with other practices thought to be primitive or immoral, such as suttee and temple "prostitution"—a goat or the image of a winged warrior was substituted for the human hook-swinger. Like earlier British colonial officials, Hindu reformers in Penang want to prohibit hook-swinging. They argue that the Birdman invented hook-swinging in an exhibitionistic gesture of individual grandiosity, and they maintain that this form of vow fulfillment has no place in authentic Hindu worship. In 1985 they issued a rule limiting the height of a kavadi in an effort to restrain the Birdman.

When I spoke with him, Ramasami was preoccupied with the question of what he would do on Thaipusam, given the new rules and the reformers' disapproval of his vow. Finally he decided he would find a different way to fulfill his vow.

Over the decade 1975–1985, forms of ritual vow fulfillment that involve piercing the body have become less severe. For example, in the 1970s, long skewers inserted through the outer arches of the kavadis were embedded in the skin over the ribs of the devotee. By the 1980s, strings attached to small silver hooks embedded in the skin over the rib cage had been substituted for the skewers.

There are many forms of ritual vow fulfillment to Murugan. Almost all devotees bring milk offerings, but some carry the milk in little pots that swing from hooks embedded in their chest. Alternatively, limes are suspended from hooks across the chest and in the back and shoulders, and the milk offering is carried in a pot on the head or in one's hand. Some devotees follow the example of Murugan's demon disciple, Idumban, and carry two pots of milk or bunches of coconuts suspended from the ends of a pole borne on the shoulder. The most dramatic form of vow fulfillment combines the chariot pulled by hooks embedded in the back, limes and milk pots hung from the chest, and a six-foot vel (lance) that pierces the cheeks and has pots of milk suspended from it.[17]

There are also less spectacular forms of vow fulfillment. As at Palani, the vow of head-shaving (pirarttanai mudi) is common. Head-shaving is a ritual of purification, for hair (like bodily secretions) is thought to absorb and contain pollution. On Thaipusam, parents frequently bring their infants for head-shaving. This removes the pollution of birth. Among adults, both women and men interpret head-shaving as a renunciation of one's vanity and ego. As a form of pollution, hair also may symbolize sin, and head-shaving the purification from sin (Trawick 1990a, 159; Dumont 1966, 51; Babb 1975a, 76–78). After the head has been shaved, it is covered with saffron-colored turmeric paste, which is "cooling" and purifying.

Some parents make the pilgrimage to the hillside shrine carrying their infant in a sling suspended from sugarcane stalks, which they support on their shoulders. This act is often in fulfillment of a vow made when the child's life was threatened by illness or when the child's birth was desired.

Women and girls usually carry their milk offerings in a brass pot on their heads. Some also have small vels inserted through their tongues or in the skin of the forehead. Many fall into trance. Other women make a vow to prepare cooked sweet rice or curry for distribution to worshippers. This act is appropriate to festival days, when traditional caste restrictions on communal eating are suspended.

Every year, a few Westerners, Chinese, and Indians from other parts of India join the Tamil devotees of Murugan in fulfilling vows.[18] Some speak, as Tamils do, of promises made to the god upon seeing others fulfill vows the previous year. The Western devotees, however, usually have not asked the god to help them but say that their vow fulfillment was inspired by the religious or spiritual intensity they saw in the ritual.


The pilgrimage to the hillside shrine of Murugan is made barefoot. The distance may be from four to twelve miles, and the journey usually takes several hours. If the road becomes so crowded that passage is blocked, the devotee carrying a kavadi may be given a stool to rest on and offered water to drink. Someone may also bring water to wash the feet of one who fulfills a vow, for by fasting and meditation the devotee has purified his body and become like the statue of the god that has been sanctified so that the god can enter into it. Murugan then possesses his devotees and enables them to fulfill their vow without experiencing pain. Caring for the devotee becomes an act of worship.

The mood of ritual vow fulfillment is festive. Many devotees perform their pilgrimage in the company of friends and family. They bring drummers who play while the devotees perform the kavadi dance. The dipping, swirling steps of the dance are modeled on the courtship dance of the male peacock, Murugan's mount, which like Murugan provides an image of masculine beauty and sexual attraction. In this spirit, the kavadi dance often appears to be a display of masculine prowess and beauty. The men sing the kavadi songs and dance, circling around the devotee, while women dressed in saris of rich and brilliant hues— orange, purple, green—look on. Golden chains and bangles shine on their necks and arms, and they wear fragrant jasmine in their hair. The mood is joyous, and the air is full of the scent of blossoms. Western tourists are often invited to join in the celebration.

On Thaipusam, the scene at the shrine of Muniswara is even more chaotic than at other shrines and temples. Many devotees gather here to begin their pilgrimage to the temple on Penang Hill. Those who pass by the shrine also stop to break a coconut before Muniswara, and some of them fall into a violent trance as they enter the shrine. A man, who appears to be a laborer in his fifties or sixties, takes a stylized martial pose in front of the deity and then moves to the tray that holds the sacred ash and a piece of burning camphor. He picks up the cube of camphor and places it on his extended tongue, so that the flames leap out of his mouth. He shows no pain. People do not interfere or even take much notice as he dances, tongue aflame, until the camphor is burnt up. One bystander explains that the heat of the flame, manifesting the power of the goddess, will drive out the spirit that has possessed the man.

Next to the shrine a young man dances in a jerky manner and grabs leaves from the tree, which he chews. Onlookers say he is possessed by Hanuman, the monkey god. Hanuman is a celibate deity, but he nevertheless possesses all the characteristics of an idealized masculinity (because his energy is not dissipated in sexual intercourse). He is extremely strong, and his body ripples with muscles. He is the devoted ally of Rama and a paradigm of the devoted servant of a high god in the form of a king (Babb 1975b, 115–20). Possession by Hanuman may suggest this young man's wish to show himself as virile and manly.

A thin, work-worn woman begins to dance before Muniswara, using the stylized violent gestures of possession by a fierce spirit. She dances in front of Arumugam, the pujari of the shrine, who is standing quietly, dispensing sacred ash to those who pass by. When the woman gestures to her tongue, Arumugam takes ash from his tray and places it on her tongue. She shakes her head violently and gestures to another tray in front of the deity. Arumugam takes some ash from that tray and places it in her hand, but she insistently points at the tray and again at her mouth. This time Arumugam takes the cube of burning camphor and places it on her tongue, but she shakes her head, spitting out the burning incense. Now she points to her forehead, and Arumugam seems finally to understand. He takes *kunkumam* (red powder) from the tray and puts this on her forehead. She extends her tongue, and he places kunkumam on her tongue as well. She now seems satisfied and continues on her pilgrimage. Kunkumam represents blood and symbolizes the presence of the goddess, which appears to be what this woman wanted to convey.[19]

Then another middle-aged woman, who had been standing inconspicuously at the edge of the crowd, suddenly strides provocatively up to Arumugam, almost as if she were about to attack him. Her chest is flung forward, and her arms outstretched. He extends his hand to put vibhuti on her forehead. Then he places his hand firmly on top of her head until she relaxes into her previous state of mild composure. Such violent trances seem to happen fairly frequently among middle-aged women. To a Western observer, these trances may appear to vent pent-up anger or sexual frustration. The women fling their arms and heads about with abandon, their usually well-groomed long hair becoming tangled and unkempt as they dance until spent. Then the pujari places vibhuti on their foreheads, and they come out of their trance.

Arumugam adjusts his manner and posture intuitively for each encounter. Most of the time, he is calm, quiet, and authoritative as he gestures devotees to continue on their journey to the hillside temple or gives them vibhuti or a lime from the trident of Muniswara. However, on occasion, he appears to enter a trance. As a group of men struggled to restrain a man in his fifties, dressed in a silk shirt, who appeared to be possessed by a very fierce martial deity, Arumugam put down his tray and stood in front of the devotee.[20] He also took a martial stance and began to breathe in and out rapidly through his nose. Then, in a deep rough voice quite unlike his usual one, Arumugam asked the identity of the spirit who had entered the body of the worshipper. He gestured to those who held the man to fall back. It seemed as if the two warriors greeted each other. Arumugam gave the man a lime from Muniswara's trident; then he blew his breath out violently into the man's face and made a gesture with both hands, lowering them slowly and steadily but forcefully. At this the man slumped limply and came out of his trance. One onlooker explained that the pujari had driven out the warrior spirit by blowing "cooling" sacred ash into the possessed man.[21] Bystanders cannot always identify the deities and spirits who enter into entranced worshippers in scenes such as this one; nor do they consider this important, so long as the power of the deity of the shrine, manifest in the pujari, is stronger than the power of the possessing spirit.

After leaving the shrine of Muniswara, Murugan's devotees pass by the Nattukottai Chettiar Murugan Temple. Some enter and perform a pradakshina; most simply break a coconut in front of the temple entrance. When I asked why devotees did not enter this temple, I was told that the Chettiars once attempted to raise funds for the temple by charging fees for offerings made on Thaipusam. Hindu temples traditionally charge for offerings, but the Chettiars' attempt to levy fees evidently outraged Tamil laborers, who resented the Chettiars' great wealth and their claim to high-caste status. This incident led to a partial boycott of the Chettiar Murugan Temple until the fees were abolished.[22]

At the bottom of Penang Hill, Murugan's devotees pass through a gate commemorating vow fulfillment. The funds for the gate were donated by a hospital attendant who won the lottery and invested his earnings, becoming very wealthy. Atop the gate stands Murugan, in the form of an ascetic youth, flanked by Vinayagar and Idumban and attended by a man and a woman carrying kavadis. The devotees stop at a table where they pay a fee for offerings made at the Arulmigu Bala Thandayuthabani Temple on the hillside. The charge for a milk offering *(pal abhisheka)* is one Malaysian ringgit; for a kavadi offering or head-shaving, the charge is three ringgits. The drummers are required to leave their instruments in the care of entrance guards here, for the committee that manages the temple wants to encourage a spiritual atmosphere within the temple precinct.

The crowd inside the temple compound is thick. First, the devotees perform a pradaksina of the temple of Vinayagar at the bottom of the hill. Then they pass round a shrine said to belong to Idumban, the demon disciple of Murugan. (This shrine contains only a trident, perhaps a symbol of Shiva?) Under the old pipal tree across from the shrine of Idumban there are images of entwined serpents, such as one might see in virtually any village temple in Tamilnadu or Malaysia. (Live snakes are said to live in these trees and are fed with offerings of milk and eggs.) These serpent images are associated with fertility and rebirth (because they shed their skin). Many devotees stop here to break another coconut for the serpent powers.

Finally they are ready to ascend the stairway that climbs the steep hillside to the shrine above. This is sometimes a dramatic moment. Their pilgrimage almost complete, the devotees seem to sink into a deeper level of trance. Some are filled with renewed energy and stride up the stairs rapidly, passing by those who climb with a slow, regular pace in the heat of the day. Others seem to face an inner struggle and balk at the stairs. A companion may chant, *"vel, vel, vetri vel"* so that such a devotee will feel the power of Murugan come into him. The bell in the shrine above rings out. A priest says that it calls Murugan's worshippers: "The sound of the temple bell is like the waves of the sea and the vibrations of *om*. The vibration travels down to the people carrying kavadis, and they think, the god is calling me."

Inside the hillside temple, one can barely move. The throng of worshippers pressing to the altar with offerings of milk is impassable except when all, somehow, make way for still another devotee to perform an obeisance before Murugan. (In 1984 railings were installed to channel those who fulfill a vow through the crowd to a position in front of the altar. The priests keep the file of worshippers moving, and the press of the crowds has been considerably reduced as a result.) The priests who receive offerings of milk, work without respite. Cubes of camphor incense flare brightly, and the air is suffused with the mixed scents of crushed jasmine, sweat, warm milk offerings, and the fragrance of burning incense. It is a scene of great emotional intensity: the climactic moment of obeisance before the god. Amid the press of bodies, amazed tourists hold their cameras high in the hope of catching a shot of the priests extracting one of the great spears that some devotees have inserted through their cheeks.

When a devotee arrives with a spear through his cheeks, a priest gestures to him, indicating where he should stand. If the devotee is agitated or exhausted, the priest seems to communicate wordlessly, attuning his gestures so that they match those of the devotee, and then modulating them to calm him. Several men support the devotee while the priest presses vibhuti to the wounds as he removes the spear and the hooks and skewers of vow fulfillment. I have never seen blood flow at this moment.[23]

Outside the temple, the exhausted devotees rest quietly until they are ready to set out on their journey home. They appear to have returned to the normal consciousness of everyday life. On the return journey, groups of friends greet each other gaily.

## CALLING OUT THE SHARES

The devotions and austerities of vow fulfillment and the Thaipusam pilgrimage are framed by the gala chariot processions of the Nattukottai Chettiar Murugan Temple. In the late afternoon of the day after Thaipusam, the Nattukottai Chettiars begin to gather at the temple on Waterfall Road, the men standing to the right side of the deity and the women to the left, on the *mandapa* (covered porch or hall) in front of the inner sanctum. When the priest has performed the puja before the image of Murugan that is to be placed in the chariot, the chairman of the committee that manages the temple begins to call out the names of the heads of the families who belong to the Nattukottai Chettiar lineage. As each man steps forward, he is given prasad, half a coconut decorated with flowers and set in a chalice. Temple committee members are honored by being given cloths *(pattu)* as well (on *panku kurutal,* or "calling out the shares," see McGilvray 1983, 100).

As dusk falls, the men of the temple committee prepare to take the image of Murugan to the chariot that stands outside. As on the first day, Murugan is accompanied by his musicians, and by his royal escort, bearing his scepters, fly whisks, fans, and torch, the emblems of royalty. The outer courtyard of the temple is full of worshippers. There are many Chinese families who make simple offerings. Some follow Hindu practice and offer a coconut with burning camphor; others give blossoms or a banana and put money in the collection box. Many simply light a joss stick. The signs that request visitors to remove their shoes in the temple are not observed by the Chinese worshippers, Western tourists, or the soldiers and police on duty to control crowds and provide protection for the valuable image. On this day, it seems that concern about pollution of the temple is suspended.

The streets outside the temple are also filled with worshippers. Thousands of coconuts have been piled by the side of the road, and more thaneer pandals have been erected. At the crossroads in front of the shrine of Muniswara, the chariot of Murugan pauses to receive offerings. Arumugan carries the lamp and bells used for worship in the shrine through the press of worshippers. His assistants follow with trays of offerings and garlands. The procession circumambulates the chariot three times, and then the offerings and implements of worship are passed to the priest on the chariot. The lamp of Muniswara's shrine is lighted anew from the lamp of Murugan, and the offering trays are returned with new garlands and scarves for the image of Muniswara. This ritual might be interpreted as the tribute of a lower deity to the higher deity, Murugan. However, the lighting of the lamp of Muniswara from the lamp of Murugan suggests the ultimate unity of all forms of the deity in Hinduism.

The popularity of the evening chariot procession has increased enormously in the past decade. In 1980 crowds were small, and families greeted each other as they came with offering trays to see the splendor of the chariot with its silver dome and spire, which sparkled in the gleam of electric lights. The women of the Chettiar caste, richly dressed in a glorious array of gold-brocaded silk saris and their necks and arms aglitter with gold jewelry, walked together just in front of the chariot under the glow of pressure lamps. These were carried by the poorest Tamils of Penang, so that this procession almost seemed a pageant portraying the uneven distribution of wealth among Murugan's worshippers.

By 1985 the Nattukottai Chettiars were lost in the large crowds that had gathered outside the temple, which each year included more and more Penang Chinese families. The Chettiar women no longer formed a procession in front of the chariot. A few devotees who had chosen this night for their pilgrimage to the hillside temple followed the chariot in the early evening and then circled back to the Penang Hill Murugan Temple. Throughout the night, the procession wends its way through George Town until it arrives at the shop-house on Penang Street where the chariot will be stored. As day breaks the priest of the Nattukottai Chettiar Murugan Temple performs a final puja, and Murugan's worshippers begin their journey home.

## 5

## RITUALS AND POLITICS

During the Japanese occupation of Malaysia, the Thaipusam festival was not celebrated. After the war, the British banned the procession of Murugan along with the festivals of the Chinese community, because they feared that "communist agitators" might use them as a cover for civil disturbances.[1] In the late 1950s, toward the end of the so-called communist Emergency (June 1948–July 1960), the Nattukottai Chettiars petitioned for permission to conduct a small-scale chariot procession on Thaipusam. This was granted, on the condition that the chariot did not stop for offerings. After the Emergency, restrictions on the festival were discontinued as the Malaysian government came to regard religion instead as a safeguard against the spread of communism. The Thaipusam festival has now become an important tourist attraction.

Since the early 1960s, when the celebration was resumed, every year more and more of Malaysia's Hindu Tamils have participated in the worship of Murugan on Thaipusam. The number of people fulfilling vows at the Batu Caves in Kuala Lumpur increased sixfold in twenty years, from roughly five hundred in 1961 to over three thousand in 1980 (Kirkup 1963, 249; *New Straits Times*, January 28, 1980). In Penang, over one thousand devotees fulfilled vows at the

Penang Hill Murugan Temple in 1980, and two hundred thousand people participated in the celebration. This was far more than twice the number reported ten years earlier (*Straits Echo* and *Times of Malaya*, January 23, 1970).[2] During this period, Thaipusam festivals had also been established in other cities, such as Ipoh, where the number of people fulfilling vows increased from one hundred fifty in 1970 to eight hundred in 1980. The increasing popularity of the festival has led to Thaipusam being declared an official holiday in the state of Kedah (*National Echo*, January 28, 1980).

When I asked those who attended the festival why more and more people were choosing to fulfill vows to Murugan at Thaipusam, people explained that the festival reflected Murugan's power (that he answered the prayers of his worshippers), and this attracted still more people to become his devotees. However, a member of the committee appointed to oversee the Penang Hill Murugan Temple and the Thaipusam festival offered a different explanation when he explained to a reporter: "The stresses and strains of modern living, with its attendant anxiety, fright and restlessness are turning more people to religion" (*New Straits Times*, January 21, 1980).[3] Following this suggestion, I decided to see how the changing political and social conditions of Tamils in Malaysia were connected to their religious practices.

My investigations led me to see that the increase in popularity of the Thaipusam festival was due in part to the decline of vow fulfillment to an Amman goddess and the disappearance of the goddess festival on many Malaysian estates. To understand the decline in the tradition of goddess worship, I turned to studies of Indian estate laborers in Malaysia by the sociologists R. K. Jain (1970) and Paul Wiebe and S. Mariappen (1978), and to anthropological works on the village goddess festival in India, particularly that of M. Moffatt (1979). They show how the tradition of village goddess worship and the institution of the goddess temple served to legitimate and to enforce social relations based on caste, and the power of a dominant caste or of estate owners and managers. Viewed from this sociological perspective, the turn to Murugan appeared a practice through which laborers could resist the hegemony of powerful elites and evoke the egalitarian values associated with pilgrimage temples and bhakti devotionalism.

I then looked at the role of goddess temples in Penang. The histories I collected of urban temples showed that these temples were the locus of a potentially democratic politics, in which community leaders sought election to the temple committee. Communities organized on the basis of temple membership could be mobilized to obtain political goals, such as the establishment of a Tamil school or the eradication of practices of caste discrimination. This analysis recalls E. P. Thompson's study of the role of Protestant sects in *The Making of the English Working Class* (1963). Thompson showed how class consciousness is shaped by culture—"embodied in [culturally given] traditions, value-systems, ideas, and institutional forms" (1963, 10).[4] According to Thompson, class consciousness arises when changing social relationships, institutions, and ideas lead people to feel and to articulate the identity of their collective interests, as determined by the productive relations to which they are subject. Thus, class is not perceived as a significant component of people's identity until the operation of a capitalist economy affects their lives in a way that leads them to see their problems in terms of their class position. This is an uneven process of growing political awareness, reflected in the growing popularity of Murugan and the decline of the goddess tradition among Malaysian Tamils.

## THE AMMAN GODDESS AND CASTE

### The Amman Temple: Ethical Order and Relations of Oppression

The village Amman goddess of southern India—like Durga and Kali, the warrior forms of the Great Goddess—is a fierce goddess. She is portrayed with her lance and a defeated demon under her feet, and usually she demands blood sacrifice. She is also goddess of the land and of the water that brings fertility. This is reflected by her green color (in many images) and in rituals associated with her worship. For example, at the fire-walking festival of the Sri Kaliamman Temple in Penang, the mood of the goddess is tested by a ritual that involves sprouting seeds scattered at the base of the temple flag pole. The priest explained, "If the sprouts grow graciously and healthily, it is a good sign to go ahead with the festival. If they are weak and dull, it is a bad omen" (see also Babb 1975b, 134).

The Amman goddess is addressed as Mother, and all villagers worship the Amman goddess of their settlement as her children (Daniel 1984). However, as patrons of her temple, the dominant land-owning lineage claimed a special relation to her and (usually) worshipped her as their lineage deity (Moffatt 1979, 246–89; Pfaffenberger 1982, 165–66). The lineage deities of low and untouchable service castes are the semi-demonic warrior deities who guard the Amman temple (see Moffatt 1979, 271). These deities—typically portrayed with bulging eyes, vigorous mustache, and protruding belly (all signs of a greedy and violent nature)—are hot, angry, potentially dangerous spirits, but when subdued by the goddess they become her devotees, guardians of her temple, and protectors of the village. The imagery of the victorious goddess who has defeated dangerous demonic spirits, and transformed them into protective ones, can be interpreted as representing and legitimizing the social and political relations by which powerful, high status groups in the village dominate those of low or untouchable caste, who work the land (Dumont 1959b).

The festival of the village goddess temple appears to have functioned to mediate relations between high-caste and service-caste villagers with different political and social interests. Celebration of the goddess festival required the cooperation of all castes, high and low, and thus a certain degree of social harmony among castes. All villagers had to contribute to pay for the expenses of the celebration.

Furthermore, each caste had a traditional role in the festival; indeed, members of some untouchable castes had particularly important roles. If the necessary cooperation of the whole community could not be obtained, the festival might have to be postponed (see Dirks 1994). This would place the prosperity of everyone in jeopardy, for personal suffering and widespread misfortune due to drought and disease were understood to be consequences of the failure of villagers to accord respectful worship to their goddess (Moffatt 1979, 246–89; Pfaffenberger 1979, 253–70; Pfaffenberger 1980, 196–219).

The relationship of lower-caste villagers to the Amman goddess—and the social and economic institutions of caste hierarchy she represented—was ambivalent. As described by Moffatt, goddess worship in a Tamil village was characterized by a dynamic relation of coercion and cooperation between dominant and subservient groups. Strain between dominant and lower castes often led to dissension over preparations for the annual festival of the goddess temple. If lower castes were treated badly, they could refuse to cooperate in the festival. Moffatt (1979) records a dialogue between villagers and a pujari who is possessed by the goddess that reflects the relations of cooperation and coercion that characterize village life. The goddess complains about the worship offered her in the village: "You only worship me when you need me. You do not come when you should." Another pujari speaking for the villagers responds, "That is not so great a fault. Are you worried about your car festival [being omitted this year]? We will do that properly for you next year. . . . If there is no rain . . . if there is nothing in this village, then nobody will light even a quarter-anna light for you. If not even drinking water exists, who will bother to spend a quarter-anna?" (279), reminding the goddess that, although the villagers owe the goddess worship for her bounty, she too is dependent on her worshippers.

The villagers try to secure the love of the goddess by showing her their devotion. When they think she is angry, they try to appease her. They try to control her through ritual, and if necessary, they may humiliate and insult her. As villagers try to bribe or shame the goddess into caring for them as a good mother should, they can symbolically express resentment against the dominant caste, reminding them that the high castes are also dependent on the lower service castes and should care for them appropriately.

Recruitment of Tamil laborers to go to colonial Malaya to work on rubber estates was organized under the kangani system, named for the title of the Tamil boss who recruited a work crew in India and then acted as the crew's overseer on the plantation in Malaysia. The laborers arrived indebted to the kangani for their passage and the expenses incurred in setting up a household (Wiebe and Mariappen 1978, 6). Few had any chance of finding other employment, even after the expiration of the indenture period (usually from five to seven years). Only very gradually was this system reformed (Arasaratnam 1979, 60–65). In 1907 the Tamil Immigration Fund was set up, assessing estate employers to pay for transportation, medical aid, and repatriation of laborers. The practice of treating a laborer's passage as an advance to be deducted from wages was made illegal in 1913. The Government of India Emigration Act of 1922 suggested wage guidelines and welfare safeguards for immigrant laborers in Malaya, but its impact was minimal.

In the 1930s, under the impact of worldwide economic depression, the profitability of plantation agriculture in colonial Malaya declined steeply, and wages for plantation workers were cut 40–60 percent. In the following two or three years, 130,000 immigrant laborers were repatriated to India (Hatley 1969, 460). Only in 1935 did the colonial government pass legislation aimed at correcting abuses in labor relations on the estates. In short, on the plantations of colonial Malaya, Tamil laborers found themselves dependent on European estate owners or managers and their intermediaries, the kangani overseers and kirani clerical staff, just as they had once been dependent on land-owning castes in India (Jain 1970). Like the dominant land-owning caste in a Tamil village, the kangani and kirani wielded power primarily through the institution of the goddess temple. They organized the collection of funds for building the temple and formed the temple management committee. When a laborer committed an offense, the temple committee would decide on a punishment or would levy a fine payable to the temple.

The annual festival of the goddess temple was the most important social and religious occasion of the year on the estate. Jain (1970) has shown how the festival reflected the power relations to which Tamil plantation workers were subjected. He quotes a rubber tapper's account:

> On Tipavali [Dipavali] day, each tapper had to pay a sum of $5 to the head kangany. At the time of worship only he [the kangany] should get into a trance; if anyone else went into it, the head kangany would beat him. The head kangany collected from the coolies a sum of $3,000 or $4,000 but he would buy a goat for $7 only. He would cut the goat into many parts and each coolie would be given one latex-cup full of meat as his share. Should a coolie ask for more, he would be beaten. (277)

Jain shows how the role of the European boss in the annual goddess festival paralleled the role of the dominant caste in a southern Indian village (see also Wiebe and Mariappen 1978, 143; Arasaratnam 1979, 172). The estate manager paid half the expenses for the festival, and he, along with other colonial officials whom he invited, were guests of honor at the fire-walking ceremony. On the second day of the festival the laborers carried offerings, which might include gold jewelry, to the manager, who like the god of the festival "was garlanded with jasmine and marigold and sprayed with attar of roses" and entertained with folk dances (Jain 1970, 291). Jain quotes the account of Faucounnier, a French visitor to Malaya in the 1920s:

> Suddenly from the forest edge burst forth a machine-gun volley of tomtoms and the strident arrows of trumpet calls. A joyous crowd scattered beneath the palms.

> The handsome Mukkan, clad only in a scarlet loin cloth, balanced upon his head a large tray of presents: goat flesh, bananas, shaddocks, little green limes that bring good luck and bottles of beer and gin, without which latter it would seem that happiness for Europeans is incomplete. (1970, 291–92)

The celebration concluded with a presentation by the estate manager of sweets and money to the laborers and their families. This counter-presentation was modeled on the concluding act of worship of a Hindu deity, the distribution of prasad, the food offering that symbolizes divine grace given to worshippers by the deity (Stutley and Stutley 1977, 232). Thus the manager symbolically reaffirmed his role as protector and provider for his laborers. Jain (1970) describes these rituals as "a symbolic reaffirmation of the tie between the laborer and the European boss" (292). He points out that Tamil laborers addressed a good manager as *amma appa* (mother father) and that the ritual of the goddess festival, in which Tamil plantation laborers were represented as children, accorded with the paternalistic values of the colonial planters and helped to mask the abuses of the colonial system (285; see also Wiebe and Mariappen 1978, 103). One could find no better illustration of the Durkheimian perspective on religion, which emphasizes the way a religious tradition provides a model "of and for the social world" (in Clifford Geertz's apt phrase).

The Japanese occupation of Malaya was devastating in its impact on the Tamil plantation labor force. The meager security offered by the plantation disappeared, and for many—especially women, children, and the elderly—life was reduced to a struggle to secure food and survive. Between 1940 and 1947, the Indian proportion in the population of the colony of Malaya dropped from 14 to 10 percent (Arasaratnam 1979, 111). The annual festival of the estate temple and other religious observances were abandoned under the pressure of Japanese demands for greater amounts of labor. The Japanese conscripted healthy laborers for work on the Siam Railway. Very few survived. An estate laborer interviewed by Jain reported that he was one of three survivors out of the one hundred laborers sent to "Siam" from the estate where he had worked (1970, 306). To escape conscription, some plantation workers fled to the jungle and mounted low-level resistance to the Japanese occupying army. Others joined the Indian National Army, sponsored by the Japanese to liberate India from British rule. Limited as these options were, they were the first significant choices most Tamil laborers who immigrated to colonial Malaya had ever been able to make.

The experience of the Japanese occupation was very different for the white-collar kirani. The Japanese made them managers of the estates where they had worked as clerks. Many were attracted by the pro-Asian propaganda of the Japanese administration and preferred to identify with the Japanese rather than with the Tamil laborers on the estate. As the war progressed, the Japanese applied ever greater pressure on the kirani to wring further sacrifices from Tamil laborers, which exacerbated tensions between estate laborers and the kirani. The Tamil laborers remaining on the plantations gave such clandestine support as they could to the guerrillas, who were dependent on them for supplies and cover. In return, the guerrillas often attacked kirani who abused the power given them by the Japanese and harassed rich Chinese and Indian businessmen who supported the Japanese (Jain 1970, 304). By the end of the war, however, because of many incidents of public humiliation and cruelty by the Japanese, the kirani generally welcomed the return of the British. The ironic fiction of kirani loyalty to British interests in colonial Malaya was perpetrated by British planters, who were faced with a severe shortage of trained personnel and who therefore needed to retain the kirani as managers of the estates (309). The kirani were given credit for saving the plantations from Japan's scorched-earth policy.

On the other hand, the guerrilla fighters, when they emerged from the jungle to claim the reward they believed was due them for their anti-Japanese activities, found they were viewed with suspicion. The estate laborers who had joined the Indian National Army (INA) had been exposed to the anti-Western and nationalist propaganda of the Japanese-sponsored Indian Independence League and, like the guerrilla fighters, no longer took for granted the superiority of the British or the legitimacy of British colonialism.[5] Many Tamil laborers returned to the plantations with a new political awareness. They organized to protest the inadequate food and low wages on the plantations.

British anxiety about "communist" guerrilla forces remaining in the jungle shaped their response to Tamil estate workers' efforts to organize unions and reform conditions on the plantations. The British accused the leaders of being communist agitators. Jain interviewed estate laborers in the 1960s, who reported that the guerrilla leaders invited to London for the victory celebration were arrested after their return to Malaya because they began to organize unions on the plantation (1970, 317–18). Fueled by the French Indochina War, fears of a communist uprising grew, and the so-called communist Emergency was declared. General Secretary of the National Union of Plantation Workers (NUPM), P. P. Narayanan, described the period of the Emergency as one of "fear of terrorist activities; fear of arrests and deportation by Government; [and] fear of employers" (quoted in Jain 1970, 322).

Supported by a boom in rubber prices in the 1950s, British estate managers set up management-sponsored unions and attempted to reclaim the loyalty of plantation laborers through traditional means (Arasaratnam 1979, 137–40). On the estate studied by Jain in the 1960s, kangani-kirani elites held prominent roles in the management-sponsored union and dominated the committee *(panchayat)* established to govern the estate. One of the first acts of this panchayat was to raise funds by deductions from the laborers' wages to build a new temple for the estate. However, these efforts to reestablish traditional structures of domination were resisted by Tamil laborers, who were now more politically sophisticated. In 1953, an organizer from a union banned under the Emergency organized a protest against the power wielded by the kirani and kangani through the estate temple.

Alleging that the temple committee leadership had misappropriated funds contributed for the celebration of the annual festival of the goddess, he attempted to organize the celebration of Thaipusam as an alternative to the festival of the Amman goddess. This conflict was only resolved three years later when the organizer was fired for being a troublemaker (Jain 1970, 324–27). Without his leadership, the celebration of Thaipusam on the estate was abandoned.

Similarly, on a plantation studied by Wiebe and Mariappen (1978), an ongoing controversy over the role of Adi-Dravida (Original Dravidians, a title given to formerly untouchable castes) in the festival of the goddess was a pretext for local resistance to the management control of the labor union and to the dominance of kirani and kangani in the estate temple. In 1974 a young man first challenged the kangani-kirani leadership in a union election, arguing that the "old guard" was more attuned to the interests of the management than to the interests of the estate laborers.[6] With the support of the laborers, he won the election. He then accused his kangani opponent, who was also the chairman of the management committee for the estate Amman temple, of financial mismanagement of temple funds. The young man, who was of "clean" (or Shudra) caste, argued for reforms that would permit *Adi-Dravida* worshippers to participate in the serving of food at the festival of the goddess. On this estate, the kirani—who followed a reformed Hinduism rooted in bhakti devotionalism, which rejects caste distinction—supported reform of the festival. In this instance, as in the events described by Jain, the estate management succeeded in defusing the movement to unseat kirani-kangani leaders. The kirani reformer was made chairman of a new temple committee, and the young man who had initiated the protest eventually left the estate to find employment in the city. However, Wiebe and Mariappen report that estate laborers continued to turn away from the ritual tradition of the Amman temple of the estate. By 1975, one-third of them preferred to go to nearby towns to participate in the celebration of Thaipusam (1978, 142–60).

The estate laborers' resistance to participating in an institution implicated in the relations of domination persisting on estates thus seems to have resulted in the decline of the tradition of Amman worship in the estate temple. In some cases worshippers have retained their allegiance to an Amman goddess, but they now choose to worship and fulfill vows to her at a temple in town rather than at estate temples. This is shown by the increasing popularity of the festival of the Mariamman Temple in Bukit Mertajam (a town on the mainland about thirty minutes from Penang), which has replaced the fire-walking festival in many of the surrounding estate temples and is second only to the Thaipusam celebration in the number of devotees it attracts for vow fulfillment.

In worship of the Amman goddess, the power of dominant castes and the forces of nature were symbolically conflated, so that protest against the suffering of low-caste and untouchable villagers was fused with a resentment against fate. An incident on a Malaysian rubber estate, described by Wiebe and Mariappen (1978), makes this point:

[A drought had caused hard times on the estate] so the Indians made a representation of a woman, an effigy hugely proportioned in bosom and bottom, then dragged it around the community on a cart. The young and the men made lewd remarks as it passed, the women spat at it and threw things. A good deal of humour was involved. But so too were other things. One of our respondents explained the consequences of the action of the people like this: "The (goddess of rain) saw what we were doing and was ashamed of the way we were suffering. So the rains came." (143)

We might imagine that implicit in this ritual is an appeal to the estate owners and managers that they do something to mitigate the suffering of estate workers due to the drought. However, in the tradition of goddess worship, the natural order is not distinguished from a social and political order established by human beings, and consequently, dominant groups cannot be held directly responsible for the ways they benefit from—and low status people suffer from—existing political and social relations.

## Urban Temples: Community and Conflict

In the urban environment of Penang, Amman temples have sometimes become a locus of community organization and political activism. One example of this is the Sri Raja Mariamman Temple built by the followers of Swami Ramadasar in Kampong Java Baru. Another is the campaign of the Hindu Mahajana Sangam to promote the celebration of Citraparvam. In urban Amman temples, different groups struggle to control the temple through the temple management committee, and decisions about ritual practices made by the temple committee reflect the values that organize community relations. The conflict over the hiring of a new priest for the Sri Muthu Mariamman Temple in Lorong Kulit is an example of how much the form of ritual matters. In all these cases, temple politics reflect tensions over caste (and class) differences, and disputes suggest that people implicitly understand the ways in which caste or class hierarchy is ritually legitimated.

The recent history of the Amman temple of the Bukit Glugor estate shows how social change has affected the lives of estate workers and rendered obsolete the tradition of goddess worship as practiced in an estate temple. However, in this case, the temple of the Bukit Glugor was reestablished as a focus of community organization on a more autonomous basis. Bukit Glugor is located at the edge of George Town by the side of the road leading to the airport. When the estate was enveloped by the urban sprawl of George Town on one side and by the establishment of the University Sains Malaysia on the other, the land was sold, to be subdivided for a housing development. The estate laborers were given housing sites near the temple. As the community was gradually absorbed into the urban labor force, attendance at temple worship declined, and the temple fell into disrepair.

After a few years, a wealthy Tamil businessman approached the community and offered to build a new hall for the temple. When I asked why he would donate money to a temple where he did not even worship, a member of the temple committee explained that the new temple hall would bear the donor's name. With the status of temple patron, the businessman would deserve honor and respect and acquire privileges that enhanced his power. As Washbrook puts it:

> The rewards for making donations consisted of rights to participate in certain ceremonies in certain ways and to receive gifts and honours from the gods. These, in turn, established the position of the recipient families and *jati* groups in the local social hierarchy and underwrote their relative positions of privilege. (In Frankel and Rao 1989, 234)[7]

Consequently, the small group of worshippers who still attended the Bukit Glugor temple viewed this offer of patronage with considerable suspicion. Appealing to the idea that, as they put it, their "fathers and grandfathers had built and worshipped in the temple," they decided to decline the patron's donation.[8] Fortunately, one of them won a sum of money in the lottery (which was undoubtedly interpreted to be a sign of the will of the goddess). He contributed this to the temple so that a new statue of Amman might be purchased and the building repaired. The community spirit generated by these events led to a revival of support for the temple and the reintroduction of the fire-walking festival in honor of the goddess.

In urban temples, as in the goddess tradition of estate temples, there is often a tendency to interpret political and social problems in religious terms as punishment of the community for violations of morality. An example of this is a dispute that broke out in 1980 over the failed fire-walking ceremony for the goddess of the Sri Maha Mariamman Temple on Ayer Hitam Road.[9] This temple is said to have been built in 1920 by a group of deserters from the Indian Army, a story that suggests the founders were nationalists who opposed the policy of Gandhi and other nationalist leaders who had decided to support the British war effort in World War I.[10] During the Japanese occupation in WWI, guerrilla fighters hid in the temple, and Chinese Malaysians also sought shelter there.[11] After the war, the community that worshipped in the temple was gradually enveloped by the expansion of George Town. Today the temple stands next to a major thoroughfare leading out of the city and is surrounded by blocks of working-class flats. By the end of the 1970s, unemployment among Tamil youths in Malaysia was becoming a serious problem, and groups of unemployed youths had taken to hanging out at the temple. In 1979, the temple management committee decided to do something about the situation and began to raise funds to make improvements in the temple. During the fire-walking ceremony the following year (1980), a rainstorm occurred. One committee member used this unpropitious event, which was taken as a sign of the anger of the goddess, to attack the jobless youths. He claimed that the goddess was offended because "gangs consorted at the temple planning revenge on their enemies." This provoked another faction of the community to accuse the temple committee of being responsible for the anger of the goddess because they refused to "admit mistakes" and correct them (the mistakes referred to were rituals distinguishing among worshippers on the basis of caste).

Another example of divine intervention comes from the Sri Kaliamman Temple on Air Hitam Road. This temple was built at the end of the nineteenth century by laborers who worked in road construction and as toddy tappers, shepherds, and milk sellers—all untouchable occupations.[12] The first temple was a simple shrine with a thatched roof. Later, the community raised money and built a more permanent structure. Those who worship at the temple today take pride that their ancestors built the temple without the aid of the colonial government or any other authority. The first fire-walking was held in 1943, when a devotee went into trance and was possessed by the goddess, who demanded ritual vow fulfillment be included in her festival.[13] During the war, the temple was used for storage and as a shelter during the bombing of Penang. In the 1950s, the temple committee raised money and bought the land next to the temple to build a school. In 1957, the Rajaji Tamil School was incorporated into the national educational system.

In the 1970s the Penang State government decided that the Sri Kaliamman Temple, which was located just beside a major traffic artery, had to be moved so the road could be widened. The temple management committee could not find a site in the neighborhood to build a new temple. (If the temple were built too far away, it would no longer function as a community temple.) The conflict with the city government was exacerbated by restrictions that the city placed on the procession of the goddess. Traditionally the chariot procession began at dawn and lasted until midnight or into the early hours of the next morning. The city restricted the procession to within three or four miles of the temple and required that it return to the temple before dusk, on the grounds that it contributed to traffic congestion.[14]

As the community prepared for the annual festival of the goddess in 1980, conflict with city government led to concerns about the future of the temple and the community. Worshippers recalled that the previous year a gray cat had run across the burning embers of the fire-walk pit. While in a state of trance, one of the fire-walkers had interpreted this as a bad omen, and the other fire-walkers had not been allowed to cross the fire pit. To ensure the support of the goddess for the forthcoming year, the committee decided the festival must begin with a week of purificatory rituals *(punniathanam)* "to wash away pollution." A Tirukaliamman Maha Abhisheka was to be performed. This would involve the whole community in a ritual that required their organized cooperation and that enhanced the prestige of their temple. The committee also decided to add a second chariot with images of Ganesh and Murugan to the procession of the goddess. Like estate laborers, urban Tamils see these deities as increasingly relevant to their lives.

Both the tradition of Amman worship and the worship of Murugan emphasize devotion and involve vow fulfillment, and differences between the traditions are not always well defined.[15] A vow to Amman typically follows the formula, "O Amman, see to it that such-and-such illness leaves, and I shall present a special cooling offering for you, at such-and-such a time" (Pfaffenberger 1977, 199), as does a vow to Murugan, "If you, O Murugan, will do such-and-such, I shall, upon receipt of the benefit *(palan)*, journey personally to your abode in Kataragama and give vow fulfillment" (309).[16] Appeasement of demonic spirits involves a similar kind of bargain. A pujari possessed by a semi-demonic warrior spirit demands blood sacrifice: "Give me a goat at such-and-such a place, where I am staying, or else I will take a life myself" (270). When properly worshipped, such a spirit is expected to respond to the needs and requests of his devotees and become their protector.

However, there are important differences in these ritual interactions. The Amman goddess and the semi-demonic spirits that possess people are pictured as demanding worship, and they must be appeased. The relationship of the goddess to her worshippers is oppressive, mirroring the oppressive social relations of caste hierarchy. When the pujari is possessed by the Amman goddess, he speaks with her authority. In the goddess festival, every person has a prescribed role according to their caste status, and the ritual is meant to benefit the entire community. Amman's worshippers seek to appease her or to earn merit *(punya)* so that they will be granted a better life in the future.

Vow fulfillment to Murugan rests on a very different conception of the relationship between the deity and the worshipper, and different social relations among his worshippers. Murugan does not demand worship. No one speaks with his authority when possessed. Rituals in the bhakti tradition do not require community participation and do not discriminate on the basis of caste. Each devotee has a direct and individual relationship with the god. Devotees seek (or repay) a boon that will bring them a better life in this world. Worshippers say that the goddess shows her mercy when she throws the end of her sari across the fire pit so that her devotees will not be burned (see Babb 1974; Pfaffenberger 1979, 259–60). By contrast, Murugan's devotees demonstrate their worthiness to receive the trance-blessing of the god.

Whereas the poorest and least educated Tamils have tended to stay on estates, where they hope that the traditional relations of dependency will provide a minimal security, a significant proportion of the Tamil working class have become wage laborers in a capitalist market economy. Success in this environment requires that they be more assertive, more self-reliant, and individually responsible for their families. These values can be seen in the legends of Murugan. For those who successfully compete with others for good jobs, wage labor has created the possibility for upward mobility and the rejection of the stigma of low-caste or untouchable origin. The egalitarianism of bhakti devotionalism fits well with the egalitarianism of the wage labor market in a capitalist economy.

## MURUGAN AND CLASS

### The Temple Reform Movement

Bhakti devotionalism has also proved to be an excellent vehicle for upper-class efforts to reform the religious practices of working-class Tamils. The Pan-Malayan Dravidian Association (PMDA) for the reform of Hinduism in Malaysia was established in 1931. Inspired by the Dravida Kazhagam (predecessor of the Dravida Munetra Kazhagam [DMK], the Dravidian progressive party that has dominated politics in Tamilnadu), the PMDA opposed the idea of untouchability and supported the temple entry movement to allow people of all castes to enter temples. In 1938–1939, the reformers also initiated a campaign to abolish animal sacrifice in major temples. After the war, they renewed their efforts and largely succeeded in eliminating animal sacrifice.[17] The large-scale slaughter of goats that formerly took place at the Amman temple in Butterworth, for example, no longer occurs. However, at Amman temples where the annual festival of the goddess is celebrated with ritual fire-walking, animal sacrifices are still performed, though often after dark and away from the eyes of most worshippers. For example, in 1980, a black goat was sacrificed at midnight after the fire-walking at the Sri Kaliamman Temple in Penang. The pujari explained that the blood of the goat mixed with white rice was an offering to the fierce deities who guard the goddess. Chickens are also sacrificed at small shrines throughout Malaysia.

The reformers have also attempted to convince temples to ban fire-walking and forms of vow fulfillment that they regard as "primitive." However, these campaigns have met with resistance. One reason temple committees resist reforms is economic: a major source of income in temples not owned by a subcaste lineage are the fees associated with offerings that accompany vow fulfillment. The committees that manage such temples argue that if they banned vow fulfillment (with a consequent loss of income), worshippers would simply go to some other temple with their offerings (or they would build new temples). Another reason for the failure of the reformers' campaign was that they had no way of enforcing a ban on particular practices without seeking government sanctions, and as members of a religious minority in an Islamic state, they were reluctant to involve the Malaysian government (Arasaratnam 1979, 172–74). The reformers chose instead to promote education in modern interpretations of Hindu philosophical and religious writings that emphasize the spiritual aspects of worship.

In order to create a more "religious atmosphere" on Thaipusam, the reformers on the committee that manages the Penang Hill Murugan Temple and oversees the Thaipusam festival have convinced the Chettiars to give up the amusement park concession that formerly was set up in the yard of the Nattukottai Chettiar Murugan Temple.[18] They say that this will encourage a more spiritual focus in those who attend the festival. They also claim that the practices to which they object—such as vow fulfillment, which involves piercing the body—are not part of authentic Hindu tradition.[19] Unable to ban such practices, the reformers have made rules limiting the height of kavadis and restricting the length of spears used by devotees to pierce the cheeks, rules that they say will protect devotees from harm in the thick crowds.

However, the reformers express considerable frustration over the limited impact of their educational campaigns. In 1980, the Mentri Besar (or prime minister) of Selangor State appealed to Hindu religious leaders to set up a council "to help control temples from mushrooming all over the place." Referring to a recent Thaipusam celebration where pleas to devotees "not to use spikes to fulfill penance were totally ignored," the minister said that it was particularly disheartening that "the younger generation . . . fail to understand the true concept of penance. Standing on razor-edged steel cutters, using rope whips to swirl in the air, screaming and jumping sky high are not religious acts of penance" *(Star Mail,* March 10, 1980). A leader of the reform movement, R. Karthigesu, acknowledged in an essay on Thaipusam: "It has been suggested by reformers that devotees should be encouraged to carry simple kavadis without elements of self-torture. However, the fact remains that the severity of the penance is on the rise and there seems to be no way that such exhibitions of devotion can be curbed" (n.d., 7). In the view of the reformers, working-class Tamils engage in forms of ritual vow fulfillment that involve piercing the body because they are uneducated. The reformers do not understand the ways in which working-class Tamils speak with their bodies in the language of ritual.

The devotees who pierce their body with the lance of Murugan demonstrate that they are worthy in the eyes of God and they show that Murugan can empower his devotees. Some of the images associated with ritual vow fulfillment may be interpreted as symbolic representations of the violence that holds the working-class (and low-caste) devotees of Murugan in submission, such as the coolie-demon who is subdued by Murugan or the devotees who pull chariots like beasts of burden. However, these images are subverted by the devotees' superhuman strength when they are possessed by Murugan. Every year at Thaipusam, national and local papers feature photographs of Murugan's devotees and recount the number of people who attend his festival; these articles and photos can be taken as a vivid reminder of the potential power of the oppressed.

When Hindu Tamil reformers in Malaysia stigmatize fire-walking and vow fulfillment that involves piercing the body as primitive, they lay the ideological foundations for the social control of the body that is required of workers in a capitalist society—in the apt phrase of Foucault (1980), "docile bodies" are shaped. With their claim to know the authentic Hindu ritual practices, the reformers promote values rooted in the authority of Western scientific knowledge that legitimate the power of educated elites. Looked at in this way, we can see how Hindu festivals such as Thaipusam and the annual festival of the goddess temple provide occasions for the symbolic statement of political claims and representation of the ethical principles that underlie these claims. However, the political claims symbolically embedded in the ritual practices of Thaipusam are not made explicit but "remain hidden, even from the eyes of those engaged in it, under the guise of religious or philosophical oppositions" (Bourdieu 1977, 168). For this reason, the religious traditions of Malaysia's working-class Hindu Tamils may be described as proto-political. The representation of political understandings in a symbolic form permits differences to be glossed over as merely matters of theology. This works to the advantage of elite groups.

## The Political Uses of Thaipusam

In Malaysia, under the National Front Coalition (formerly the Alliance party) that has been in power since independence, politics have been conducted on the basis of ethnically based interests represented by the United Malays National Organization (UMNO), the Malaysian Chinese Association (MCA), and the Malaysian Indian Congress (MIC).[20] Politics grounded in class-based interests have been severely restricted.[21] The strategy of the MIC has been to "play the game on racial lines" (*FEER*, July 26, 1984). The participation of the MIC in the Alliance helps establish the legitimacy of the Front as a multiethnic party. In return, MIC leaders are granted cabinet positions, so long as they do not challenge the status quo of Malay dominance and so long as they deliver the votes of working-class Tamils in national elections. The implications of this situation for Malaysian Indians have been spelled out by the Malaysian Tamil economist R. Thillainathan:

> In addition to the market mechanism, employment and wealth distribution in Malaysia are now determined through the political process. . . . how much each group can get depends on its relative bargaining strength. The Malays do not only enjoy numerical superiority but also know how to remain united . . . the Chinese, though somewhat disunited, [have] a solid economic foundation to see them through many a crisis. On the other hand, the Indians are numerically weak and are overwhelmed emotionally and psychologically by their own petty differences and squabbles. . . . We can, of course, continue to play the game on racial lines in settling national priorities: otherwise we can work for the re-alignment of forces along lines of class . . . where the distributive shares are determined by reference to considerations of equity rather than of numbers. Or alternately, we have the option of going it alone, depending on our self-reliance and ingenuity to cope with our problems and respond to the challenge as best as possible. *(ibid.)*

MIC leaders have opted for a "corporate investment strategy," which primarily benefits Tamil elites. Critics within the party warn that this distracts the MIC from the "urgent and more necessary task: persuading the [UMNO] dominated government to give Malaysia's 1.3 million Indians a better educational and welfare deal" *(ibid.)*.

Having failed to provide leadership that would represent the interests of the poorest Tamil estate workers and laborers, who form the majority of Tamil voters,

MIC leaders have sought to win support through the medium of religious ritual. Mines and Gourishankar (1990) have observed of contemporary southern India: "Clearly, temple festivals are the stuff of politics, and the popularity of temple rituals depends on their value to secular leaders, who use them to establish their instrumental role among their fellows and their individual reputations as patrons of the public" (773).[22] Like the ruling party in Tamilnadu (the DMK), the MIC legitimates its leadership by a promise "to protect the temples and shrines of the 'Tamil' gods" (Washbrook in Frankel and Rao 1989, 255).[23] The MIC has worked to have Thaipusam declared a national holiday. In 1980, MIC president Datuk Samy Vellu addressed five hundred thousand worshippers at the Thaipusam celebration in Kuala Lumpur, saying that he would instruct all MIC members of parliament and state assemblymen to attend Thaipusam celebrations "to show that this is a festival they respect" (*New Straits Times*, February 5, 1980).

The analysis of the Thaipusam festival in terms of its political significance cuts many ways. On one hand, elites use the festival to secure the support of working-class Tamils and to legitimate their leadership. On the other hand, ritual vow fulfillment to Murugan on Thaipusam (and the egalitarian values it implies) can be interpreted as a nascent class consciousness, "embodied in [the] traditions, value-systems, ideas, and institutional forms" of bhakti devotionalism (Thompson 1963, 9–11). From a Marxist perspective, the liberal-pluralist state in Malaysia has become a venue for the pursuit of elite interests. However (and ironically), under the constitutionally guaranteed protection of religious freedom provided by the liberal nation-state, religion becomes a venue for protest by groups such as working-class Tamils, who are effectively excluded from participation in political decision making.[24] This analysis has significance for understanding the widespread phenomena of neo-fundamentalism in secular regimes controlled by elites.

## CONCLUSION

The reasons why more and more Tamils are choosing to fulfill vows to Murugan on Thaipusam are complex. In contrast to the Amman goddess who represents the relations of dependency in which a community appeals to a mother to care for her children, Murugan provides the model of the son who makes his own place in the world. This image has great appeal to the Tamils of Malaysia, not only as immigrants who have established themselves in a different country but also because, as the Malaysian economy develops, even relatively uneducated Tamil estate laborers can hope for a better life if they leave the estate and make a new life in the city. Just as the Amman goddess was associated with the power relations of the estate and the promise of dependent security, Murugan is associated with a more individualistic ethos in which each devotee has a personal relationship with the god and takes individual responsibility for his livelihood. The turn to bhakti devotionalism bears comparison to the Protestant Reformation in that it inculcates values that help people adapt to the individualism and competition that is required by a capitalist system.

In the tradition of devotional worship that is associated with Murugan in Malaysia, the moral worth of individuals is judged not by their status in society but, rather, by the sincerity of their love for god and their determination to prove themselves worthy of his love. This egalitarianism represents a challenge to the power relations of the estate and accords with the liberal democratic values that legitimate the modern Malaysian state. Thus political and professional elites also voice respect for the values represented by the worship of Murugan. However, these elites, claiming that they stand for the values represented by Murugan and bhakti devotionalism, also use the Thaipusam festival to appeal to working-class Tamils for their loyalty and political support and to justify their own power and high status.

Bhakti devotionalism also represents a challenge to the power structure instantiated by the political system of the modern Malaysian state in which elites control political power and enjoy the economic benefits that such power brings. In this regard, the turn to religion among working-class Tamils is a form of political protest. Thus bhakti devotionalism is like other religious movements, such as the Islamic Dakwah movement in Malaysia, that oppose the secular elites who control the state and maintain that social justice will come from obedience to god and the fulfillment of the ethical obligations set forth in a religious tradition. The ethical basis of the political protest implicit in the Thaipusam festival will be explored more fully as we turn our attention to the personal meanings of vow fulfillment to the devotees of Murugan.

6

## ARUL

## The Trance of Divine Grace

When I was leaving Penang in 1984, I went for a last visit to the shrine of Muniswara where I had watched the pujari Arumugam perform many exorcisms. This night I watched him induce a trance in each of the young men who regularly attended his services. As each youth approached the image of the deity to receive the sacred ash, Arumugam placed his hand on the youth's forehead. Some simply closed their eyes; others shuddered violently and appeared to be possessed by the fierce deity of the shrine. The trance usually lasted only a few minutes. On this occasion the priest beckoned to me to approach the deity and placed his hand on my forehead. I lowered my eyes and tried to pay attention to how I was feeling, but I did not close my eyes. I was not willing to give up my role of detached observer, and I was afraid of the angry explosions and stylized but violent drama of possession trance. After a few minutes I quietly returned to my place among the circle of onlookers, wondering what I had been afraid might happen.

What is trance? This question is strangely difficult to answer, not just because we do not understand human consciousness, but because trance is a phenomenon shaped by what people believe it to be. The anthropological literature shows that the capacity for trance is part of the human psycho-physiological heritage.

A recognized form of trance exists in virtually all societies, although (as Erika Bourguignon points out) the forms of trance vary widely, ranging from the highly stylized movements of the Balinese trance dancer to the chaotic howling and running about on all fours seen in trances at Kentucky revival meetings, the development of full-fledged secondary personalities among the Yoruba and Fon peoples, and the fugue states of the Ashanti shrine priests.[1] This chapter explores the relation of culturally given understandings of trance to the intra-psychic dynamics of individual selves. By comparing and contrasting the culturally constructed paradigm of hypnosis to the paradigm of possession trance that is part of the culture of the Hindu Tamils of Malaysia, we can better understand the meaning of the divine trance of arul to the devotees of Murugan.

Viewed from the outside, the defining characteristics of trance are structural—that is, they are culturally constructed. As Van der Walde has pointed out, a cross-cultural perspective shows that "trance and hypnotic states are nonspecific and are characterized by behavior which is molded by the preconceptions which the individual acquires from his culture about the nature of trance" (1968, 64; see also Kapferer 1983, 10).[2] In Enlightenment France, where the discoveries of Copernicus, Galileo, Kepler, Torricelli, and Newton had created the expectation that all mysteries would be explained by science, Franz Anton Mesmer "discovered" the principle of animal magnetism. Those who were convinced of his theory responded to Mesmer's magnets with trance states. However, scientists ordered by the French court to investigate Mesmer's work observed, "Imagination, without magnetism, produces convulsions [but] magnetism, without imagination, produces nothing."[3] The scientific commissioners reported of Mesmer's subjects, "Some are calm; tranquil and unconscious to any sensations; others cough, spit . . . or [experience] an universal burning and perspiration; a third class are agitated and tormented with convulsions . . . by shrieks, tears, hiccuppings and immoderate laughter" (quoted in Bliss 1986, 12; see also Darnton 1968). When the behavior characteristic of trance is not defined by a widely shared cultural construction of the phenomenon, the forms of trance are idiosyncratic, as is illustrated by Mesmer's experiments.

Cross-culturally, the most common explanation of trance is possession by some sort of supernatural agent—a demon, the devil, a god, or an ancestor spirit (Bourguignon in Spindler 1978, 502). Other culturally constructed explanations include witchcraft, divine ecstasy, mental illness, and hypnotism. These culturally given understandings determine to a large degree which people go into trance, on what occasions, how they behave while in trance, and how others will respond to an episode of trance. In cultures where trance is highly valued as a mystical experience or as a way of contacting the ancestors, people will seek out trance experiences, and their experience will be molded by the culturally recognized patterns of sacred trance. In such a culture, sacred trance may be restricted to a selected group of religious adepts or community leaders, and outbreaks of spontaneous trance that do not accord with this pattern will be seen as inspired by either the devil or demonic spirits. Thus the phenomenology of trance is extremely varied and deeply embedded in the social and cultural fabric.

Psychological studies also fail to provide a definitive characterization of the phenomena of trance. In *Theories of Hypnosis: Current Models and Perspectives* (1991), the editors write: "There is no question that hypnosis has eluded a single, simple definition. This is not surprising; the field is far from reaching a consensus about how to explain hypnotic phenomena" (3).[4] From a psychological perspective, the most striking characteristic of trance is the dissociation from normal consciousness. The term *dissociation* was first used by William James, who was referring to the work of Pierre Janet on hypnotic amnesia (1890, 1:682). For Janet, dissociation described systems of ideas that "are split off from the major personality and exist as a subordinate personality, unconscious but capable of becoming represented in consciousness through hypnosis" (quoted in Hilgard 1977, 5). If memories are brought to consciousness by way of the association of ideas, then memories and ideas not available through association are dissociated.[5] However, whereas trance typically involves a dissociation, not all dissociation is trance-related.

Psychological theories show that trance is related to our everyday experience of the world and culturally acceptable states of dissociation—such as slips of the tongue, states of reverie or daydreaming, highway trances in which we "wake up" at our freeway exit but do not remember having driven the last ten miles, and falling in love (when we recognize an attraction but cannot fully identify its nature). Trance can be a pathological symptom reflecting mental and emotional conflict, but it may also be used in many other ways that are personally productive and positively valued, such as meditation and trancelike states of artistic creativity. In this chapter, we explore what the anthropological and psychological literature can teach us about arul, the trance of divine grace experienced by the devotees of Murugan when they fulfill their vows on Thaipusam.

## AN ANTHROPOLOGICAL PERSPECTIVE ON TRANCE

### Trance as Performance

In anthropological studies, the metaphor of a dramatic performance is often applied to trance, because trance episodes appear to follow cultural scripts. I. M. Lewis, for example, describes Haitian voodoo ceremonies as "theaters, in which problems and conflicts relating to the life situations of the participants are dramatically enacted with great symbolic force" (1971, 195; see also Kapferer 1983). Those who are possessed by spirits appear to relax their normal inhibitions. However, the trance enactment creates only the illusion of a transgression of social norms, for the behavior that would normally be deviant is now not just permitted but prescribed and scripted. As Stanley Brandes puts it, in spirit possession performances and other culturally shaped expressions of disorder such as festivals and fiestas, "the display of bodily processes and the assumption of a presumably liberated, chaotic mode, in reality are closely associated with powerful social demands for conformity" (1988, 173).

The Hindu Tamils of Malaysia also recognize that trance rituals are like dramatic performances. Some of them, usually those with a Western education, even take a rather cynical view of trance as simply a performance, as in this anecdote related to me by a Brahmin friend. The annual celebration of Sri Rama Navami in the Persatuan Brahmin Malaysia Temple (Malaysian Brahmin Association Temple) in Kuala Lumpur included a ritual known as Anjanayar Utsavam (*Anjanayar* or *Anjaneyar* is an epithet of Hanuman, the monkey king who served Rama in the *Ramayana*), during which about thirteen men of the temple community would perform a dramatic foot-stomping, monkey-like dance, circling around an altar with a lamp, while the rest of the community chanted and clapped. Every year for as long as people could remember, one of these men would go into trance and dance wildly as if possessed by the monkey god Hanuman, until he fell in exhaustion. Then the sacred ash vibhuti would be applied to his forehead to bring him out of the trance. One year the man who went into trance could not participate, and the temple committee met to decide what to do. They felt that the trance performance was an expected part of the festival and that children needed to see such performances so that they would be convinced of the existence of the gods. Finally one man agreed to "go into trance" (*sami ati*, literally, "god-dance") for that year's Anjanayar Utsavam ritual. When the festival took place, however, a different man went into a real trance in which he made frightening monkey faces and danced so wildly that the committee members decided he must be restrained. My friend explained with some irony that this man was deeply religious so the god had chosen him to be possessed.

## The Social Functions of Trance: Divine and Demonic Possession

As this story suggests and as many ethnographic accounts confirm, trance has social functions as well as personal meanings. In her study of spirit possession in Haiti, Erika Bourguignon emphasizes the ways individuals may use trance to meet personal needs or to engage others in their problem:

> One of the principal rewards [of culturally sanctioned spirit possession] consists in the fact that the dissociated individual, playing the role of spirits, has a considerably enlarged scope of action. This may not be used only for immediate impulse gratification and for compensations for the frustrations of every day life, or to deal with the problems of others. More importantly, this enlarged scope of action provides the individual with a means of dealing with his own situation in the real world of everyday life. One of the most striking findings to come from the examination of my data concerns the continuity of motivation of dissociated individuals, in spite of the break in consciousness and the discontinuity of personal identity. Ritual dissociations are notably self-serving and self-enhancing. (In Spindler 1978, 486; see also Crapanzano and Garrison 1977)

As many anthropologists have pointed out, trance often provides a release mechanism that preserves the social order in the face of individual dissatisfaction (I. M. Lewis 1971, 176; Walker 1972, 143; Spiro 1987, 159; Van der Walde 1968, 57–58). As Bourguignon puts it, "in a world of poverty, disease and frustration, ritual possession, rather than destroying the integrity of the self, provides increased scope for fulfillment" (in Spindler 1978, 487).

Early anthropological studies tended to highlight the social functions of culturally patterned forms of trance, showing how trance was used to enhance the status or authority of an individual or to call attention to a personal problem.[6] More recent studies have emphasized the ways in which culturally recognized forms of trance are constructed as forms of power and control. Not long after I began to read and think about trance, I came upon an early classic study of possession trance, T. K. Oesterreich's *Possession: Demoniacal and Other Among Primitive Races, in Antiquity, the Middle Ages, and Modern Times* (1930). This work reminded me that possession trance was part of European cultural history and that it was women and primitive peoples who were most generally considered to be subject to demonic possession.

The work of I. M. Lewis (1971) is especially helpful in showing how possession trance functions as a form of social control. Lewis distinguishes two sociocultural patterns of possession trance. In central possession cults (which are associated with small, fluid social units), a shaman or medium is possessed by a god or an ancestor spirit and speaks to the tribe (or his followers) with the voice of divine authority (170–72). In the religious practices of Tamil Hindus, this pattern appears in the possession of the priest by the Amman goddess on the occasion of her annual festival. By contrast, in peripheral possession cults, which are associated with large-scale hierarchical societies, "persons of marginal status" carry on the worship of deities peripheral to the official pantheon (35). Peripheral possession cults can be viewed as the response of the oppressed to the powerful, and Lewis notes that peripheral possession trance allows individuals to vent feelings of helplessness, frustration, and (repressed) hostility toward those who possess high status and power in ways that would normally be unacceptable. In some cases the powerless may even be able to exert pressure for change in their situation, as when an exorcist or shaman bargains with the spirit that possesses a person (Crapanzano, in Crapanzano and Garrison 1977). However, Lewis concludes his study by defining possession trance as "essentially a philosophy of power . . . tinged with a kind of Nietzschian desperation."

Hindu Tamil beliefs construct a hierarchy of peripheral possession cults. In relation to the worship of Brahmanic deities, who require the intermediation of ritually pure Brahmin priests, worship of the goddess and the warrior deities who guard her temple is a peripheral possession cult. However, in the Tamil village, worship of the Amman goddess is a central possession cult, whereas possession by the semi-demonic warrior deities who are deities of low-caste lineages belongs to a peripheral cult. Finally, the priests of these warrior deities are able to exorcise the demonic spirits that possess members of the lowest status (most polluted) groups—who are thought to attract the attention of such spirits because of their polluted and disorderly condition (see Pfaffenberger 1982, 121).

Lewis notes that where central and peripheral possession cults exist alongside each other, a possession episode is likely to be accepted as divine if the person belongs to the stratum of society from which established shamans are drawn. If similar symptoms occur in people from lower social strata, however, their possession will probably be attributed to peripheral spirits, and attempts will be made either to exorcise the spirits or to domesticate and establish them in their rightful place in the hierarchy, that is, below the high gods of the central cult. Similarly, "where central and marginal possession religions exist side by side in the same society, the first is primarily reserved for men, while the second is restricted essentially to women, or men of low station" (1971, 135).

## The Tamil Construction of Trance

Tamils use many different words for trance, which vary from area to area, reflecting a taxonomy of possession states with differently ranked status and meaning. Hindu Tamils in Penang generally recognize three categories of trance: the trance of a pujari when he is possessed by the goddess or a warrior deity, which is usually called *sami ati* (or *sami attam*, literally, "god-dancing"); the trance of those possessed by ghosts or demonic spirits, known as *pey pirichu*, or "having a ghost"; and *arul*, the trance of divine grace experienced by those who fulfill vows during religious festivals.

The trance of the priest of an Amman temple is understood as a dramatic manifestation of divine power intruding into the world through the medium of the pujari. Diehl (1956) describes the trance of the *samiyati (camiyati)* that he observed in Tamilnadu.

> When the time comes for the "possession" to take place . . . the drums are being beaten with increasing rapidity. The *Cāmiyāṭi* [the priest who is a god-dancer] moves around by small hopping steps in a quick tempo. With the increasing tempo his movements become more jerky and shaky. This may go on for a while and means that he is letting himself in for a "descendence" of the god. He uses this means when a "possession" is required, but the ecstasy may spread and persons who were not intent on taking part in the seance are caught by the urging music and whirl around with frenzy. This proves that the god is approaching. . . . Then there comes a moment when the god actually takes him in his grip. A sudden change takes place. His body becomes stiff and he would have fallen if people did not support him, his eyes have a fixed stare, and suddenly he becomes violent and several persons must hold him. He soon calms down, and now people will ask him questions. . . . This is in plain words what people see happening, and their explanation is obvious: "A god has descended on him." (222)[7]

Diehl's description could be aptly applied to the possession of the pujari at the goddess festivals I witnessed in Malaysia.

By contrast, a woman or a low status man claiming to be divinely possessed is treated with cautious suspicion. According to Diehl such a claim is tested:

> A person may be possessed and claim that a god has descended on him. He is then put to tests, because it may be an evil spirit that has seized him. At Tiru-mullaivayal, Chingleput district, the "victim" is seated in front of the shrine of Paccaimalaiyamman and the Pūcari [pujari] waves a light in front of the idol. . . . If the light burns steadily, she [sic] is possessed by an evil spirit. (1956, 225)

However, sometimes trance in a woman or low status man can be used to raise the status of a person or a family. Moreno describes a case in a village in Tamil-nadu in which a young girl was initially considered to be the victim of *pey* (ghost/demon) possession. However, a female god-dancer declared that the girl was possessed by the goddess Kaliyatta and demanded that a shrine be built for worship of the goddess. The girl's parents built a shrine and sponsored a festival for the goddess, and in this way they attained a new status as temple patrons (in Waghorne and Cutler 1985, 105–13).[8]

It is more typical that the trance experiences of women—generally charac-terized by a violent and destructive abandon that suggests repressed anger and un-happiness—are treated as demonic possession. For example, Pfaffenberger (1982) writes of the Hindu Tamils of Sri Lanka:

> The spirit causes the young woman to engage in immodest, indecorous, lustful, and disobedient behavior, all of which threaten her chastity and her reputation. A possessed woman may rush into the house during her period of menstrual pol-lution and touch the kitchen's pots, an act that pollutes them so much that they have to be destroyed. She may roll about on the ground moaning, or swoon with love for an unsuitable partner. Worst of all, she may be made permanently in-fertile. (105–6; also see Obeyesekere in Crapanzano and Garrison 1977)

In such cases, the victim of possession is brought to a deity, such as Muniswara (Muniandi), for exorcism.[9] An exorcism that I watched in Penang shows how the possessed person may be intimidated so that she is made more amenable to social control. The victim was a thin, quiet, unhappy-looking girl of about seventeen. She had been brought to the shrine of Muniswara by her parents. Muniswara is represented as a formidable, mustachioed, turbaned figure who carries a sword and a club. The whip coiled around his arm, which the pujari used in the exor-cism, enhances his threatening image. As I watched the exorcism, I found myself cringing, but the girl who was being exorcised was passive and unresponsive. In my field notes I wrote:

> The *pujari* Arumugam had just finished treating a man of about forty years, who had suffered a series of misfortunes and whose business was failing. Already in a state of possession, Arumugam inclined his head, indicating that the girl

should kneel and bow her head in prayer. Then he took the whip and wrapped it around her neck. Jerking her lightly, he demanded to know the name of the spirit who possessed her. Receiving no response, he took hold of the girl's hair, knotted at the back of her head, and loosened it. Then he yanked her about quite roughly by her hair, all the while demanding that the spirit make his demands known and depart. Finally, he picked up a knife, and holding it above the girl's head, pulled up her hair and wound it round the lime. She could not see what he was doing and did not react, as if she had shut out what was happening to her. Arumugam cut the lime with the knife and discarded the pieces to the four directions as an offering to the exorcised spirits.

No one was willing to tell me what symptoms or behavior had caused the family to bring the girl to the shrine for exorcism. I wondered if she might be resisting the marriage plans of her parents. The pujari's gesture of cutting the lime he had wrapped in her hair seemed to me particularly cruel, because Tamil women pride themselves on their long, glossy black hair.

The autobiography of the untouchable Muli, recorded by James Freeman (1979), includes another story that shows how the "victim" of possession is intimidated through ritual exorcism. This example is particularly interesting because it also illustrates how trance may be used to solve a personal problem and how possession by an angry goddess reflects constraints on the expression of anger by women. Freeman observes that "demonic possession often occurs among young Indian women confronted with personal conflicts that they are afraid to discuss openly or directly" (188).

Muli lived in a village in the state of Orissa in India. His marriage was arranged when he was nineteen years old and Kia, his betrothed, only fourteen. Muli did not want to marry, but his grandfather, who was head of the family, insisted. Two days before the scheduled ceremony, Kia's father died. By custom the wedding should have been postponed (due to the pollution of death), but Muli's grandfather insisted on proceeding with the marriage just two weeks later. After the marriage, Kia, who was young and in mourning, stayed on in her parental home. Nine months later Muli still had not come to fetch his bride. At this point Kia was possessed by a spirit, who said she was an angry goddess. Muli heard the story of Kia's possession from Kia's uncle:

> [That day] many girls went to collect firewood from the mango grove. Under a thorny screwpine bush nearby they heard a sound, "khas! khas!" [Kia] was alone there; the others were a distance away. She became afraid and ran over the fields, shouting, "Oh Father, oh father, who is coming out from that place?" Suddenly she fell down. Her friends took her home. After that she became very taciturn. In the evening she suddenly started laughing in a strange way and was unable to stop. She jerked her shoulders, bared her teeth, and spoke in a strange way, saying strange things: "I am the mother of Chandi. I came from that hill. Why aren't people worshiping me? That's why I am traveling back and forth without finding any shelter." (190)

Kia's family summoned a priest to exorcise the spirit. Muli reported, "the magician lit a smokepot full of hot peppers under her nose. She sneezed; he beat her hard with a cane. Over twenty times the cane landed on her legs, back, hands, and chest. She feared, and the spirit in her called out, 'I am the spirit; I will go back.'" After more beatings, the magician ordered the spirit to carry a big bell-metal bell jar of water with her teeth. According to Kia's uncle, "Grasping a jar with her teeth, our daughter carried it out of the house and down the road until she fell senseless" (190).

Was Kia humiliated by her husband's failure to fetch her to his home? Did her girlfriends tease her? Did the spirit that possessed Kia speak for her when she protested that she had no shelter, was not treated with respect, and was forced to wander back and forth? We cannot know what set off Kia's trance, but we learn that her possession gave her family a reason to summon Muli. On his visit, Muli was asked to contribute to the care of his sick wife and was reminded of his responsibilities. A few days later Muli's grandfather fetched Kia to live with Muli.

By contrast with the case of Kia, wife of an untouchable, trancelike behavior in a high-caste male is treated respectfully, as is shown by an incident described by Margaret Trawick (1990a) in her ethnography of a Tamil Brahmin family. Trawick's informant, Ayya, was subject to attacks, which his sister described as follows: "there would be *atircci* (shock), he would tremble uncontrollably so that no one could hold him, and run out into the street. His brother would run after him and bring him back. After that, it took him an hour or two to return to his senses" (189). These attacks were called *irraipattu* (literally, "soul-touched"), suggesting that Ayya's soul was touched or punished by a god.[10] Evidently no one ever thought that these were episodes of demonic possession.

Among Hindu Tamils in India, what an episode of trance is called reflects a great deal about the social relations that define the identity of the person who exhibits trancelike or socially unacceptable behavior. However, when speaking of episodes of spontaneous trance, Hindu Tamils in Penang often use the Malay word *kemasukan* (to be entered) for trance to avoid making a distinction between divine and demonic possession. For similar reasons, Western-educated professionals prefer the English word *trance*. This means that possession trance is less important in Malaysia than in Tamilnadu as a means of social control to reinforce the social hierarchy of caste. However, the word *trance* as used by Western-educated, high status professionals often suggested a pathological or hysterical condition of women and the lower classes. In Malaysia, class differences were reinforced in this way and the cultural significance of arul, as a highly valued state with religious meaning, was denied.

The word *arul,* used for the divinely inspired trance that devotees experience during vow fulfillment, can be translated as grace or blessing. Arul can be distinguished from other forms of possession trance in several ways. Unlike spontaneous trances, arul must occur in an appropriate context—during a pilgrimage, at a temple, on a festival day, or during worship. The trance of divine grace also should be preceded by a period of spiritual preparation and ritual purification. Finally, arul is not restricted to particular individuals or groups, as is usually the case with the possession trance of the village Amman goddess during her festival (see Jain 1970, 277; Dirks 1994).

As a form of ecstatic mass possession, arul has significant political implications. Lewis describes episodes of mass possession as "separatist cults" and suggests that they thrive in periods of political instability (1971, 174–75). In Malaysia, we have seen how political and economic changes since World War II have provided the context for the emergence of egalitarian values. In this context, the trance of divine possession in the tradition of bhakti devotionalism has egalitarian implications, which transcend the protest against dominant groups that is implicit in the possession of low status worshippers by peripheral deities. Through the trance of divine grace on Thaipusam, working-class devotees from low and untouchable backgrounds may begin to reshape their understanding of their place in the world. If the Hindu Tamils of Malaysia were not a minority population, the increasing popularity of Murugan might develop from a religious movement into a political movement.

## A PSYCHOLOGICAL PERSPECTIVE

### Hypnotism and Trance

After my return from Malaysia, I set about learning all that I could about trance, but reading about trance was clearly quite different from experiencing it. Finally, I asked a trusted friend, a therapist who taught the use of hypnosis in therapy in a graduate program, to help me experience a trance. Our first experiment took place in her office. After being instructed how to sit in a relaxed posture, I was given the task of envisioning a place where I might want to return in further trance exercises. Engaged in this imaginative task, I found myself in a pleasant state of mild dissociation. While I remained aware of the therapist's quiet presence, the passage of people in the hall outside, and noises from the street below, I was so engrossed in my thoughts I felt no pressure to interact with the therapist or to respond in any way to the world outside. Indeed, at the end of the session I realized that such a trance was very relaxing, and I was eager for further experimentation.

In a short while, I mastered to a considerable degree my fear of hypnosis as a form of control by another person.[11] I then attended a series of classes (taught by a different person) for a small group of therapists who wanted to learn how to use hypnosis in their practice. At the first session, the instructor emphasized that each of us would be in control at all times and if we wanted to come out of trance at any time, we would be able to do so. He also said we would each have our own reasons for wanting to go into trance, and we would know when we had achieved our goal. These instructions removed the social pressure to conform to the hypnotist's instructions. Finally, trance was defined as a valuable tool for self-exploration and therapy, thus distinguishing therapeutic trance from stage hypnosis with its aura of exhibitionism.

This approach to the use of hypnosis in therapy is shaped by the work of Milton Erickson. In his writings, Erickson emphasized the positive side of trance, how it could be used constructively to solve personal problems. The typical Ericksonian hypnotic induction consists of a commentary of paradoxical suggestions and double-bind instructions that leave the subject free to interpret almost any response as the beginning of a trance: "I do not know when you will go into a trance, but when you do, you will raise your right hand. Or maybe it will be your left hand. . . . When you are in a trance, your eyes will close, or perhaps they will remain open." These remarks are made in a pleasant monotone that requires no response, followed by suggestions that engage the imagination, such as "Imagine your favorite color. Is that color warm or cool? What part of your body has the temperature of that color?" A therapist then directs patients to visualize their problems in metaphoric images; for example, an electrician might picture difficulties in communication as being like an electric circuit that he can repair. In another case we discussed, a woman used gardening as a way to visualize how she might control a particular behavior that distressed her. Thus the therapist's directions made the experience of trance highly individual and highlighted what the person brought to the trance, as opposed to emphasizing the hypnotist's control over the subject.

As the situation became familiar in the hypnosis classes, everyone came to look forward to the time when they would be allowed to go into trance. Each session of hypnosis was followed by a discussion period, in which the participants described their experience of trance. These discussions were very instructive. I learned that although everyone had listened to the same suggestions, each person interpreted them in a unique way. Over the weeks, as the trances became deeper, some members of the class began to be amnesiac for what they had experienced for the fifteen- or twenty-minute period of trance. They could report only that they noticed a change in mood after awakening, for instance, a feeling of being at peace with themselves and the world. On one occasion, a woman woke up in tears (reminding me of the silent tears of devotees I had observed on Thaipusam), but she could not recall why she was crying. I found that at first I had amazingly complete recall of my thoughts and could repeat in detail the instructor's entire induction (while most of the others remembered what he said only up to a certain point, when their thoughts drifted off onto a chain of personal associations). However, after a while I realized that I had instructed myself not to lose my awareness of what happened in the class, for this was *research*. When this internal prohibition on letting go of conscious awareness was removed, I found that I could not always remember the whole induction or my complete train of thought when I awoke. Nevertheless, the whole class returned to consciousness on cue, just as the teacher had instructed in the induction, so none of us ever completely lost awareness of our surroundings or the social situation of the class.

Although possession trance and hypnosis are distinctive cultural paradigms,

Van der Walde has identified the underlying structural features that they share when considered from a cross-cultural perspective:

1. The given form of trance is accepted, tolerated, or encouraged by a given culture or society, either for the entire culture or for specific individuals or groups within the society.

2. The behavior associated with the trance state is accepted, tolerated, or encouraged so long as it occurs within the trance state. Frequently the same behavior would not be tolerated by the individual or his society when pursued in a non-trance state.

3. There is a real or fantasied authoritative figure who is regarded as responsible for controlling the trance state.

4. There is a conventional ritual which serves to initiate and differentiate the trance state from ordinary social relations. (1968, 64–65)

From a psychological perspective, we may point to other similarities. First, hypnotic subjects and people in trance may exhibit extraordinary control of involuntary parts of the nervous system, so that they are anesthetized against pain or can demonstrate unusual muscular rigidity (Erickson 1980, 1:533–35, 4:9). Second, central to both phenomena is the dissociation that prevents the trance experience from being admitted to conscious awareness, hence the normal amnesia for experiences in a state of trance or hypnosis (although a hypnotic subject may be instructed to recall the trance experience).

The psychologist Ernest Hilgard (1986), who studied both hypnosis and dissociative trance states, concluded that the trance of a Malay *bomoh,* or shaman, and a Chinese medium (which he witnessed in Singapore) had much in common with self-hypnosis.[12] The psychologists Ronald Simons, Frank Ervin, and Raymond Prince (1988), who studied the psychobiology of trance as manifested in devotees of Murugan on Thaipusam in Kuala Lumpur, also compare trance to hypnosis. They observe that the pattern of arousal in trance accompanied by dancing and drumming is different from that of hypnotic trance and that the physiological concomitants of the trance state in devotees on Thaipusam are similar to symptoms exhibited by people subject to extreme stress. Nevertheless, they conclude that the states of hypnosis and trance are comparable in being defined by "a set of culturally defined expectations and learned techniques for narrowing and focusing attention" (281). Like the hypnotic subject, all subjects who entered arul experienced periods of amnesia for the events that occurred while they were in trance, although there were also "islands of recollection and awareness of pain." At such times, the drumming and singing of companions helped the trancers return to the trance state (263).[13]

In drawing on my own experience of hypnotic trance to understand the trance of Hindu Tamil devotees of Murugan on Thaipusam, I treat trance as a cultural practice that may serve people in a variety of ways. Although trance is structured by shared conceptions, people will have unique experiences, which are motivated by conscious and unconscious concerns about their personal lives and shaped by the situation in which the trance occurs—that is, the ritual or suggestions of the hypnotist.

## A Psychoanalytic Theory of Trance

In *Hypnosis and Related States: Psychoanalytic Studies in Regression* (1959), Gill and Brenman provide an extensive discussion of trance and hypnosis in terms of the theoretical constructs of Freudian psychology. They explain that in the framework of ego psychology, the ego is understood to be operating under the pressure of stimuli from both the external environment and the id, impulses and desires experienced as an internal upsurge of emotion. The relatively autonomous ego is aware of both external expectations and internal motivational urges but has the capacity to assess them and choose its response to them. This autonomy of the ego—a characteristic of the healthy, well-adapted personality—may be disturbed by increased pressure from either the environment or the id, or by a great decrease in information or pressure from one or the other. Thus, in sensory deprivation when the press of environment is eliminated, the id tends to dominate the ego and the subject experiences hallucinations. A situation of emotional crisis also produces strong pressure from the id, reducing ego autonomy, and a trancelike state may occur (in an extreme case, a state of catatonia). Gill and Brenman hypothesize that the remembering of long-forgotten episodes from one's childhood in hypnotic trance results from a relaxation of defenses against the id (1959, 49). By contrast, in brainwashing we have a state of compliance in which the ego is dominated by increased pressure from the environment.

Hypnosis is also considered a case of decreased ego autonomy from the environment. Hypnotic induction produces this loss of autonomy by strong pressure from one part of the environment (the hypnotist), combined with loss of input from other parts (the hypnotist's suggestion that his subject focus attention on a single object). The subject may respond to conscious or unconscious anxiety about surrendering control to another person and choose not to obey the instructions of the hypnotist to enter trance. If, however, the subject is motivated by pressure from the id as well, the normal conscious desire to comply with the hypnotist's authoritative directions tends to result in a trance state emerging. Freud refers to this as a form of transference, reminding us that the hypnotic subject has invested the relationship with the hypnotist with special (unconscious) meaning. Thus, id (unconscious motivation) and environment (hypnotist) reinforce each other (Gill and Brenman 1959, 189).

According to Gill and Brenman, in a hypnotic state the ego surrenders partial and temporary control to the hypnotist through the agency of a regressed subsystem of the ego (1959, 191). However, the ego continues to monitor trance behavior and retains the ability to terminate the trance.[14] To support this conclusion, they cite the fact that a hypnotized person normally does not walk into chairs or perform other injurious acts while in a trance state. Gill and Brenman compare trance to a sleep state in which the ego also continues to function, acting as censor of dreams (and awakening a person in case of noises in the night). A major difference between sleep and trance states is that fantasies are depicted symbolically in disguised and compromised forms in dreams, whereas in trance, thoughts and impulses may be acted out (in symbolic or disguised forms) rather than merely envisioned. Gill and Brenman point to another parallel between trance and dream states—their characteristic hypermnesia (abnormally complete memory loss or recall). According to Freud, a person normally cannot remember dreams due to the expression of powerful wishes or impulses of the id that are unacceptable to the conscious self. Similarly, the events of a hypnotic trance are normally not available to conscious recall, as the subject has surrendered to a transference wish to be controlled by the hypnotist. However, Freud was also impressed with the ability of a person in a hypnotic state to remember long-forgotten events. Indeed, he developed his earliest theory (1895) of conscious, preconscious, and unconscious mental systems in an attempt to understand the dynamics of "cathartic cures" achieved through hypnotic recall of forgotten childhood memories.

The theoretical constructs of Gill and Brenman are helpful in showing how one might discriminate between trance as a form of pathology and trance that is "ego syntonic," that is, under control of the ego and in service of aims acceptable to the ego (or conscious self). From the perspective of ego psychology, when the ego suffers a loss of autonomy from either id or environment, regression is said to occur. This regression may be pathological (as in schizophrenia, which occurs when the ego is overwhelmed by the id) or "in the service of the ego," as in artistic creativity and dreams (1959, 157–67, 181; see also Kris 1952). When a trance-like state involves regression in service of the ego, unconscious fantasies (id impulses) are tolerated by an ego that has the capacity to end the regression. The deciding factor in determining whether the regression or trance state is ego syntonic is whether the person is able to choose the circumstances in which the trance is experienced and to control trance behavior so it is in accord with a culturally acceptable pattern. Thus, Gill and Brenman would concur in the diagnosis of spontaneous episodes of trance as pathological "demonic possession," and in seeing arul (the divine trance of ritual vow fulfillment) and the trance of a pujari as being ego syntonic. These trance states demonstrate ego control because they occur under socially sanctioned conditions, and they are ego syntonic because they enhance the social status of an individual while providing an outlet for repressed feelings and fantasies.

Gill and Brenman compare hypnosis to trance, taking as their example the ritual trances of Bali described by Bateson and Mead (1942):

> a seer or priestess . . . in the trance state exhibits emotions never otherwise appropriate except on the stage—tears and intense expressions of grief and

> striving. All these are lived through, until again vacancy and awayness supersede. . . . The Balinese character . . . is curiously cut off from inter-personal relationships, existing in a state of dreamy-relaxed dissociation, with occasional intervals of non-personal concentration—in trance, in gambling, and in the practice of the arts. (47)

Bali is famous for the trance performance of the Chalonarang, a religious performance in which the witch-goddess Rangda causes men to turn their kris, a curved dagger, against their own breast and stab themselves until the paroxysm passes or they are restrained. Comparing the frenzied emotion of Balinese in such trance enactments to the compliant behavior of hypnotic subjects, Gill and Brenman argue that the ways trance is culturally shaped may be related to the kinds of personality characteristics that are valued and encouraged in a particular society. Thus, "in our culture, in which autonomy from the environment is fairly well maintained, trance may result in domination by the environment after the loss of autonomy, while in the Balinese culture, in which autonomy from the id is fairly well maintained . . . trance may result in domination by the id after autonomy has been lost" (1959, 318). In general, Tamil culture, like Balinese culture, requires people to be less direct and open in the expression of their emotions than Westerners tend to be.[15] From the perspective of Gill and Brenman, Tamil trances appear to allow for the expression of wishes and feelings that are normally not acknowledged or are forbidden (that is, defined as bad or identified with demons).

### Transference: Trance and Empowerment

Freud (1921) describes the relationship between subject and hypnotist as a form of transference, that is, a relationship in the present that is modeled on an earlier relationship of great emotional intensity, usually that of child to parent (also see Erickson 1980, 3:6). In his most extensive discussion of hypnosis he suggests that hypnosis reactivates the oedipal relationship of father and child, which elicits the compliance of the subject with the commands of the hypnotist.[16] In his later works, *The Future of an Illusion* (1927) and *Civilization and Its Discontents* (1930), Freud treats all religion as a kind of culturally induced transference fantasy. When his friend Romain Rolland drew his attention to the ecstatic religious trance of mystics, Freud (1930) traced the feeling of religious ecstasy and the experience of an "oceanic oneness" with the universe back to infancy when the child did not yet feel separate from its mother and the gratification of all desires seemed possible (S.E. 21:64). Religion, he argued, provides the illusion that an omnipotent parent continues to watch over one and also the illusion of participation in the omnipotence of this all powerful being. As the psychoanalyst Otto Fenichel points out, this fantasy of sharing in omnipotent power can take many cultural forms including hypnosis and participation in political movements, as well as ecstatic religious experience:

One important way of once more sharing in the lost omnipotence (of the infant whose needs are fulfilled) seems . . . to be in the fantasy . . . of somehow dissolving in [the powerful one], being devoured *by* him [*sic*]. All those later narcissistic feelings of well-being in which one's own insignificance feels sheltered within a something infinitely great which nevertheless has an ego quality, are of this sort. Such are: patriotism ("my nation is infinitely greater than I, and yet is I"); religious ecstasy (God is infinitely greater than the self, yet the believer is one with Him); hypnosis (the hypnotist is infinitely greater than the subject, and yet he now fulfills functions which are otherwise those of the subject); and the relation to authority in general (the authoritarian leader is infinitely greater than any single individual of his nation—and yet he himself is a single individual of the nation). (1953, 2:142)

This analysis can be applied to arul, the ecstatic trance of the devotees of Murugan, which is understood as a kind of participation in and empowerment by the divine. In a study of the trance of devotees who fulfilled vows to Murugan at the Thaipusam festival in Kuala Lumpur, Simons, Ervin, and Prince (1988) interviewed subjects who were practicing going into trance at the shrine of a skilled pujari.[17] They recorded what these devotees could remember about the onset of trance:

After a period of time . . . they began to feel "something" moving up from their feet or legs. Some described this as a feeling of heat, or of cold, or of lightness. Some described their bodies as feeling larger than usual and some [described] a feeling of strength. Almost all remarked that their arms, legs, and bodies were shaking, and some noted that the hairs on their arms stood up. Several spoke of seeing Murugan or another god. Most reported dimness of vision, saying that they were unable to see clearly when they opened their eyes. (262–63)

These comments reflect the popular understanding that, during trance, Murugan enters into a person's body. After awakening from trance on Thaipusam, these subjects reported that they "felt exhausted but elated" (263). Although they could not find words to explain the reasons for their feeling of elation, the trance of vow fulfillment had clearly been an intense and meaningful emotional experience.

The souvenir program for Thaipusam explains, "Phenomenal *existence* or 'creation' as such begins with the fall of *Arul*—a power of consciousness emanating from Shiva-Sakti" (italics in original, Longanathan 1985). On one hand, the trance known as arul is interpreted as manifesting an enlightened consciousness; on the other hand, this divine emanation of consciousness is understood as a form of primordial energy or divine power, known as sakti.

The word *arul* has suggestive parallels with the English word *ecstasy*, which is defined in the *Oxford English Dictionary* as "blissful, rapt absorption in the divine." Like *arul*, the ancient Greek *ekstasis* referred to a trance in which either the soul left the body to unite with the divine, or the god dwelt inside a person, who thereby became an oracle (Murray 1926, quoted in Lewin 1950, x).[18] In early Tamil texts *arul wagui* was used to refer to a divinely inspired utterance. By extension, *arul paidan* referred to the executor of royal or divine commands (Tamil Lexicon 1936). Thus, the word *arul* expresses the claim that one is filled with the grace of God and also refers to the power of Murugan that is manifest in his devotee. Murugan has become one with his devotee in trance.

## Transference, Dissociation, and Multiple Personalities

Freud's interpretation of trance as a reenactment of the relationship of the child to the powerful father, both loved and feared, is derived from hypnosis in which typically a male hypnotist controls a younger male or a female subject. However, Freud (1921) noted Ferenczi's suggestion that two sorts of hypnotism should be distinguished: "one coaxing and soothing . . . modeled on the mother, and another threatening . . . derived from the father" (S.E. 18:127). He also compared the transference relationship of hypnosis to erotic love, describing it as "the unlimited devotion of someone in love, but with sexual satisfaction excluded" (ibid., 115; see also Gill and Brenman 1959, 136–45). Such transference relationships are fantasies that may be enacted in relationship to a person (such as a hypnotist, therapist, or priest) or to an imagined personality (such as a deity).

Freud's suggestion that a variety of transference relations can be enacted in trance states can be connected to the work of psychologists who treat trance and hypnosis as states of dissociation related to the development of multiple personalities. Like Freud, Hilgard (1977) and Bliss (1986) emphasize the continuity between normal consciousness and the pathology of multiple personalities. They treat dissociation as a natural state consequent to "divided consciousness" or as a form of "focused inattention." Hilgard holds that conscious representation of normal mental activity is never complete and "the unity of consciousness is illusory" (1).[19] Normally a person's awareness shifts back and forth from what is currently happening inside the body, and what is impinging on it from without, to events that are remembered or imagined:

> Because conscious awareness is partial, we speak of paying attention, which implies that some things that are happening may not be attended to. Such divided attention . . . may be illustrated by what happens in a conversation between two people. . . . Several things may be going on in parallel, with sufficient attention given to listening to register what is being said, with enough surplus attentive effort remaining to allow for the simultaneous preparation of the intended reply. Even more intriguing and puzzling is the possibility that in some instances part of the attentive effort and planning may continue without any awareness of it at all. When that appears to be the case, the concealed part of the total ongoing thought and action may be described as *dissociated* from the conscious experience of the person. (2)

In the view of Hilgard, minor dissociative states are frequent occurrences in our experience of everyday life: "Such events as forgetting the keys to the office when you prefer to stay at home, or slipping in an unintended negative that tells the truth when you were trying to falsify to be polite, are minor dissociations of familiar experience, with the interpretations often obvious to the person who is exhibiting them" (251). Hypnosis and trance are simply more extreme instances of focused inattention.

Bliss describes dissociation as due to focused inattention. He writes, "A fixation of the eyes was only one aspect of the riveting of the mind on one idea, and this concentration on a single idea was the essence of the process. This narrowing or focusing of attention internally continues to be viewed by some as the essential element in the induction and the state of hypnosis" (1986, 102).[20] Aldous Huxley also speaks of focused attention in describing a state he called Deep Reflection, which he cultivated for his writing. In such a state, Huxley could take a telephone message or respond to others in an acceptable manner, but later he had no memory of these interactions. He explained that he had acted "automatically" (in Erickson 1980, 1:85). This state resembles hypnosis or trance in that Huxley did not pay conscious attention to the world around him, but Huxley was not amnesiac for the thoughts that absorbed his attention. This way of looking at trance suggests its relation to all those times when we "forget where we are" or "find ourselves" acting in unexpected ways.

Hilgard proposes that the personality (ego-state) that emerges in a hypnotic trance is actually "an enduring fraction of the total personality, like a covert or incipient multiple personality," which has lost communication with the "dominant control and information system" of the personality (1977, 17). He argues that "multiple personalities may be more prevalent than commonly believed" (299–300). Bliss (1986) observes that patients with multiple personalities are excellent hypnotic subjects and theorizes that these patients have long employed, unknowingly, a capacity for self-hypnosis to isolate early traumatic experiences of sexual or psychological abuse. Through self-hypnosis, these patients could keep a relatively healthy personality established in relationship with one parent, which is isolated from the emotions, memories, and role expectations experienced in a traumatic or abusive relationship either with another parent or with the same parent split into good and bad aspects (117–63). For Bliss, hypnosis or trance is "a certain kind of role enactment" along with amnesia for this role. However, the role-playing of hypnotic trance is not "sham behavior . . . since the subject at the moment experiences [it] as real. There is a deep involvement in the role" (98).

## Multiple Selves and Secret Selves

These observations about the relation of trance to multiple personalities and to the enactment of different transference relationships may be developed to open a psychodynamic account of personality to the organizing effects of culture. In Western cultures, the expectation of a consistency of character or personality imparts a kind of predictability to social relations, which makes social life possible.[21] The psychoanalyst Erik Erikson (1950) has outlined a model of psychological development in Western cultures, in which the autonomous maturity of the adult rests on the establishment of "ego identity" (recognized by others as character or personality) as the result of an adolescent "identity crisis."[22] However, as anthropologists have pointed out, the "selves" of people in non-Western cultures may be experienced quite differently (Dumont 1966; Geertz 1984; Shweder and LeVine 1982; White and Kirkpatrick 1985; Stigler, Shweder, and Herdt 1990). In a classic formulation of the cultural relativity of "selves," Geertz (1984) writes:

> The Western conception of the person as a bounded, unique, more or less integrated motivational and cognitive universe, a dynamic center of awareness, emotion, judgment, and action organized into a distinctive whole and set contrastively both against other such wholes and against its social and natural background, is, however incorrigible it may seem to us, a rather peculiar idea within the context of the world's cultures. (126)[23]

India has been cited frequently as a culture that rejects the values associated with Western individualism and the patterns of individual autonomy and personal identity cultivated in Western societies (for example, Barnett 1975; Fruzzetti, Ostor, and Barnett 1976; Shweder in Shweder and LeVine 1982). For example, positing "homo hierarchicus" of the caste system, Dumont (1966) writes:

> To say that the world of caste is a world of relations is to say that the particular caste and the particular man have no substance: they exist empirically, but they have no reality in thought, no Being. . . . I regard it as fundamental and would therefore firmly posit, at the risk of being crude, that on the level of life in the world the individual *is* not. (272)[24]

According to Dumont, people in India emphasize their relatedness, their interdependence, and their shared identity as members of families, clans, villages, and so on.[25] Similarly, the southern Indian poet and scholar Ramanujan writes:

> The [Indian] social structure does not permit the emergence of a cogent adult role as perceived in Western societies. Subordinating one's individual needs to the interests of the group, be it a family, a kinship group, a clan or a class is upheld as a virtue. . . . Thus self-assertion becomes selfishness, independent decision making is perceived as disobedience. The response from the in-group is tacit disapproval if not outright condemnation. Under such circumstances it is easier to play safe. The only way this can be accomplished is by passive aggressive behavior or regression into total passivity. (Quoted in Mines 1988, 570)[26]

Margaret Trawick's intimate ethnographic description of a Tamil Brahmin family (1990a, 1990b) allows us to see what these rather general and abstract statements might mean when applied to people's lives. Trawick illustrates the way in which involvement with others is taught to children. "Padmini (the mother) taught Jnana Oli (her son) the value of closeness to others by threatening to withdraw this closeness. And conversely, Oli learned that he could elicit interaction by stubbornly withdrawing himself" (1990a, 223). Trawick observes that a child who withdrew from social interaction might fear that he or she was unloved, for "the true sign of love's absence might be the absence of any interaction at all" (1990b, 48). The way that the lives of different members of the family were inextricably intertwined is perhaps best illustrated by the manner in which children were punished: "In general, a child could never know if or when or even upon whom the punishment would fall for a mistake that was made. One person would err and another would be punished for a mistake the other had committed in the past and thought forgotten. . . . Or alternatively, the same person would punish and comfort, punish and comfort, until the child completely lost its bearings, and began to weep" (1990a, 77).[27] From such interactions the child learned to master the theatrics of daily interactions and to cultivate an inner self or "secret identity" that was protected from the assaults of others. Trawick writes:

> It seemed to me that behind all these deceptions, illusions, and inversions, each child treasured a secret identity, which he or she would mysteriously guard. How successful the child was, both at theatrics and at guardianship of the self, depended ultimately on what truth came through the drama—how hard or how gentle were the beatings, how many the chances for secret kisses, how much the milk entered the belly. (1990a, 218)

Alan Roland (1988), an American psychoanalyst who has described his practice in northern India, was struck (as Trawick was) by the sense that "beneath the observance of an overt etiquette of deference, loyalty, and subordination, Indians keep a very private self that contains all kinds of feelings and fantasies that will not be revealed in the usual hierarchical relationship with an elder" (64).

This secret inner self should not be conceived of as a pathological development, nor is such a self necessarily the unconscious consequence of repression. In Indian society, the point is that this self remains "inner"—ordinarily there is no demand that others acknowledge it, for that would disrupt customary social interaction. Thus a sense of an inner identity, quite different from one's socially ascribed identity, may be consciously maintained. Trawick's informant, Ayya, told her, for example, "that he really was a female at heart, who had been born as a male just in order to be able to go out in the world and teach" (1990a, 36).[28] The idea that Indian culture and society encourage the development of a protected, inner, secret self would probably not strike most Westerners as so strange.[29] However, the contrast between American and Indian culture becomes evident when we think how often people in Western societies are encouraged to "be themselves" or to "express themselves."

We may hypothesize that in Indian society the ability to shift smoothly from role to role as one interacts with superiors and inferiors may be more highly valued than the expression of one's "true" feelings. In particular, there are many instances recorded in the ethnographic literature that point to taboos on open and direct expression of anger, especially anger toward those of higher status.[30] Such an angry self might find expression in possession by an angry goddess or warrior deity. More significant, the highly valued inner self that is not recognized in the society of caste hierarchy may find expression in the trance of divine possession in vow fulfillment to one's *ista deva* or chosen deity.

The rich variety of culturally given forms of trance developed in different societies is, perhaps, one of the clearest illustrations of the power of culture to shape human behavior. Among Hindu Tamils, culturally given understandings of trance reinforce the constructs of caste hierarchy and gender difference that stigmatize women and those of low-caste or untouchable heritage as polluted and vulnerable to demonic possession. The discussion of divine and demonic possession trance shows how these cultural constructs are imposed as forms of social control and how they are internalized so that women and those of low-caste or untouchable heritage see themselves as dangerous or evil. However, ritual vow fulfillment also provides a medium for individual self-transformation through ascetic self-mastery. In choosing to fulfill their vows to Murugan on Thaipusam, Hindu Tamils resist the culturally inscribed identities that stigmatize them as morally inferior and express their commitment to the egalitarian values of bhakti devotionalism. Ritual vow fulfillment empowers the devotees of Murugan and brings public acknowledgment that they have been found worthy of his blessing, which takes the form of trance. Collectively the working-class devotees of Murugan demonstrate their power and the power of the god they worship.

# SYMBOLIC ACTS

## The Meanings of Ritual Vow Fulfillment

Don't take it as a matter of course, but as a remarkable fact, that pictures and fictitious narratives give us pleasure, occupy our minds.

("Don't take it as a matter of course" means: [do] find it surprising, as you do some things which disturb you. Then the puzzling aspects of the latter will disappear, by your accepting this fact as you do the other.)

—*Ludwig Wittgenstein*, Philosophical Investigations

In *Philosophical Investigations,* Wittgenstein observes that when we pay attention to what we generally take for granted—in this case, our human interest in pictures and stories—what most puzzles us about an action or event may seem less disturbing. I must admit it took me a long time before I really grasped the significance of the stories that I was told so frequently by the devotees of Murugan as they tried to help me understand the Thaipusam festival. These stories gave meaning to the acts of ritual vow fulfillment that so puzzled me. These stories also gave meaning to the lives of the people who told them to me. As the psychoanalyst Sudhir Kakar has also noted, "Cultural ideas and ideals . . . manifested in their narrative form as myths, pervade the innermost experience of the self. One cannot therefore speak of an 'earlier' or 'deeper' layer of the self beyond cultural reach" (Kakar 1990, 443).

In Western societies a sense of self is organized by the constructs of folk psychology and, for most people, by the conceptual framework of Freudian psychology. Whether or not one has read Freud, the concepts of ego, id, and superego, the idea of unconscious motivations, and the idiom of the Freudian slip, all provide a vocabulary for people's understanding of themselves and others. For Malaysian Tamils, the narratives of Hindu myths and legends and of Tamil folktales function in a similar way, providing cultural paradigms and a vocabulary for people's self-image, their image of others, and their relation to those others. Kakar (1990) writes: "Vibrantly alive, their symbolic power intact, Indian myths constitute a cultural idiom that aids the individual in the construction and integration of his inner world" (439).[1] Thus, the legend of the founding of the Palani Murugan Temple provides a cultural template for oedipal rivalry directed at a brother, rather than at a father figure. Legends about the ascetic practices of hermits, gods, and demons describe how mastery of the body is converted into mastery of the world, a pattern of meaning that contrasts sharply with Christian narratives about ascetic practices based on the paradigm of penance for sins or of redemption from original sin. Images of gender are linked in Hindu myths to cultural conceptions of purity and pollution, to a conception of female power and anxiety about female anger. These constructs have various consequences for individuals. Tamil women may fear their own power, despite their relative powerlessness in social relations, and Tamil men may entertain a conscious identification with the "good" feminine that does not threaten their sense of masculinity.

At the same time that these legends show us the culturally shaped meaning of experience from a Hindu Tamil perspective, we also find that these myths reflect universal human questions. What is the nature of God? What is the relation of humans to the divine? Although the sacred narratives of the Hindu tradition answer these questions in particular ways, they give expression to universal human longings—the desire for union with the divine, the desire for submission and protection, the wish to steal divine power or command it for oneself, the desire for revenge over powerful beings who have humiliated or oppressed one. Thus Hindu tales may speak across the gaps created by cultural differences, and people from other cultures may find meaning in these narratives and the rituals associated with them.

In the heritage of myths, legends, and tales, Tamils find a symbolic vocabulary that allows them to give expression to their deepest selves, as well as to unconscious desires and proscribed emotions. In this chapter we will see how Tamil trance experiences may be interpreted in terms of transference fantasies or symbolic enactments: expressions of an inner identification with one or more of the various images of Murugan (the indulged child-god in relation to his adoring parents [or mother]; the jealous but triumphant rival of his brother; the victorious warrior who is recognized by the high gods and rewarded with marriage) or of an inner self in relation to Murugan (as Valli, the beloved of Murugan; as the good nurturing mother of the infant god; or as Idumban, the rebellious demon who is defeated by Murugan and transformed into his chief devotee). My aim in this chapter is to illustrate the dense complexity of detail and layering of meanings that make ritual vow fulfillment a rich medium for the representation of an inner self that is not acknowledged by the world of caste and class hierarchy. Each devotee chooses a vow that is personally meaningful; symbolically that vow may have multiple meanings through its relation to the many myths, legends, and tales that are associated with Murugan and the Thaipusam festival. These meanings may even be contradictory, for, like dreams and symptoms, rituals allow people to express contradictory wishes.

### THE DEMON DEVOTEE: MASTERED BY MURUGAN

The legend of the Palani Temple, which is the model for the Arulmigu Bala Thandayuthabani Murugan Temple on Penang Hill, identifies the worshipper who fulfills a vow by carrying a kavadi with the demon Idumban, Murugan's chief devotee. The theme of conquest, submission, and service also appears in the other legend most commonly told in connection with the Thaipusam festival, the story of Murugan's victory over the demon Surapadma. Having been granted the boon of immortality by Shiva because of his great austerities, Surapadma led a rebellion of the asuras against the high gods. The gods realized that only a son of Shiva would be able to defeat the powerful demon, and they conspired that Murugan be conceived. Murugan is given an invincible weapon by his mother, the goddess, and he then sets off to fight Surapadma and his allies. Throughout the battle, Surapadma takes different forms in order to gain an advantage over the god. Murugan strikes back at each form, but he cannot destroy the demon because of the boon granted by Shiva. Finally, Surapadma takes the form of a tree, which Murugan splits with his lance. One part of the tree becomes a rooster and the other a peacock. In these last two forms, the demon is subdued and comes to serve Murugan.[2] The cock appears on Murugan's banner, and the peacock becomes his mount or vehicle (see Clothey 1978, 55–56). According to Obeyesekere (1978), among the Hindu Tamils of Sri Lanka, the possession trance of Murugan is known as *avesha* (to alight or rest). When the god "mounts" or "rests" on the devotee as his peacock vehicle, his force is experienced as trance (468). Thus the devotee of Murugan who carries a kavadi decorated with peacock feathers can also be identified with the conquered demon Surapadma, who has become Murugan's peacock vehicle.

Like Idumban and Surapadma, the devotees who fulfill vows to Murugan on Thaipusam have been pierced with the lance of Murugan. They are vanquished by the god and transformed into his faithful servant-devotees. This identification of the worshipper with the demon can be understood in two different ways. First is the association of the demonic asuras (cur in Tamil) who are at the bottom of the divine hierarchy with untouchables and tribal peoples, who are at the bottom of the hierarchy of caste. They are considered polluted and undisciplined and similar to the asuras. They would presumably rebel against the rule of the high and mighty if they could. This identification is most frequently seen in those of high-caste heritage who believe that, because people of untouchable and low-caste background eat meat, they are brutal and aggressive, like the demonic meat-eating asuras. Second, the demons who embody sexual desire and aggression are symbolically equated with the part of the self that feels unacceptable lust, greed, and anger, and that must be mastered in order for the self to be made worthy of the god's grace, the divine trance arul.

This identification of demons with the lower self of desire and aggression appears in the way Tamils understand dreams. According to tradition, Prajapati, the creator, formed the devas from higher life energies and the asuras from lower energies (Danielou 1964, 140). Originally the devas and the asuras were equally powerful, but their power was divided, with the gods exercising power by day and the asuras by night (Stutley and Stutley 1977, 23). Therefore the demonic asuras visit people at night in their dreams.[3] When a child has a nightmare, parents will mark the child's forehead with the sacred ash vibhuti to drive out the demons.

In his autobiography, the religious teacher Vivekananda provides another illustration of the theme of the inner demon. He writes, "When I was naughty [my family] would say, 'Dear, Dear! So many austerities, yet Shiva sent us this demon after all, instead of a good soul.' . . . Even now, when I feel mischievous, that word [demon] keeps me straight. 'No!' I say to myself, 'not this time'" (quoted in Kakar 1981, 169). Trawick describes how the image of the demon as an unruly child appeared in a play that she observed in a Tamil village. In this play "the goddess Adiparasakti was created to destroy a demon. This goddess was huge and green; she bit her bright red tongue angrily and stomped about the stage wielding a sharp trident" (1990b, 57). To the delight of the audience, the child-demon immediately fell in love with the goddess. In this humorous form, the figure of the demon who acts with inappropriate and uncontrolled desire is ridiculed. In a more serious tone, Zvelebil (1981) describes demons as "symbols of the most devastating, most destructive quality which man in his human condition must struggle against: of ANGST, of Fear, of the feeling of alienating terror, apprehensions, and anxieties arising from the unknown around us, in the universe and in our future. . . . Cur [the asura] is the great symbol of chaos and disorder, of formless matter, of dangerous, wild, untamed, inimical nature" (35).

In the theology of Shaiva Siddhanta, the demon is explicitly recognized as a metaphor for impulses and desires that destroy the possibility of liberation and union with the divine. The asuras are said to personify the three *malas* or *pacas*, the forces that bind human spirits to this world (Clothey 1983, 109): *anava* (ignorance), *karma* (the inevitability of an action's consequences), and *maya* (worldly ensnarement). According to Danielou (1964), the discipline of the yoga adept is described metaphorically as a battle between the gods and the demons in which desires must be defeated so that the true ascetic, represented by Skanda (Murugan), may be born (299). Shulman (1980) also interprets the story of the demon-devotee as representing a victory over the self, which leads to redemption:

> The demon . . . symbolizes the evil within man (preoccupation with a false "self-hood," the lust for power, opposition to the divine ideals); this evil must be destroyed before redemption becomes possible—indeed, redemption is directly consequent upon the destruction of egoism and wrong desires. For the human devotee, this process need not culminate in actual death (as it does on the symbolic level for the demon devotee); it does, however, require a form of self-sacrifice. (320)

Devotees who are pierced with the lance of Murugan thus symbolically represent their victory over the demonic part of the self.[4] However, this symbolic act may have different meanings for particular individuals. Depending on caste heritage and class, a man may identify with Idumban, the coolie, or with Surapadma, the rebellious asura, or with the victorious warrior god Murugan. Or he may identify with all three.

## ANIMAL SELVES

### The Dance of the Peacock

The dipping, swirling dance of devotees who carry a kavadi decorated with peacock feathers imitates the trancelike dance of the male peacock when he courts his mate. The devotee's identification with the peacock introduces the motif of sexual beauty and courtship. In Hindu iconography, the major deities are generally associated with an animal vehicle. Shiva rides Nandi, the bull; Vishnu rides the Garuda (a mythical figure with the beak and talons of a predatory bird and the body of a man); Murugan rides the peacock; and Ganesh, the elephant-headed god, rides the rat. These animal vehicles can be seen as representations of the sexual energies of the gods. For example, the symbolic associations of the bull make it an appropriate vehicle for the god consort of the Great Goddess, for the bull plows the earth (mother) and is the male counterpart of the great Indian mother symbol, the cow. By contrast, Ganesh, who is represented iconographically as phallically crippled (his face distorted by the limp phallic trunk, his tusk broken off), rides the rat, which inhabits secret holes underground (see Obeyesekere 1978, 469–70; Courtright 1985). In contrast to Ganesh, Murugan is like Kama, the god of love who rides a parrot or a peacock. The male peacock, who courts his mate by displaying his tail, is frequently employed in Tamil poetry as a symbol of masculine beauty (Clothey 1978, 32; Shulman 1980, 168). The rooster that appears on Murugan's pennant is another symbol of masculine beauty. These animals aptly reflect the sexual energy of the young and handsome lover of Valli.

On the day of vow fulfillment, young women dressed in their finest saris and wearing gold bangles and chains watch the devotees of Murugan whirl to the beat of the drums in what could be aptly described as an exhibitionist display of erotic male beauty. The young men who perform the *atta kavadi* (dance of the peacock) and who impale their bodies with the lance of Murugan appear to enact a double identification, first with the peacock as a symbol of male sexual beauty and second with Murugan, who subdues the peacock demon with his lance, thereby winning as his bride the heavenly Deviani. For these youths, the ritual of vow fulfillment might be described as a rite of passage into manhood, during which sexual impulses are symbolically represented and controlled at the same time.[5]

## The Serpent and Sexuality

The peacock that serves as Murugan's vehicle grasps a snake in its claw or beak.[6] Clothey reports that there is a strange lack of myths or even references in the mythology of Murugan to this snake (1978, 187). I was told that the serpent was to the peacock as the peacock was to Murugan: a dangerous enemy that had been defeated and tamed. There is a striking replication of imagery in that the cobra, like the peacock, performs a trancelike dance in an erect state (see Clothey 1978, 32).

Although the image of the snake is not prominent in rituals associated with Thaipusam, the serpent motif is worth briefly exploring for its potential meanings, because the serpent is perhaps the most complex and ubiquitous animal symbol in Hindu legends and iconography. In most societies, snakes have been objects of fear and veneration and have been used as symbols.[7] They make excellent symbols because of their strange and unusual characteristics. Snakes shed their skin and may therefore appear immortal (and thus provide a symbol for the idea of rebirth).[8] They walk without legs (see Genesis). Snakes inhabit holes in the ground and seem to appear from nowhere and to disappear quickly. Some snakes bring death with their poisonous bite (in this regard, the serpent as a sexual symbol bears comparison to the Western use of the pistol as a sexual symbol); some snakes stand erect and have a hypnotic stare. Some snakes bear live young; others devour their prey live. Some snakes lay eggs; snakes also feed on eggs (and thus may appear cannibalistic).

As animals with no obvious sexual characteristics, serpents can stand for both sexes.[9] The erect cobra is a common phallic symbol, but the snake that devours its prey live may suggest the vagina as a devouring, potentially castrating organ. The association of serpents with female sexuality and its dangers appears frequently in Tamil poems and tales: in the poem *Shilappadikaram,* for example, the courtesan is said to have a pubis like a cobra's hood, and the Shaivite poet Pattirakiri writes:

When will come the time
when I rid myself from the spreading hoods
of their greedy cunts gaping like red wounds?
(in Zvelebil 1973a, 89)

Trawick cites a myth in which Shiva says to his spouse, Parvati, "Your body against my body is like a black snake coiled around a white tree" (1990a, 31), and a poem in which a girl is described as having a "small belly [like] a snake." Trawick's informant commented on this image: "As a snake spreads its hood in anger, the heroine spreads the place at the lower end of her snake-like waist in desire" (1990a, 29).

The most common representation of the serpent in Tamil temples and shrines is found under a banyan tree that grows in the courtyard of a temple or in the household compound. These images—which usually consist of an erect serpent or of two intertwined serpents—are associated with fertility.[10] When a woman wishes to have a child, she makes offerings of milk and eggs to the serpent deities, and she may mark the fulfillment of her prayer by hanging a miniature cradle containing a doll in the branches of the tree that shelters the shrine. The association of serpents with fertility is also represented in Manasa, the snake goddess of Bengal, who causes her worshippers to be "blessed with wealth, sons and fame" (Gupta 1965, 48).

The serpent is also represented in the figures of the Naga Raja (Cobra King) and his wife, who have the upper bodies of humans and the lower bodies of snakes. Like the gods, the Nagas have both a human and an animal aspect, but these are conjoined. There is no representation of conquest and mastery. Tales about these Naga spirits portray them as both sexual and aggressive creatures. They are potentially malevolent, like the demonic asuras and rakshasas, but they may be subdued and turned into guardian deities, as when Krishna subdues the Naga Raja Kaliya.

Another prominent symbolic use of the snake is in the goddess Kundalini, who personifies the energy (sakti) or divine power that pervades the universe. In human beings this energy is said to lie coiled like a serpent in the area of the genitals. In yogic practices, Kundalini is awakened and made to rise through the seven chakras (literally, "wheels") that are located between the base of the spine and the forehead. These practices transform sexual energy into spiritual power and lead to liberation (moksha) or enlightenment (see Eliade 1969; Zvelebil 1973a; Bhagat 1976). In the image of Kundalini, the serpent is explicitly associated with both sexual and spiritual powers.

As symbols in Hindu myths, legends, and theology, serpents conjoin sexuality with dangerous aggression (as in the erect cobra with its poisonous bite), both basic human energies that can be transformed into spiritual power.[11] These associations are reflected in the images of Shiva and Kali, which are adorned with serpents, suggesting that these deities can control the dangerous serpent energies. Vishnu is also represented as a god who controls the serpent powers. He is frequently portrayed resting on the serpent Sesha (or Ananta), who was tamed by Vishnu because the serpent demon had poisoned the oceans and terrorized the people, bringing chaos to the world.

Religious use of the serpent symbol may allow worshippers to invoke the protection and assistance of the gods to help them confront their anxieties about the dangers of sexual contact and violent anger. Just as the god or goddess handles serpents with comfort, so may the devotees. Maity reports that after worshipping Manasa, the snake goddess, "a man gets no fear from snakes" (in Gupta 1965, 48). The snake, like the god's animal mount, may represent potentially dangerous energies—fused sexual and aggressive wishes—that are brought under control and transformed into spiritual powers.

## ASCETICISM: POWER AND PENANCE

The symbolic meanings of asceticism *(tapas)* in Hindu tradition are rich and varied. According to the theory of yoga, ascetic practices can be used to master sexual desire and to convert sexual energy into spiritual power. The equivalence of sexual and spiritual energy is a central paradox in Hinduism, represented symbolically by Shiva, the "erotic ascetic," who is worshipped in the form of the phallic *lingam* (O'Flaherty 1973). The power derived from ascetic practices is manifested as heat. (The word *tapas* is derived from the Sanskrit root *tap,* which means heat.) While *kama* (desire) generates the heat of sexuality, which is dissipated in sexual intercourse, the requirement of celibacy in tapas transforms the energy of sexual desire into spiritual heat. Thus, renouncing sexuality actually produces both spiritual and sexual potency (O'Flaherty 1973, 35; see also Danielou 1964, 299; Eliade 1969; and Obeyesekere 1981).

The theme of empowerment through ascetic practices also appears in tales of religious hermits and demonic asuras and rakshasas, who perform ascetic practices (tapas) with the aim of obtaining boons from the gods. For example, the ascetic austerities of Ravana—king of the rakshasas and antihero of the *Ramayana*—forced Brahma to make him invulnerable and enabled him to assume any form he pleased. The horrible man-eating rakshasa Viradha—"wearing a tiger's skin, dripping with fat, wetted with blood, terrific to all creatures, like death with [an] open mouth"—also obtained the boon of invulnerability by tapas (see Dowson 1961, 358, see also 264). Ascetics in the *Mahabharata* are empowered by their tapas or yoga and shake the very throne of Indra, who sends down *apsaras* (heavenly nymphs) to seduce and distract them from their ascetic discipline. In these legends, the ascetic is able to compel the gods to grant him (the hermits are invariably male) a boon through control of his own desire (Bhagat 1976, 210–12). The symbolic equivalence of self-mastery and mastery of the world has frequently been noted by scholars of yoga and Hindu asceticism. For example, Eliade comments that "one always finds a form of yoga whenever there is [a] question of *experiencing the sacred* or arriving at complete *mastery of oneself,* which is itself the first step toward the magic mastery of the world" (Eliade 1969, 196; see also Menninger 1938, 119; and Masson 1976, 624).

In Hinduism the theme of empowerment through ascetic practices is linked to ideas about caste. In the *Mahabharata,* for example, the sage Parasara says to King Janaka: "O King! those great souled ones who have made themselves pure by austerities even though born of low parentage cannot be considered low, only because of their low birth" (cited in Bhagat 1976, 203). In the tale of the famous ascetic Vishvamitra, we see how asceticism provides a symbolic means of triumphing over those who claim high status in the caste hierarchy.[12] Vishvamitra was a warrior who fought his rival the Brahmin Vasishtha in battle many times, only to be vanquished in each encounter. Finally Vishvamitra realized that his strength as a warrior was nothing as compared with the spiritual strength of a Brahmin, so he resolved to gain spiritual strength by performing ascetic practices. He practiced tapas of the most demanding and awe-inspiring kind, eating only roots and fruits and meditating day after day. However, when the heavenly nymph Menaka was sent to seduce him, he could not suppress his desire. After this failure, Vishvamitra added the vow of chastity to his tapas. Another beautiful nymph, Rambha, was sent to seduce him. This time he resisted temptation but gave vent to his anger by turning the heavenly nymph to stone. This impulsive act deprived him of a great deal of accumulated ascetic merit. So Vishvamitra again increased the severity of his tapas: "he never opened his mouth, never spoke, never ate, and held even his breath." He was in a *samadhi* (meditation trance) for a very long time until he had subjugated lust, greed, anger, and all the "passions and lower propensities of his nature." As a result of this unparalleled tapas, Vishvamitra became a Brahmasari, the paradigm for all ascetics, not only a Brahmin by caste but an exemplar of the ideal Brahmin (following Bhagat 1976, 15–16). In this tale the Kshatriya warrior ultimately prevails, but he does so by becoming a Brahmin, thereby providing further proof of the ultimate superiority of Brahmins. What begins as a refusal to recognize the superiority of Brahmins is converted into an ascetic conquest of the self. The message is that the lowly prevail over the powerful by conquering their own impulsive and desirous natures and acquiring the virtues of the powerful. They fulfill the aims of their aggression by turning that aggression back against themselves.

As Bhagat (1976) explains, while *tapas* is often translated as penance, "the idea of sin and its expiation is not always present behind the austerities of most ascetics . . . . In some cases the penance is performed, as in the case of Vishvamitra, not only to atone for moral lapses but also to transmute his lower nature of lust and passions into a higher state of perfection" (15). Frequently, the sole aim of ascetic practices is revenge, as in the tale of the corrupt raja cited by Karl Menninger (1938). When this raja ordered the house of a Brahmin destroyed and his lands confiscated, the Brahmin retaliated by fasting at the palace gate until he died. He then became an avenging ghost who destroyed the raja (110). Menninger points out that a familiar form of this fantasy occurs in the angry but powerless child who thinks, "They'll be sorry when I die." He comments, "It seems at first contrary to human nature that one individual could force another person to do his will simply by compelling his antagonist to witness his suffering and thus force him to assume the moral but illogical obligation for it. Yet this appeal has often proved effective where more direct aggressions have failed" (110).[13] Like the ascetic *rishis* of the *Mahabharata* who shook the throne of the high gods, Mahatma Gandhi demonstrated that passive-aggressive asceticism can be an effective political technique for protesting the unjust acts of those who can enforce their will through greater strength.

The theme of ascetic withdrawal leading to restitution for wrongs committed against one appears also in the legend of the founding of the temple of Murugan at Palani, which is associated with the Thaipusam festival. The divine brothers Murugan and Vinayagar (Ganesh) both wished to have the golden mango that the sage Narada had brought to their parents. Outwitted by Vinayagar, who won the mango by avowing his devotion to his parents, Murugan stripped off the sacred thread of the high, twice-born castes and left home. In his retreat on a hilltop in Tamilnadu he became an ascetic. The power he thus accumulated eventually compelled Shiva, his father, to acknowledge Murugan as a powerful deity and his true heir.

In the closely knit Tamil family, the appeal of culturally sanctioned ascetic withdrawal from the world may be very strong. The psychoanalyst Sudhir Kakar (1981) has suggested that the ascetic fantasy is a defensive one in which a denial of bodily needs is equated with denial of a need for supplies of love and gratification from others in the world, according to the formula "I do not need anyone's love, nor do I need anything from the world, not even food" (156). In her ethnography of a Tamil Brahmin family, Trawick provides an illustration of this need for withdrawal as expressed by her chief male informant, Ayya, who "liked to point out that he was separate, not closely related to anyone in the household, and that he avoided the bonds of 'attachment'" (1990a, 73). Ayya also cultivated such detachment in the male children in his household, saying approvingly of them that they (unlike their sisters) would not cry when beaten. In this last comment a stoical response to physical pain is equated with the denial of emotional pain.

## THE LEGEND OF PALANI: OEDIPAL THEMES AND THE RIVALRY OF SONS

For Shaiva Tamils, the divine family consists of Shiva, his consort Parvati, and their sons, Vinayagar (also known as Ganesh) and Murugan. (Usually, Vinayagar is said to be the elder brother, but sometimes Murugan is said to be older [see Courtright 1985, 123].) The relationships among these figures are

richly developed in the literature of the Puranas and in legends such as the popular story that tells of the rivalry between Murugan and Vinayagar, which is associated with the founding of the Palani Temple. In this legend, Murugan is bested
by Vinayagar through the latter's declaration of devotion to his mother (parents).
Vinayagar thereby wins the coveted prize, a golden mango.

This legend has been analyzed for its oedipal themes by Obeyesekere
(1978), who points out that the mango is a symbol of the vagina in Sri Lanka
and in Tamilnadu (469).[14] A variant of the legend found in the *Shiva Purana*
(Courtright 1985, 123) confirms this interpretation by making the prize a
bride.[15] In yet another variant, in the *Padma Purana* Vinayagar is given food as
a prize for worshipping his parents (Courtright 1985, 126–27). In the symbol of
the mango, then, both oral and sexual satisfaction are suggested. This allows for
the expression of a consciously unacceptable sexual desire for the mother in the
sublimated form of a desire for food. In this way the mango is associated with
the breast and the mother. In the Tamil village where she did her fieldwork,
Trawick (1990b) says:

> A mango was like a breast. You kneaded it between the palms of your hands un-
> til the pulp was a creamy juice, then you cut a small hole at the tip and sucked
> out the juice. In our village, it was a sin to cut down a fruit-bearing mango tree,
> just as it was a sin to kill a pregnant cow. I cannot help but think it significant
> that the mango tree was called *ma*. (45)

Vinayagar, the devoted son, is portrayed with a bulging potbelly that is said
to be the result of his childish love of sweets and the overindulgence of his
mother. His satisfactions thus remain at the oral level. Kakar observes that the
potbellied, elephant-headed deity "embodies certain 'typical' resolutions of de-
velopmental conflicts in traditional Hindu society. . . . In effect, the boy expresses
his conviction that the only way he can propitiate his mother's demands and once
again make her nurturing and protective is to repudiate the cause of the distur-
bance in their mutuality: his maleness" (Kakar 1981, 101–2). This repudiation of
male sexuality is depicted symbolically in the displacement of the phallic trunk
upward to the mouth (Obeyesekere 1978, 469–70; see also Ramanujan in Edmunds and Dundes 1983, 245). I also found Ganesh's fixation on his mother represented in the story I was told, to explain the images of Vinayagar that are found
at public bathing places throughout Tamilnadu. People said that Vinayagar is
continually looking for a woman as beautiful as his mother, but since he never
finds one, he remains a perpetual bachelor.[16]

The tale of Vinayagar's birth also emphasizes his close relationship with his
mother, Parvati, who creates him by mixing the skin that she washes from her
body with unguents. This story not only denies that any father participated sexually in the conception of this son but also gives Vinayagar the wish-fulfilling fantasy of guarding his mother's chamber against his father's entry. When Shiva returns home, he is barred from entering Parvati's bath chamber by her new son.

Before he learns the boy's identity, Shiva cuts off the youth's head. In response to Parvati's pleas to restore her son to life, Shiva agrees to replace the boy's head with that of the first living creature he encounters. That creature is the elephant.[17] In addition to the motif of decapitation, other signs of Vinayagar's symbolic castration are his "exaggerated but perpetually flaccid trunk" (Courtright 1985, 109) and a broken tusk. According to some accounts of the legend, his injury was the consequence of eating the symbolic mango (Obeyesekere 1984, 471).[18]

If Vinayagar represents the son who is sexually fixated on his mother, Murugan is a virile son who is identified with his father.[19] We see this first in the myth of Murugan's birth, which provides a striking contrast to the story of Vinayagar. The rebellious asuras are making war on Kailasha, and Parvati is sent to Shiva's retreat so that a son may be born to fight them. But Shiva, engaged in ascetic practices, does not respond to Parvati's seductive advances. Even after their marriage, no child is born. Finally the dove obtains the seed of Shiva and deposits it in the River Ganga, who gives birth to six children. When Parvati gathers them in her arms these children are made into one child with six heads. It is significant that Murugan is born of his father's seed without the participation of his mother (although the female's role as carrier of the male's seed is represented by the River Ganga, who is known as a goddess in her own right). This myth may be said to express the wish-fulfilling fantasy that men do not need women but may produce children by themselves (Dundes 1962a). As in the story of Vinayagar's birth, sexual intercourse between the parents is denied, but in this case the son does not have a mother who is his rival for the affection of his father.[20]

The identification of Murugan with his father is emphasized in the legend of the Palani Temple. When Vinayagar is given the mango for his demonstration of devotion to his parents, Murugan goes to southern India, where he takes up ascetic practices. In asceticism the body, where incestuous wishes and aggressive and hostile feelings lodge, is both punished and at the same time mastered. Through his asceticism Murugan compels his father—Shiva, the great ascetic—to recognize him as his true heir: "You are the fruit." At the pilgrimage temple of Palani this ascetic solution to oedipal desire and jealousy is commemorated.

Oedipal conflict in Indian tales and myths has a different pattern from the Greek form that we take to be paradigmatic (see Goldman 1978; Kakar 1981; Ramanujan 1983; Obeyesekere 1984, 1990). There are very few narratives in which sons express hostility toward (or murder) a father or father figure. More commonly, fathers or father figures (and mothers or stepmothers) express hostility or act aggressively toward their sons or daughters.[21] Kakar (1990) writes: "The Indian context stresses more the father's envy of what belongs to the son including the mother—and thus the son's persecution anxiety—as a primary motivation in the father-son relationship. It is thus charged with the dread of filicide and with the son's castration, by self or the father, as a solution to the father-son competition" (443). In Indian tales that treat the relationship of the son to the father, the son commonly renounces the kingdom and/or reproductive sexuality so that the father may continue to indulge his desires fully.[22] The most famous example comes from the *Mahabharata* where Bhishma becomes a lifelong celibate, renouncing both the kingdom and his reproductive sexual life, so that his father may marry a fisher girl. Later Bhishma, the celibate and submissive son, becomes powerful in his own right as a result of his austerities. In the mythology of Murugan and the legend of the founding of Palani we find a variant of this theme. The son's hostility toward the father is internalized and directed at the self through asceticism. His love for his father is unsublimated, and by mastering his hostility, the son wins the love and acknowledgment of the "father" (god).

For Hindus, as for the Greeks, the expression of a son's hostile and rivalrous wishes toward his father is culturally disapproved. However, in India, oedipal rivalry with the father may be displaced to a brother, as in the tale of Murugan and Vinayagar.[23] In the traditional Indian family, when the father is dead or absent, the elder brother stands in the position of father, as the authority to whom respect and obedience are owed. Brenda Beck has pointed out that, whereas Indian epics celebrate male sibling cooperation as exemplified by Rama and his brothers, rivalry between brothers is a common theme in Indian folktales (Beck in Blackburn and Ramanujan 1986, 99; see also Courtright 1985, 123–26). Trawick tells us of an incident that suggests the powerful emotions associated with sibling rivalry. According to his sister, Trawick's chief informant, Ayya, ran away from home after an angry fight with his older brother. Their father sent the older brother to Madras to find Ayya. When he failed, the father himself went and convinced Ayya to return (1990a, 227). In the personal history of Ayya and his brother, we hear echoes of the story of Murugan, who also left home because of rivalry with his brother, forcing his father to seek him out and demonstrate his love for his son.

Kakar (1981) has described a common pattern of relationship in Indian families, in which fathers tend to be emotionally remote from their sons (whom they may envy), whereas the emotional bond between mother and son is intimate and deep.[24] This pattern contributes to friction between mothers and their daughters-in-law and leads men to search for the ideal father, who may be represented in the figure of the guru (138–39). Trawick points out that the most popular male gods in Tamilnadu—Murugan, Kannan, Ayyapan, and Pillaiyar (another name for Vinayagar or Ganesh)—are all represented iconographically as children (1990a, 159). She suggests that their worshippers, the majority of whom are men, identify with these gods as sons. If a worshipper is looking for an ideal father who will recognize the power and virtue of his son, identification with Murugan can offer the fantasy (or hope) of winning the father's love and approval, as did Murugan, through ascetic practices. The relationship with one's mother may also be involved in identification with Murugan. Trawick describes a magazine article, *Ammavai Tedi* (In Search of Mother), that tells how the boy-god Murugan appeals to his own mother to help "all the mother-seeking souls" (Trawick 1990a, 166). In this way, the themes of Amman worship, in which devotees seek the protection and nurturance of the mother goddess, also appear in the worship of Murugan. Identification with Murugan may suggest to a young man the wish that the mother goddess care for him and also give him the powerful spear, the sign of manhood, through which a bride is won.

The story of the rivalry of Murugan and his brother Vinayagar may be told from different points of view. Among those of high-caste heritage who stress the importance of education, the tale is frequently told to emphasize the cleverness of Vinayagar. As Paul Courtright (1985) points out in his study of Ganesh, the story has been used theologically as a metaphor representing different traditions within Hinduism, distinguishing the path of devotion to one's parents and fulfillment of caste duty, from the ascetic's path of self-denial and rejection of family responsibility (128). For example, in the *Padma Purana* Murugan performs a pilgrimage, and Parvati exclaims, "All the pilgrimages and sacrifices are not worth a sixteenth part of the worship of one's parents" (quoted in Courtright 1985, 126–27). Thus, Vinayagar's devotion to his parents may be used to make a theological point about the superiority of the orthodox tradition of Hinduism (respectful worship of authority figures) over the heterodox tradition of pilgrimage temples and bhakti devotionalism. However, as told by the devotees who fulfill vows to Murugan on Thaipusam, the story celebrates Murugan's victory over his brother, the father's recognition of the son's power and independence, and the tradition of devotional worship in a pilgrimage temple.

## THE CELEBRATION OF EROTICISM

At the annual festival of the temple of Kataragama in Sri Lanka (where Murugan is addressed as Kataragama), the god is taken in procession to a temple where Valliamma (Mother Valli) is said to abide, so that the divine couple can have sexual intercourse (Wirz 1966; Obeyesekere 1978, 1984). On the climactic third day of the festival, when the union of Murugan and Valli has been consummated, devotees go to a nearby river for a ritual bath, which Obeyesekere describes as a display of riotous erotic release (Obeyesekere 1984, 473).

Among Tamils, Murugan differs from his rival Vinayagar in having freed himself from his attachment to his mother. He not only wins Deviani for his bride, he also woos the sensuous Valli. Some worshippers in Penang say that Murugan is taken in the Thaipusam procession to visit his wife (or mistress), perhaps echoing the theme of erotic power that is played out at Kataragama. But the story ends differently, and in Penang, shame and anxiety over sexuality prevail. Murugan is said to return on the third night under cover of darkness because he has not succeeded in having intercourse.[25] To understand this sexual anxiety, we must turn our attention to images of gender and female sexuality in Tamil Hinduism.

## The Dangerous Goddess: Unmarried and Untamed

In the warrior goddess Durga, slayer of the buffalo demon Mahishasura, and in Kali, who wears a necklace of skulls, we find powerful images of the destructive energy (sakti) and dangerous sexuality of female deities. In some parts of southern India, the demon Mahisha is said to be the suitor of Durga, her would-be husband. David Kinsley (1986) writes: "A central point of the South Indian myths about Durga and Mahisa is that any sexual association with the goddess is dangerous and that before her sexuality can be rendered safe she must be dominated by, made subservient to, defeated by, or humiliated by a male" (1986, 115; see also Babb 1975b, 216–24).[26] The theme of the violent goddess who conquers and marries her (demon) husband is also represented in the celebration of the annual Amman goddess festival in parts of Tamilnadu (Beck 1981). Indeed, anxiety about the power of the malevolent goddess appears to underlie the rituals of the festival of the Amman goddess, which have the purpose of transforming the goddess into her benevolent form, either by appeasing her appetite with offerings or by bringing her powers under control through marriage (Moffatt 1979, 246–89). It is the unmarried goddess who is dangerous and out of control. As Kinsley (1986) puts it, "Independent in her unmarried state, Durga is portrayed as possessing untamed sexual energy that is dangerous, indeed, deadly, to any male who dares to approach her" (115).[27]

In her dangerous and threatening forms (Durga, Kali, and the Amman goddesses), the goddess rides a maned lion. Although apparently a masculine symbol, the lion (or tiger) can also be interpreted as a frightening iconographic representation of the devouring mother and of the female genitalia that may castrate.[28] The vehicle of the goddess provides a striking contrast to the animal vehicles of male deities, which suggest sexual energies that have been domesticated or brought under control. It is significant that in her benevolent form as Parvati, wife of Shiva, the goddess is usually not represented with an animal vehicle, or her lion is shown sleeping at her side, like a giant pussy cat. Parvati may also be represented with a parrot or a dove on her shoulder, symbolizing her gentleness and beauty.

Even more frightening than the sexually devouring goddess is the representation of the devouring mother, as in the image of Kali, with her necklace of skulls, gaping mouth, and lolling tongue that drips with blood (see Chaudhuri 1956, 142). Kali is most frequently addressed as Kali-ma, or Mother Kali. Similarly, the village Amman goddesses are often represented with fangs and with dead children under their feet.[29] The violent images associated with women and the goddess are puzzling because the picture of unrestrained female hostility stands in sharp contrast to the ideal of the devoted Indian wife and mother. In his commentary on the *Catakantaravanan Katai* (the story of Sita's conquest of the demon Satakantharavana, Ravana with one hundred heads),[30] Stuart Blackburn asks, "Why does the folk source prefer to identify violence with the woman, passivity with the male? ... Does the aggressive Sita, happily lopping off the limbs of her male opponents, represent a masculine fear of female sexuality? Is this the source of the male's impotence in this story? Or does Sita embody *female* fantasies of power, experienced imaginatively in the medium of the story?" (Shulman in Blackburn and Ramanujan 1986, 121; see also Wadley 1980, 1–34, 153–70).

There are, of course, no simple answers to these questions, for different individuals may draw very different meanings from the imagery of the violent goddess. However, the split in the image of the goddess—who in her benevolent form as wife and mother is all good and in her malevolent form represents death and danger—has profound significance for both men and women. Sudhir Kakar (1981) suggests that "underlying the conscious ideal of womanly purity, innocence and fidelity, and interwoven with the unconscious belief in a safeguarding maternal beneficence is a secret conviction among many Hindu men that the feminine principle is really the opposite—treacherous, lustful and rampant with an insatiable, contaminating sexuality" (93). Anxiety about female power in its malevolent form may also haunt women, causing them to fear their own feelings, especially anger.

Tamil men may see women as devourers of energy and life force because they believe that in intercourse men lose sakti (power or energy) to women through their semen (Daniel in Wadley 1980, 90; see also Carstairs 1958). Even if a woman behaves in an exemplary fashion, she presents a danger to her husband, for she drains off his sexual energy. Fear of sexual contact with women and the image of women as seducers who destroy one's spiritual power are themes that appear in connection with the Thaipusam festival in the devotional songs of the Bhakti poets. In the following hymn, for example, the Murugan *bhakta* Arunakiri implores the god to save him from temptation of women who lure him from the path of enlightenment:

> Those women
> with swaying breasts
> lovely red hands
> filled with bangles
> as they jingle
> with dark cloud-like tresses
> where bees sing
> and soft beseeching words like the *kuyil*
> lovely as the five-colored parrots
> their voices honey
> fish-like eyes
> vying
> warm with fear
> their forehead a crescent moon
> By them I was lured
> in their magical ways

into this sea of birth
Your slave am I
Help me reach the shore
of your brave noble feet
Conquer and bless me.
Arunakirinatar, *Tiruppukal* 2 (in Zvelebil 1973b, 242)

## The Devotee as Beloved: Fear of and Identification with Female Sexuality

One way of avoiding the dangers of sexual contact with a woman is by identifying with the Valli, Murugan's beloved. The male devotee's feminine self may
then win the love of the god through submission, as a Tamil woman submits herself to her father and her husband and thereby wins their love. In another poem
Arunakiri pleads in the voice of Valli to be rescued by Murugan:

Lord with the spear
worshipped by
the spouse of the mountain king's daughter
the spouse of the daughter of learning
the spouse of the daughter of wealth
You
with the deer of the millet fields
with the deer of the heavenly groves
in love embraced
in your merciful arms
Rescue
this daughter of the earth
where great poets stray
with your golden-rayed spear
residing on the hills of Tiruttani
You redeem those lonely followers
all day mounted
on your beautiful peacock
O pride of prides!

Those bedecked women
with luring words
mingled with the sounds of horns
and the call of black *kuyils* from the shore
echo of the sea
merged with thoughts
From the murderous arrows of Manmatan
rescue this woman with creeper-like waist
from being destroyed in sorrows
You adorned with the *kura* flower
grant me your garland of katappa blossoms

strung round your wide arms!
Arunakirinatar, *Tiruppukal* (in Zvelebil 1973b, 245)

Of course, men may also identify with Murugan as the lover of Valli, the dark, sensual tribal girl, the forbidden woman. Obeyesekere has pointed out that this fantasy may have special appeal for some Tamil men, because the ideal marriage to the daughter of their mother's brother increases the likelihood that a man unconsciously will equate his wife with his mother, with the consequence that sexual desire is repressed (1978, 470). However, both men and women also identify with Valli and participate in the metaphor that describes union with the divine in the language of erotic love and sexual union.[31]

Identification with Valli may have a variety of meanings to the male devotees of Murugan. In recent psychoanalytic writings exploring the cultural and psychological construction of gender difference, theorists have pointed out that a boy first identifies with his primary caretaker, that is, his mother.[32] This feminine identification must be suppressed later and replaced with a masculine identification. In many cultures the transition is marked by male initiation rites that isolate young men from the rest of society. In other societies, the feminine is denigrated, and there is a hypervaluation of masculinity, as in the culture of machismo (see Slater 1968; Parsons 1969; and Carroll 1986). In Western culture there is suspicion and fear of a feminine identification in boys as indicating a homosexual tendency. A boy who does not repress his feminine identification is likely to be taunted as a sissy (sister) and encouraged to "act like a man."

The data on India suggest another pattern. The mother's intense idealization of her male child appears to ease the transition to a masculine identification for the boy. And in some cases, the primary feminine identification may be consciously maintained and valued as an inner "true" feminine self. For example, Trawick's informant "Ayya was a preacher who taught about the ideals of Tamil womanhood as he saw them—softness, meltingness, subtlety, mystery, modesty. 'As I teach,' he said, 'I become what I teach'" (1990a, 74).[33] According to Kakar, "the wish to be a woman is one particular solution to the discord that threatens the breaking up of the son's fantasized connection to the mother, a solution whose access to awareness is facilitated by the culture's views on sexual differentiation and the permeability of gender boundaries" (1990, 439).[34] He cites Gandhi's statement "that he has mentally become a woman." In the view of Gandhi: "There is as much reason for a man to wish that he was born a woman as for woman to do otherwise" (439). One reason that Indian men may be able to consciously retain a feminine identification may be because the feminine has been split into good and bad aspects, and it is only the positive side of a feminine identification that is consciously maintained. For example, Trawick's informant Ayya was also liable to taunt his wife with deprecatory remarks, such as "All women are dogs" (1990a, 192).

In vow fulfillment on Thaipusam, some male devotees carry milk offerings in small pots of milk hooked into their chests (as symbolic breasts). Here we find a feminine identification with the mother who receives the love of the god because of her nurturing devotion to her infant son. In this identification, the erotic element of the feminine is disguised (or denied) by a representation of the female as supplier of food rather than sexual satisfaction (an oral as opposed to a genital mode of relationship). Kakar suggests that identification with the feminine may also mean a loss of masculinity that is reassuring. "In psycho-sexual terms, to identify with one's mother means to sacrifice one's masculinity to her in order to escape sexual excitation and the threat it poses to the boy's fragile ego" (Kakar 1981, 102).

The son who renounces his male sexuality is no longer a threat to his father in an oedipal rivalry for the mother. In traditional Tamil families, the emotional bond between mother and son is complex, but usually a deep and lasting one. Ramanujan has observed that in Tamil folktales, the mother's love or desire for her son is relatively unrepressed (1983, 252; see also Kakar 1981, 90). According to Trawick, on the son's side, "Erotic love for the mother is, of course, strongly repressed. However, an interesting bit of Tamil ideology . . . claims that children before puberty have no sexual feelings. Hence close physical relations with the mother are allowed up until that time. Many adults, especially men, remember having been nursed for years, even to the age of five or beyond" (1990a, 171). Trawick gives an example of the kind of intimate and sensual interaction that occurred between a "mother" and son in the family that she lived with: "Anni [Jnana Oli's mother's sister] was Jnana Oli's most subtle teacher. Sometimes she would sit in the afternoon with Jnana Oli on her lap, one hand cradling his head, the other cupped over his penis, talking with him. When he said something charming, she would squeeze his penis gently, as one would squeeze a friend's hand, in a sudden small burst of affection" (1990a, 219). In the world of Jnana Oli, as Trawick describes it, there was "a plurality of mothers. Many laps cradled him, many hands fed him. He slipped without friction in and out among them as though they were all interchangeable" (1990b, 228). In an extended family, Trawick reminds us, the intensity of relationship between a mother and a son was diffused over many mothers, as reflected in the idea that "all mothers are one" (see Kurtz 1992). Nevertheless, for men who did not have a plurality of mothers, oedipal rivalry with a father might be very threatening. In Malaysia extended families are rare.

For some devotees, then, the piercing of the tongue with a vel may be a symbolic castration that is meant to reassure the devotee that he has controlled (denied) or destroyed unacceptable sexual desires. Jones (1929) has described the characteristics of the tongue that make it a phallic symbol: "the fact that it is a red pointed organ, with dangerous potentialities, capable of self-movement, usually discreetly concealed but capable of protrusion (as in the defiant and forbidden exhibitionism of children), which can emit a fluid (saliva) that is a common symbol for semen" (312). If the phallic tongue is a source of temptation and sin, then a ritual that involves cutting it off or piercing it may be interpreted as a renunciation of temptation and a cleansing oneself from pollution and sinful thoughts. Such an interpretation makes sense of the story of "a fanatic self-torturer [who] makes a vow to cut half his tongue off, executes it coolly with his own hands, puts the amputated portion in an open coconut shell, and offers it on his knees to the divinity [the Amman goddess]" (Dubois and Beauchamp 1906, 606). For other devotees, symbolic castration of the phallic tongue may be meant to reassure the powerful representatives of the father—the god, high-caste leaders, and political leaders—that the rebellious sons are not a threat.[35]

## PURITY, POLLUTION, AND GENDER

The association of pollution with bodily products shapes the Hindu conception of gender difference. Women are polluted by organic processes that men do not experience—menstruation and the act of giving birth. Since greater pollution leads to less self-control, women are thought to be less virtuous than men and therefore in need of control and protection by fathers, brothers, or husbands. Like untouchables, women are thought to pose a dangerous threat to the moral order of society. Holly Reynolds writes: "[Tamil] culture decrees that woman left to her own devices is unpredictable, capricious, wily, fickle, voracious in sexual appetite, disrespectful of boundaries, limits, and categories. As such, woman is a being in need of control" (in Wadley 1980, 46).[36] By protecting and controlling women, men preserve their honor and ensure their prosperity and happiness. In the Tamil classic *Shilappadikairam* (The Ankle Bracelet), one is told, "Where a woman's virtue is safe and unsullied, the blessings of rain never fail, prosperity never declines, victory is ever a slave to the monarch" (Adigal 1965, 103).

In traditional Tamil society, a girl was prepared from a young age for a life of self-sacrifice and subservient deference to men. She was expected to care for her siblings and to help with cooking and housework while her brothers were free to play (S. Daniel in Wadley 1980, 72–73). She was taught to protect others from the danger to their purity that she represented. At puberty when a girl began to menstruate, a strict behavioral code requiring self-restraint was imposed on her. She began to wear a sari six yards long, wound around and covering her body, especially breasts and loins, the loci of female generative power and the source of pollution; she began to keep her hair bound up and was expected to stay near the vicinity of the courtyard and have only females as companions (see Wadley 1980, 35–60, 153–70). These restrictions and prohibitions implied both the danger of the girl's blossoming sexuality and the danger that she posed to her family through the contaminating contagion of menstrual pollution.

In Malaysian Tamil families, restrictions on girls are far less severe than in traditional Tamil society, yet all girls learn that they must not enter a temple during a menstrual period or have sexual relations with their husbands; nor can they prepare food for the family. In English-speaking families, girls are sometimes told that the restrictions on menstruating women are to allow a woman the rest that she needs during her monthly period. Yet ritual practices ensure that girls also learn the traditional reasons for the self-control and the restriction of women. In some families of Brahmin heritage, girls are taught that menstruating women must never water plants, because this would damage or kill them. And the ritual in which a girl who has her first menstruation is worshipped as a goddess is conducted by many families in Malaysia, as in Tamilnadu. Thus Malaysian Tamil girls become aware of the dangerous power and pollution that characterize women, and they are generally told that a woman should marry an older man who will have greater wisdom than she and who can take responsibility for her. Then a wife will look up to her husband and allow him to guide her.

A Hindu girl is taught that she should be devoted and respectful to the husband that her father chooses for her, and in ritual practice she should worship him as a god. As a wife, she is expected to take Sita—the chaste, loyal, and submissive wife of Rama—as her model (Kakar 1981, 63 71). Even when the actions of her husband or father endanger her security or cause her hardship, she should show him respect and never express anger or resistance to his control. As a mother, a Tamil woman must be prepared to sacrifice everything to protect and nurture her children. The banana plant—which dies after bearing one bunch of fruit and produces shoots that grow into new trees around the stump of the mother plant—is used as a metaphor for motherhood. A Malaysian Tamil woman told me that the banana plant "sacrifices its body to feed people and asks nothing in return. When one tree dies, another comes from the root. Even after death, a mother thinks only of her children."

Stories of heroic women and goddesses teach women that they will be rewarded for their virtue and chastity and the sacrifices they make, with the power of a goddess. Thus:

> Sītā . . . the prototype of the Indian wife . . . is spiritual sister to the proverbial Savitri, who because of her chastity and devotion had the power to snatch her husband from the jaws of death. She is sister to the medieval Bengali Behula, who, as the story is told in *The Manasā-maṅgal,* . . . conquered by chastity and devotion that fierce goddess who had taken her husband's life, and brought about his resuscitation. She is sister also to the famous Rajput princesses, the *satī* (Suttee), "true wives," who leaped onto the funeral pyres of their husbands rather than risk dishonor at the hands of their conquerors. The complexities of life in modern India sometimes obscure the ancient ideals, but they are never lost. Sītā is *pativratā,* a chaste woman, true to the vows she made to her husband. (J. A. B. van Buitenen in Dimock et al. 1974, 79)

These images impose a heavy burden on Tamil women, for the corollary to the belief in the power of the virtuous woman is the understanding that any misfortune that befalls a family reflects a woman's lack of virtue and her failure to obtain the gods' protection for her family.[37] Reynolds quotes a Brahmin informant who told her that "a woman at the death of her husband mourns not so much for the husband but for the status she has lost," because the death of a husband reflects a wife's lack of virtue (in Wadley 1980, 50).

The anxiety that Tamil women may feel about being good permeates Trawick's account of the women of the family with whom she lived. For example, the schoolgirl Arivaraci "strove to be good. She would sweep the house, scrub the dishes, run errands for her parents. While the other children were playing, she would stand apart, or she would join them for a while and then leave them early to go home" (1990a, 235).[38] Trawick's ethnography shows also that in Tamil families women are not supposed to express anger (especially at a husband), but a man's anger is accepted and understood. In the family with whom Trawick lived the husband and the wife, Ayya and Padmini, quarreled constantly. Trawick comments:

> In Ayya's case, no explanation seemed needed; anger was just a quality he was born with. . . . But for Padmini's angry nature, they sought explanations. . . . An uncomfortable silence fell over the family when Padmini lost her temper, scolded an adult, beat a child or servant. Attai said, distressed, that no matter how much they told her that it was wrong to get angry like this, when they told her, she would pout and her anger would not go away. (193–94)

The prohibition on a woman's expressing anger tends to lead a wife to experience conflict with her husband as the consequence of her own bad nature.[39] When Ayya threatened to leave Padmini because she spoke harshly to him, Padmini exclaimed to Trawick through her tears, "My husband says I'm no good, my sister says I'm no good, my uncle says I'm no good, my brother says I'm no good" (198).

Freeman (1979) records that the marriage of Muli, the untouchable, was also characterized by violent quarrels. Muli was unfaithful and left his wife and son without support for two years while he lived with another woman. The breach in the marriage was finally healed with the help of Muli's brothers. But later when Muli's wife berated him for his inability to support his family, he beat her. After this quarrel, Muli's wife tried to commit suicide. Again relatives intervened to mediate between the couple, and Muli's wife was advised, "You should not get angry at your husband. Instead, you should pout. By pouting, a woman can make a curve straight. Go back to your house . . . you should go back to your husband and run your lives happily" (319). This advice is typically given to women who must deal with a difficult husband. They are taught to repress anger and to control their husbands through passive-aggressive demonstrations of suffering.

Fasting in fulfillment of a vow, or *nonpu* (Sanskrit *vrata*), is a practice that ritualizes the suffering of Tamil women and demonstrates their self-control and virtue, thereby protecting from danger their husbands, sons, and brothers. In Tamilnadu, the fast of Savitri Nonpu is performed to avert the death of one's husband; the fast of Gauri Nonpu safeguards the health and well-being of a husband; and that of Auvaiyar Nonpu is performed for a brother. In an essay on

"The Auspicious Married Woman," Reynolds describes these rituals as "power events," in which women ritually become the goddess or appropriate some of the goddess's power (in Wadley 1980, 50). Like the hermits who practice tapas, women are symbolically empowered through practices of self-denial such as fasting. Such ritual practices have deep psychological roots in the belief that human beings can compel the gods and powerful humans to respond to their needs through passive-aggressive suffering, just as an infant seemingly forces his parents to respond to his needs by his helplessness (Dundes 1963). Men (especially those of Brahmin-caste background, to whom violence is forbidden) also may use passive-aggressive suffering to control people. Trawick observed that when Ayya's wife Padmini did not respond to his criticisms and instruction in the way that he wished, "he would punish himself (and, indirectly, her) by fasting for days." His mother-in-law said that he fasted "because people will not do what he says."[40] In this way, Ayya eventually compelled others to comply with his wishes without direct expressions of anger. Gandhi acknowledges in his autobiography that his mother's devotion and ritual observances were the model for his own fasting.

## VOW FULFILLMENT BY WOMEN ON THAIPUSAM

In the myths and legends associated with Murugan and the Thaipusam festival is a variety of images of womanhood that may appeal to women at different stages of their life cycle. These include Valli, the lowly tribal maid who is beloved of God; Valli, the jealous maid betrayed by her unfaithful lover; Parvati, the good, nurturing mother; and the dangerous, angry, violent mother represented by the Amman goddesses. A young girl who is worried about the husband that her parents will choose for her may identify with Valli and yearn to be rescued by a divine lover. No matter how low her birth, she will be redeemed by the purity of her love. A married woman who has outgrown romantic dreams may identify with the jealous Valli, who berates her lover for his fickle ways and demands that he renew his loving concern for her. In a "Praise Poem for Murugan," this Valli protests that her lover has lost interest in her:

> Why are these hugs and kisses bitter for you now?
> When we were alone in the forest in the evenings,
> You used to look at me and say,
> Your lips, are they sweet honey or a sugar crystal?
> Did you not say all these things (to me)?
> (Beck 1975, 100)

The poem continues as Valli bitterly charges that the god despises her for her low-caste background. There are striking parallels between the role of Valli in the cult of Murugan and that of Radha in the worship of Krishna, who is also an unfaithful lover.

As a mother, a Tamil woman can identify with the good mother whose devotion to her child is unlimited. In worship of the infant deity, the metaphor of maternal devotion is employed as an image of the devotees' love for the god. Kakar (1981) describes the significance of motherhood for Indian women in this way: "For an Indian woman, imminent motherhood is not only the personal fulfillment of an old wish and the biological consummation of a lifelong promise, but an event in which the culture confirms her status as a renewer of the race, and extends to her a respect and consideration which were not accorded to her as a mere wife" (79). In an arranged marriage, a Tamil woman may have to compete with her mother-in-law for her husband's affection. However, when she becomes a mother, she has a new object for her love and also wins a new status in the household. In motherhood, "the wish to be loved can be transformed into the wish to love; hostility [toward a woman's in-laws] can be directed towards the protection of her child from the environment; the longing of her reawakened sensuality can be temporarily sublimated, given over to physical ministrations to her child" (Kakar 1981, 78).

The birth of a male child is especially significant. If a woman still competes with her mother-in-law for the love of her husband, she knows that someday her son will empower her, making her ruler over a domestic world of daughters-in-law and grandchildren. Furthermore, the emotional bond between mother and son appears an especially deep one, in which the ideal of unambivalent love is preserved by a denial of feelings of hostility on both sides. Beck notes that in tales sons may rebel against cruel stepmothers (dangerous, violent, bad mothers) but not against biological mothers (idealized good mothers), and the most common mother-son story in folktales involves a son who either rescues his mother from danger or rights an injustice done to her (Beck in Blackburn and Ramanujan 1986, 96). In worshipping Murugan as an infant deity, then, a woman can be reassured of her essential goodness (as an ideal mother) and perhaps also enjoy the (unconscious) fantasy that the god as son will right the wrongs she suffers (Kakar 1981, 79).

## THE APPEAL OF THE INFANT GOD

The similarity of the Krishna and Murugan cults is also apparent in the increasing popularity of Murugan worshipped as an infant deity. Prints of the infant Krishna are frequently used in the decoration of kavadis. Most people seem unaware that the deity represented is Krishna, because both Murugan and Krishna are associated with peacock feathers. The committee that oversees the Penang Hill Murugan Temple have encouraged this emphasis on worship of the infant deity by constructing a pond in which the six infant-forms of Murugan float on lotus petals.

For both men and women, the most common form of vow fulfillment on Thaipusam is *pal kavadi*, an offering of milk.[41] The milk is poured over the image of the deity by the priest and then flows out a small drain in the side of the temple, where worshippers gather to collect the flow in the palms of their hands so that they can drink it or fill vessels, which they will take home as prasad. In this ritual act, worshippers seem to identify with the youthful god who is offered an abundance of good milk.

The symbolic importance of food and eating is not unique to Hindu ritual. In a footnote to his first lecture in *The Varieties of Religious Experience,* William James writes, "Language drawn from eating and drinking is probably as common in religious literature as is language drawn from the sexual life. We 'hunger and thirst' after righteousness; we 'find the Lord a sweet savor'; we 'taste and see that he is good,'" continuing in this vein for a full page of quotations (1906, 11). As the psychoanalyst Bertram Lewin observes, "Christian devotional literature quite floats in milk, thought of from the point of view, not of the mother, but of the greedy babe" (1950, 148). Devotees of Murugan may also identify with the beloved child who is cared for by all-powerful parents, while at the same time enjoying the fantasy of omnipotence because, as an infant, one is adored and all one's needs are met without one having to exert any effort.[42]

The ritual of consuming prasad may also involve the fantasy that by ingesting the food of the gods one incorporates them, that is, becomes one with them. A. K. Ramanujan quotes a bhakti poet who says of his god: "I, by his leave, have taken him entirely and I have him in my belly for keeps" (Nammalvar 8.7.1, quoted in Ramanujan 1989, 51). The anthropologist Harper tells a story that suggests some Hindus understand that, in the ritual of taking prasad, one is obtaining (or stealing) the power of the god.[43]

> The Havik woman *sadhu* (holy person) whom I knew was, when she visited our village, given a "*pada puja,*" in which her feet were bathed in a mixture of *pañchamrita* (a mixture of five sacred fluids) and water. The solution was then passed around to those present, in a special silver vessel used only for worshipping, and poured into the right palm to be drunk as *tirtha* (sacred liquid), indicating that she was being accorded the status of a god rather than a mortal. . . . It was reported that these disciples "stole" and ate the food left on the sadhu's leaf "in order to absorb her qualities." (1964, 182)

In this context the taking of prasad also includes gestures of respect and humiliation that serve to counteract the image of "stealing" from the god.[44]

The symbolic significance of milk for Tamils is illustrated in Trawick's ethnography by women who told her that "mother's milk was a special substance because it was mixed with the feelings of the mother and transmitted them to the child. In particular, mother's milk contained the mother's love" (1990a, 94).[45] This imagery reflects the mood of bhakti devotionalism, suggesting that the human soul longs for (and is in need of) God, just as the infant is in need of a mother. Worshippers who identify with the child-god may return to the experience of being a beloved child, or they may be trying to fill a void left by the relative neglect they experienced. At the same time, the imagery of the infant god identifies the devotee with god. Tamils say they pamper children because their innocence makes them worthy of worship. Tamil sayings also equate children with gods: for example, *Kulantai devamum, kanta itathule* (Child and god reside where they are praised). Rituals of vow fulfillment that involve such deep emotional needs and the symbolic fulfillment of a desire for omnipotence may fill the worshipper with elation and triumph.

Vow fulfillment originates from the feeling that one is powerless to affect a situation, or as a response to persistent misfortune that is understood as due to the loss of God's love. In rituals of vow fulfillment, devotees acknowledge their unworthiness through complete submission to the god. They ask for the god's help in mastering the worldly or sinful parts of the self, and they punish the body-self for wishes and impulses that they believe are bad and may have caused their misfortune. As Freud (1930) puts it:

> As long as things go well with a man, his conscience is lenient and lets the ego do all sorts of things; but when misfortune befalls him, he searches his soul, acknowledges his sinfulness, heightens the demands of his conscience, imposes abstinences on himself and punishes himself with penances. Whole peoples have behaved in this way, and still do. . . . Fate is regarded as a substitute for the parental agency. If a man is unfortunate it means that he is no longer loved by this highest power; and, threatened by such a loss of love, he once more bows to the parental representative in his super-ego—a representative whom, in his days of good fortune, he was ready to neglect. This becomes especially clear where Fate is looked upon in the strictly religious sense of being nothing else than an expression of the Divine Will. (S.E. 21:126–27)

Ascetic practices reflect a sense of powerlessness, but they also involve an attempt to gain power. Thus Murugan's devotee may communicate complete submission to the god and devoted love of him, and at the same time express a wish to seize power, to compel the god to grant a prayer, to become the god. Such unconscious meanings of ritual vow fulfillment, which might otherwise threaten to disrupt the mask of civility and compliance that people must wear in the world, are accommodated both in ritual vow fulfillment (which allows worshippers to demonstrate their moral worthiness of the god's blessing and raises a devotee's status in the eyes of self and society) and in arul, the trance of possession by Murugan, which is experienced as a divine blessing and empowerment.

Symbols can be interpreted in many ways, so that we do not always know what a particular symbolic enactment means to an individual. Symbols also encompass the ambiguity of experience, which is never simply positive or negative. They allow for the expression of multiple meanings that are ambivalent, complex, and saturated with deeply felt emotions. Linking concepts through association and metaphor (so that manhood may be identified with warrior and nation, and women with pollution and danger), symbols may appear to become forces in themselves, evoking a sometimes tragic pattern of unrecognized associations and responses. This ambiguity is richly represented in ritual vow fulfillment to Murugan on Thaipusam.

8

## A CEREMONIAL ANIMAL

One could almost say that man is a ceremonial animal. That is perhaps partly false, partly nonsense, but there is something correct about it.

*—Ludwig Wittgenstein,*
Remarks on Frazer's Golden Bough

In this study of Thaipusam, we have seen how asceticism and ritual vow fulfillment function in Hindu tradition as moral practices—bodily means of moral discipline (Asad 1993). Through the language of ritual, the self of the devotee is identified symbolically with the rebellious, immoral demons, which Murugan or the Amman goddess defeat in battle and transform into devoted guardians. Through ritual vow fulfillment the devotee seeks the aid of the deity in conquering his or her demon self and achieves moral redemption. These conceptions give ritual vow fulfillment both its psychological meanings and its political significance.

As Wittgenstein suggests in the passage chosen as an epigraph for this chapter, rituals and ceremonies are distinctive and central to all forms of human life. In this chapter, a theoretical perspective is developed that shows how the ethical capacities of humans are grounded in ritual practices, drawing on Wittgenstein's later philosophy, particularly his somewhat enigmatic *Remarks on Frazer's Golden Bough* (1979).[1] Wittgenstein's general approach to the study of ritual has been followed in this study of ritual vow fulfillment on Thaipusam. His idea of a perspicuous presentation is illustrated again with a vignette of vow fulfillment at a fire-walking festival for Mariamman. To deepen our understanding of the significance of Wittgenstein's later philosophy for thinking about ritual, we turn to Susanne Langer's *Philosophy in a New Key: A Study in the Symbolism of Reason, Rite, and Art* (1942), which anticipates ideas that are central to Wittgenstein's thought. In that work, Langer argues that language and conceptual thought originated in ritual rather than as a verbal expression of emotion or as a practical or instrumental act of naming objects. As she writes, more poetically, "ritual is the cradle of language, metaphor is the law of its life" (1942, 141). To clarify her conception of symbolic thought—as contrasted with the discursive form of language—object relations psychology is used to describe the first symbols that human infants naturally invent and to show the importance of symbolic thought for the development of conceptual thought, individual identity, and moral autonomy. Herbert Fingarette's (1972) Wittgensteinian reading of Confucius' *Analects* is then drawn upon to show how rituals instantiate non-violent social relations that provide the foundation for dealing with others as morally responsible autonomous agents. This discussion of ritual as moral action leads naturally to Richard Wolheim's attempt to show in his essay "The Sheep and the Ceremony" how we can make moral judgments about rituals as ethical practices (Wolheim 1993, 1–21).

## *Explanation and Interpretation: A Perspicuous Presentation*

Ludwig Wittgenstein first turned his attention to a consideration of ritual in 1931 upon reading Frazer's *The Golden Bough, a Study in Magic and Religion* (1922). Wittgenstein was troubled by Frazer's account of the ritual life of ancient and primitive peoples, and in the margins of *The Golden Bough*, he tried to articulate what he thought was wrong with the idea of explaining a ritual as a form of magic, as Frazer did. Wittgenstein protested:

> Even the idea of trying to explain the practice—say the killing of the priest-king—seems to me wrong headed. All that Frazer does is to make this practice plausible to people who think as he does. It is very queer that all these practices are finally presented, so to speak, as stupid actions.
>
> But it never does become plausible that people do all this out of sheer stupidity. (1979, 1e)

To show how misleading it is to think of the ritual killing of the priest-king as a kind of magic, Wittgenstein suggested that one think of rituals from one's own experience:

> Burning in effigy. Kissing the picture of a loved one. This is obviously *not* based on a belief that it will have a definite effect on the object which the picture represents. It aims at some satisfaction and it achieves it. Or rather, it does not *aim* at anything; we act in this way and then feel satisfied. (4e)

What Wittgenstein means here by "satisfied" is the feeling we experience when we have found just the right word to express our thought. He suggests that rituals are representation[2] and that ritual acts are like metaphors, but the representation of an event is used symbolically not to describe, but to create, a situation. "Baptism as washing. — There is a mistake only if magic is presented as science. If the adoption of a child is carried out by the mother pulling the child from beneath her clothes, then it is crazy to think there is an error in this and that she believes she has borne the child" (4e). The symbolic gesture (along with the words that may accompany that gesture)—for example, the exchange of rings between bride and groom and the "I do" of the marriage ceremony—is simply the way one performs a particular action in that particular culture, in this case, the act of marriage. Such ritual acts may have to be performed in a particular setting, like a marriage, or they may have meaning in any setting, like a handshake or a kiss.

In suggesting that ritual acts should not be conceived on the model of magic, as a primitive (but mistaken) science with instrumental ends, Wittgenstein was criticizing the positivist view of language implicit in his earlier work, the *Tractatus Logico-Philosophicus* (first published in 1921), which rested on a conception of language as a picture of the world, words as names of things, and propositions as true or false representations of the world. In the *Tractatus*, he had argued that "the sense of a proposition is its agreement and disagreement with possibilities of existence and non-existence of states of affairs" (1921, para. 4.2). Wittgenstein now objected to the view that the only way to analyze language is in terms of the truth or falsity of its representation of reality. This is the context in which he described human beings as "ceremonial animals":

> One could almost say that man is a ceremonial animal. That is perhaps partly false, partly nonsense, but there is also something correct about it.
>
> In other words, one might begin a book on anthropology in this way: When we watch the life and behavior of men all over the earth we see that apart from what we might call animal activities, taking food &c., &c., men also carry out actions that bear a peculiar character and might be called ritualistic.
>
> But then it is nonsense if we go on to say that the characteristic feature of *these* actions is that they spring from wrong ideas about the physics of things. (This is what Frazer does when he says magic is really false physics, or as the case may be, false medicine, technology, &c.) (1979, 7e)

Wittgenstein referred to the social and linguistic conventions of a particular culture as their "form of life." He never explicitly defined the expression but, rather, left it open to a richly suggestive range of uses. Not only are the unique conventions and rituals of a particular society a form of life, but so are the characteristically human ways of being that peoples in all cultures share and recognize, despite differences in convention and language.[3] These aspects of human life include expressions of ethical thought, the idea that there is a purpose to human life, and conceptions of a society organized on principles of social justice. Such conceptions do not exist as true or false representations of the world. Rather, they are aspirations that can be represented symbolically and given existence in a shared form of life.

In the *Philosophical Investigations* (1968), Wittgenstein suggested repeatedly that the idea of explanation is misleading when one is interested in understanding what an instance of language (or ritual) *means*: "Our considerations could not be scientific ones. . . . And we may not advance any kind of theory. There must not be anything hypothetical in our considerations. We must do away with all *explanation*, and description alone must take its place" (1968, #109). For example, Wittgenstein was an admiring reader of Freud, but he criticized Freud for claiming to *explain* mental events in terms of causes. His critique of Freud helps us understand the difference between explanation and interpretation:

> When a dream is interpreted we might say that it is fitted into a context in which it ceases to be puzzling. . . . It is as though we were presented with a bit of canvas on which were painted a hand and a part of a face and certain other shapes, arranged in a puzzling and incongruous manner. Suppose . . . we now paint in forms—say an arm, a trunk, etc.—leading up to and fitting on to the shapes on the original bit; and that the result is that we say: "Ah, now I see why it is like that, how it all comes to be arranged in that way, and what these various bits are . . ." and so on. (1972, 45–46)[4]

An interpretation of this sort shows us a pattern that may help us understand how events and actions are related, but such an interpretation does not have explanatory value in the sense that a scientific hypothesis does: "One may be able to discover certain things about oneself by this sort of free association, but it does not explain why the dream occurred" (50).[5] Wittgenstein suggests that interpretation of a ritual or dream requires "the conception of a perspicuous presentation (a way of setting out the whole field together by making easy the passage from one part of it to another). . . . This perspicuous presentation makes possible that understanding which consists just in the fact that we 'see the connections'" (1979, 9e). In the *Philosophical Investigations*, he writes, "Our mistake is to look for an explanation where we ought to look at what happens as a *protophenomenon*" (1968, #655).

In one of his most often quoted aphorisms, Wittgenstein writes: "Let the use *teach* you the meaning" (1968, #212).[6] To understand what he means, it helps to look at how we learn language. Pitkin (1972) describes a vignette in which a three-and-a-half-year-old girl appeared in her parent's bedroom one morning dragging a blanket. Her parents told her to take the blanket back to her room and put it on the bed, to which she replied, "I simply can't function in the morning without my blanket." When her parents recovered from their amused astonishment, they recognized the phrase as one the little girl's mother habitually used about her morning cup of coffee. The little girl certainly did not use the word *function* in other contexts, and she undoubtedly did not know what the word meant. Rather she had picked up the expression as a whole and grasped its use. "What recurred was a context somehow familiar because a person (mother, child) was about to be deprived of something (coffee, blanket) and said something which altered the situation so that the person was not deprived after all" (Pitkin 1972, 57). Pitkin comments, "words need not be labels here at all, but like signals in a game, the appropriate thing to do under these circumstances" *(ibid.)*. This child had learned to use the word *function* in this expression and recognized the applicability of the expression to her intentions and this context. In her world, words were part of a conventional expression used to interact with others, eliciting feelings, actions, and consequences. She will eventually learn the meaning(s) of the concept *function* from this and a variety of other expressions.

A convention may at first appear to be a kind of rule that one follows in order to behave appropriately. However, the example of the little girl who could not function in the morning without her blanket should help us see that we do not simply follow rules when we speak but rather imaginatively project forms of expression and conceptual schemes from one context to another. We are liable to make a mistake and think we are "explaining" why people behave in a particular way, if we think that they simply follow rules. Bourdieu (1990b) has observed that Wittgenstein's critique of Frazer can be extended to modern ethnographies where the behavior of natives is explained as the product of cultural and linguistic patterning:

> I hadn't read the merciless criticisms addressed by Wittgenstein to Frazer, and which apply to most ethnologists, when I described what seemed to me to be the real logic behind mythical or ritual thinking. Where people saw an algebra, I think one should see a dance or a gymnastic exercise. The intellectualism of ethnologists, which only increases their concern to give a scientific trimming to their work, prevents them from seeing that, in their own everyday practice . . . they are obeying a logic very similar to that of "primitives." (73)

Pitkin cautions that Wittgenstein did not equate meaning with the use of a word.[7] She points out that "the various cases out of which the meaning of the word is compounded need not be mutually consistent; they may—perhaps must—have contradictory implications" (1972, 85). Wittgenstein's later writing shows how inconsistent or contradictory uses of a concept may give rise to philosophical puzzlement. In interpreting rituals, too (as we have seen in this study of the Thaipusam festival), symbols have inconsistent and contradictory meanings.

In this study of vow fulfillment to Murugan, I have tried to provide a "perspicuous presentation," which helps one interpret the acts performed by devotees by describing the cultural traditions of Hindu Tamils that link participation in vow fulfillment to psychological and moral concerns and by describing the social and political context of the Thaipusam festival in Malaysia. Before going on to discuss the theoretical insights that can be derived from the approach to ritual Wittgenstein has suggested, it will be useful to consider briefly another instance of vow fulfillment—this time the context is a fire-walking festival for the Amman goddess—to see how a perspicuous presentation leads to understanding. The story of Sheilah is taken from my field notes.

On the full moon day of Panguni Uttiram (March–April), when the marriage of Murugan and his divine wife Devasena (or Deviani) was to be celebrated, I left Penang early in the morning to go to the Chettiar Murugan Temple in Bukit Mertajam, a town on the mainland, just across from Penang Island. On that same day, there was also to be a fire-walking festival at the Sri Mariamman Temple, which was located a few hundred yards down the road from the Murugan Temple. After Thaipusam, this is the most popular occasion for vow fulfillment in Malaysia.

When I arrived, the Mariamman Temple was already filled with families bringing offerings to the goddess. Those who were to fulfill vows stood quietly at the back of the temple, awaiting their turn in front of the pujari who was tying a protective amulet of turmeric root *(kanganam)* around the wrist of each devotee.[8] Another priest dispensed receipts to those who had paid the temple charges for offerings. As I watched the bustle in the temple, a procession of musicians announced the arrival of the temple's patron and his entourage. The crowd of worshippers fell back so that this rich businessman might approach the altar, and I found myself standing next to a slim girl dressed in a simple yellow skirt and blouse. She leaned forward to tell me about this man, who was a distant relative of hers.

My new acquaintance, Sheilah, was eighteen years old. She lived with her mother and sister on a rubber estate near Bukit Mertajam. Sheilah told me that on Thaipusam the previous year she had been in the General Hospital in Penang, suffering from a tubercular infection in her hip. As she watched the devotees of Murugan pass by the hospital, she had prayed to Mariamman that she might be cured of her illness, and she had promised to mark her vow with a milk offering on Panguni Uttiram. Although she continued to suffer pain from the infection and was still in treatment, Sheilah was now going to fulfill her vow. This was her first experience of ritual vow fulfillment. She had never experienced arul, the trance of divine blessing, or any other sort of trance and was not expecting to go into a trance. In preparation for vow fulfillment, she had eaten no meat for several days and no food at all since the previous morning.

While we talked, another blast of music heralded the arrival of the pujari who carried the *karagam*, a pot decorated with garlands of flowers that contained the sacred fire symbolizing the goddess. The priest was still wet from the water he had poured over himself to wash away all pollution. Another pujari had prepared a pile of twigs in front of the altar, which he now set alight and tended while the priest with the karagam prayed to Mariamman. When the goddess entered into him, he demonstrated her possession of his body by stepping with bare feet onto the upturned blade of the sickle of Mariamman, which two assistants held several inches above the ground. Then the pile of flaming twigs was tipped into the (wet) cloth wrapped around his waist, and he ran out of the temple to the fire pit, where the glowing sticks were used to light the firewood in the fire-walk pit. This pit was about ten inches deep, eighteen feet long, and six feet wide. The fire that the priests had started would burn over the next seven hours, until glowing coals filled the pit.

At about noon, the processional image of Mariamman was brought from the temple and placed on a decorated chariot. Over a hundred men were lined up to pull the temple car; this was another kind of vow. A second group of men stood nearby, prepared to help balance the chariot when it went around corners and to help brake it if necessary. A cluster of temple committee members worriedly consulted each other, concerned that the pulling be well organized so that no one would be hurt. A bystander explained that an accident would be considered a bad omen, indicating that Mariamman was angry with her worshippers. Someone else added that anyone crushed under the wheels of the chariot would go straight to heaven.

After Mariamman's procession left the temple, those who were to fulfill vows to the goddess began to leave to go to a spring about seven miles distant, where the pilgrimage of vow fulfillment was to begin. I waited with Sheilah, who delayed her departure because she had to wait for her mother and sister. They were supposed to come by bus from the rubber estate where the family lived. By 2:30 P.M. all the other devotees who were to fulfill vows had left, but Sheilah's mother and sister had still not arrived. Sheilah offered excuses for her mother, saying that the buses were full of people coming in from the estates to the festival. Then she showed her dismay, angrily asking why her mother and sister had not left home early enough to arrive on time. She was upset because she did not know the prayers and rituals required to fulfill her vow correctly. She needed her mother's help.

Finally, Sheilah asked me to accompany her to the spring where the devotees of Mariamman would be blessed by the priests and begin their procession. We went first to a small house behind the temple where Sheilah had stored the items she had prepared for ritual vow fulfillment—a tray, camphor, limes, banana leaves, sacred ash, coconuts, bananas, flowers—and a container of milk to be offered to Mariamman. When Sheilah picked up her basket, she noticed that the milk had separated; the rich cream (or soured curd?) had risen to the top of the bottle. Now she became really upset, because she thought that the milk offering would no longer be acceptable. Sheilah dismissed my suggestion that we might try to find more milk. That, she said, would be impossible. She decided we should go in my car to where the other devotees had gathered. There she could find someone to advise her.

The spring was about two miles off the main road out of Bukit Mertajam. We passed a Malay settlement and stopped at the edge of the dirt road near a clearing where a bathing place had been built. Several hundred Tamils and a few Malaysian policemen stood in small groups above the spring on an open slope fringed with jungle. Sheilah found some women who were friends of her mother. They scolded her for being late but helped her arrange her offering next to theirs. They agreed that the separation of the milk Sheilah had brought was a bad omen and suggested it was because Sheilah was late (not a fair assessment, I thought).

While Sheilah prepared for vow fulfillment with a ritual bath, pouring the water from the spring over herself so that all pollution would flow to the ground, I wandered around the clearing. The pujaris from the Mariamman Temple were moving from group to group, blessing the offerings and putting into trance those who were to have hooks and spears inserted in their bodies. The atmosphere was tense, and some people were taken by spontaneous trances. As I watched a middle-aged woman who was dancing wildly, flinging her long black hair about, a bystander explained that she was possessed by one of the animal spirits that inhabit wild places like this jungle (as one could tell from her cries and wild behavior). No one interfered with her dancing, because the spirit who possessed her was clearly very fierce. I noted that no one seemed to think the woman was possessed by Mariamman. Off to the side of the crowd, a young man of about twenty-five crouched. He was slashing his tongue with a knife so that blood dripped down his face. Two women knelt before him to receive blessing, because he was understood to be possessed by Mariamman.

At around 4:30 P.M. the pujaris signaled that the procession was to leave for Bukit Mertajam. The priest who held the sickle of Mariamman in one hand—while he balanced the karagam containing the sacred fire of the goddess on his head with the other—took his position at the front of the column of devotees who had assembled on the road. The assistant pujaris hurled coconuts to the ground as an offering, and the procession set off. However, for no apparent reason, the priests would stop the procession every now and then. I wondered if they were delaying because they wanted to arrive at the place where they were to meet the chariot at a prearranged time. These unexplained delays began to irritate people. One woman with a miniature spear through the skin on her forehead began protesting: "They should not keep us waiting! They should not treat us like this!" Normally a Tamil woman would not utter such angry outcries in public, but on this occasion the woman was treated with cautious respect as if she might be a vehicle for Mariamman's anger.

After we had walked and waited for over an hour, I decided that I had better retrieve my car from the clearing in the jungle, so I would not have to trek back alone in the dark later that evening. I explained to Sheilah what I intended to do, and she nodded. After moving my car to the edge of Bukit Mertajam, I returned to the procession, which was now entering the city. When I found Sheilah, she made no sign of greeting or recognition. The procession had stopped, and she stood silently, supporting the pot of milk on her head with one hand. Her eyes were glazed over, and she seemed tired and drained. Her mother and sister had joined her, and someone must have told them about me, because they greeted me with voluble thanks. I asked about Sheilah's condition, worried about the strain of fasting and walking in the heat for someone who had tuberculosis, but they reassured me that she was fine.

I was not sure what I should do next, but before I could make up my mind, Sheilah suddenly slumped backward, and her sister and I lunged forward to catch her. She had not fainted for she writhed in our arms so that it took both of us to support her. Sheilah's sister had grabbed the pot of milk, which she handed to their mother. Together we tried to keep Sheilah from falling to the ground, while her mother searched for some vibhuti to calm her. I was surprised at Sheilah's strength and energy. The vibhuti, which a bystander offered us, was applied to Sheilah's forehead and calmed her frenzied movements. When the procession began to move again, Sheilah also began to walk. Her mother tried to hand her the pot of milk, but she would not take the heavy brass pot. After a while her sister placed the pot on Sheilah's head, and she reached up and grasped it. She seemed to me on the edge of collapse.

In Bukit Mertajam the crowds were thick, and again the procession of devotees was forced to stop. The woman who had complained earlier shouted again, "Somebody is mistaken. We should not stop like this all the time." At this, Sheilah began to dance, weaving and flinging her body about. Her sister managed to grab her milk pot before it fell to the ground. Sheilah's dancing was quite dangerous, because we were crowded together and some devotees had long spears through their cheeks. Her mother and sister looked upset, but they did not seem to know what to do. Someone in the crowd stepped forward and pressed more vibhuti on Sheilah's forehead. She slumped passively into my arms, and after that she stood waiting calmly. When the procession started again, Sheilah would not take her milk offering. Her mother scolded her, reminding Sheilah that she had made a vow she was obliged to fulfill, but Sheilah no longer seemed aware of any of us.

As we neared the temple, the procession stopped again, and Sheilah began to dance, flinging herself back and forth. I was carrying the basket of ritual equipment, which contained (among other things) several empty bottles from the milk offering. As I stepped back to avoid Sheilah, the bottles tipped out of the basket and shattered on the ground. I was horrified at what had happened, because the devotees who were fulfilling vows were walking and dancing barefoot. Several people helped me as I tried to brush the glass out of the way. A woman in the crowd took charge of Sheilah by "reining her" with a cloth passed round her waist so that she could dance but was lightly restrained from doing harm to herself or anyone else. This worked until we came in sight of the temple spire, when this woman let out a shriek and bolted through the seemingly impenetrable crowd toward the temple. Another bystander attempted to quiet Sheilah's dancing by a forceful application of sacred ash. And Sheilah's mother and sister made further attempts to convince her to carry her milk offering around the fire pit in fulfillment of her vow. But Sheilah ignored everyone as she pushed through the press of people and entered the enclosure that surrounded the fire pit.

At Bukit Mertajam only men are allowed to walk the fire. The pujari who carried the karagam had been first to walk the fire. Now he stood at the head of the long rectangle of glowing coals that the devotees of Mariamman would cross. He seemed to be the one who decided who would be allowed to cross the fire, dispensing his judgment with a gesture of his hand, which indicated that a particular man must walk around the fire. One man circled the pit three times, each time stopping to see if the pujari would allow him to cross the fire. After the third time, his companions took him by the arm and led him away in the direction of the temple. I saw another young man stumble just before the smaller pit filled with milk at the end of the fire-walk, and I followed him into the temple to see if he had been burned. But this did not seem to be the case. He did not stop to inspect his foot, nor did he limp. I could see only the gray cover of ash on his feet.[9]

I found Sheilah slumped against a pillar at the back of Mariamman's temple. Her mother, sister, and some friends were still trying to persuade her to take her milk offering to the altar, but she responded to no one. A young man (whom Sheilah had introduced as a friend that morning) finally resolved the problem by taking the offering to the altar for Sheilah. Someone else fetched her a soft drink, which she drank. I realized that it was already 11:00 P.M., and I still had to fetch my car from the edge of town. I took my leave of Sheilah's mother and sister, who thanked me and invited me to visit them. But I felt strange as I tried to say good-bye to Sheilah, who did not acknowledge me.

About ten days later there was a letter from Sheilah. She wrote to thank me for helping her on Panguni Uttiram and to invite me to visit her family. When I went to the rubber estate where they lived a week after that, Sheilah told me that she did not remember what had happened when she was fulfilling her vow to Mariamman. Her mother and sister had described to her my participation in the events of the day.


When Sheilah began to talk to me in the temple at Bukit Mertajam, she assumed that she could help me understand what was happening. I begin with this observation because the emphasis on "otherness" that is so pronounced in scholarly writings of the 1980s seems to me to obscure the fact that cultural differences are not an insurmountable barrier to friendships rooted in mutual recognition of what people share as fellow human beings. And I assume, similarly, that Sheilah's impulse to ask for the help of a god in curing her illness is one that anyone can understand.

Sheilah probably chose Mariamman, rather than Murugan, for vow fulfillment because the Amman goddess is understood to afflict her worshippers with disease (or drought) when she is angry (Bean 1975). Vow fulfillment provides a means for the "children" of the Amman goddess to demonstrate their love and devotion so that the goddess will respond as a nurturing mother and care for them. In fulfilling her vow, I believe Sheilah meant to prove her devotion to the goddess, a powerful mother figure. Given the tradition of goddess worship that explains affliction as punishment and requires a person to appease the angry goddess, Sheilah acted out of a rational plan for coping with her infection—out of a desire for health.

The image of the hostile goddess who afflicts her worshippers with life-threatening illness is culturally given. However, Sheilah did not seem to have been consciously aware of her experience of Mariamman as a hostile figure, and I never heard her express anger at Mariamman for striking her with a painful and threatening disease. The image of maternal hostility represented in the Amman goddess may reflect an unconscious fear that, if the mother is angry, she will no longer protect her children from harm and may even damage or destroy them. No mother can satisfy completely all her infant's desires, and the pains and illnesses that the infant inevitably suffers will initially be attributed to her failure to give adequate care or to her hostility. The theme of the Amman goddess who must be propitiated by her children undoubtedly reflects the frustration and rage that is inevitably a part of the mother-child relationship. In her ethnography of a Tamil family, Trawick has shown how a Tamil mother may use the threat of withdrawing her love to control her child:

> Jnana Oli [an indulged only child] had been throwing daily temper tantrums. People responded by carrying him from one place to another and offering him playthings, but daily he became more difficult to satisfy. After one such bout, his mother embraced his [male] cousin and said, "Umapathi is my darling; you are not my darling." Jnana Oli angrily stalked away and refused to talk to anyone for one and a half hours. When he returned, he found his mother again lying by Umapathi's side. He turned on his heel, went back to the side room and refused to speak to anyone for the rest of the afternoon—about three hours. (1990a, 223–24)[10]

When her mother failed to appear at the appointed time on Panguni Uttiram, Sheilah may have begun to doubt the concern of both her own mother and the mother goddess whom she hoped would cure her illness. Her trance seemed to have been triggered by the angry exclamations of the woman who kept protesting, "They should not treat us this way!" For Sheilah, this protest might express her (unconscious) feelings toward both her own mother, who had failed to get to the temple on time, and Mariamman, who had afflicted her with tuberculosis.[11] Sheilah's violent trance dancing may have been a culturally patterned expression of her anger, as the angry destructive goddess is often portrayed as dancing on the corpse of her victim. But Sheilah's expression of her anger at her mother was muted and indirect. When she resisted her mother's demands that she must carry the brass pot with the milk offering and finally refused to present her offering of milk at the temple, she clearly disappointed and frustrated her mother. These gestures may have been intended (in part) to punish her mother for being late, and they may also have reflected Sheilah's feeling that her offering was spoiled or curdled by her own anger at her mother and at the mother goddess. I think she questioned whether her offering would be acceptable to Mariamman.

Sheilah may also have seen the spoiled milk as a sign that "the mother" (a fused image of her own mother and the Amman goddess) would no longer give her good milk, but rather only poisoned milk (her tuberculosis)—just as she had offered the goddess spoilt milk. In Hindu tradition, the theme of poisoned milk appears in the well-known story of Putana, the female demon who tried to kill the infant Krishna by suckling him on poison.[12] (In the myth Putana is sucked to death by Krishna, who thus destroys the hostile demon mother.) Ethnographic accounts of the Tamils also provide evidence that milk is symbolically important. For example, Obeyesekere (1990) tells us that ascetics who worship Skanda (as Murugan is known in Sri Lanka) at Kataragama sometimes drink "bitter milk" (prepared from crushed margosa leaves mixed with milk) as a punishment for the betrayal of a loved one (12). He notes that margosa leaves, which are extremely bitter, are applied by mothers on their nipples to wean children. And Trawick gives an account of the weaning of a favored child that evokes the powerful and ambivalent emotions that may be associated with milk:

> Jnana Oli was weaned . . . by bitter *neem* [a tree] juice being rubbed on his mother's breasts. . . . At the age of two he received cow milk, one cup in the morning and one cup in the evening, and the degree of anxiety he showed with respect to the cup of milk was surprising, considering his composure in other situations. In the evening, when he saw the cup of milk coming, he would cry in fear, but he drank the milk without a struggle. In the morning, he accepted the cup of milk willingly but cried when they temporarily took it away to wipe his mouth. With this vital food alone he had no choice; making sure he drank his milk, and drank it all, was a matter of deadly seriousness to the women of the household. Milk was very expensive, and it was the only source of concentrated protein that Shaivas allowed themselves. The older children and adults in this family did not get milk at all but had occasional helpings of diluted buttermilk or, much more frequently, went without. For any child, the experience of sweet mother's milk given on demand suddenly followed by such a bitter weaning must have imbued the idea of motherhood with contrasting meanings. (1990a, 223)

Sheilah's choice of Panguni Uttiram as an occasion for vow fulfillment seems to have been shaped by the social dynamics that had led a previous generation of estate laborers to give up vow fulfillment at estate temples in favor of vow fulfillment to Mariamman in Bukit Mertajam (or to Murugan on Thaipusam). Sheilah herself was not concerned with the politics of temples or the social hierarchy of the estate. The Bukit Mertajam festival is famous for the crowds it attracts, attesting to the power of Mariamman worshipped there, and that seems to have determined Sheilah's choice of this venue for vow fulfillment—although perhaps the fact that the patron of the Bukit Mertajam Temple was a distant relative played a role in her decision. In choosing to fulfill her vow to Mariamman in Bukit Mertajam, Sheilah participated (unreflectively) in a social-historical shift away from the ritual tradition of the Amman goddess as worshipped in an estate temple and the social relations of hierarchy that were represented and legitimated by that tradition. From this perspective, the rich Tamil merchant who had replaced the manager of a colonial estate as temple patron and as sponsor of the festival of the goddess at Bukit Mertajam could be taken as a representative of the new socioeconomic order of capitalist enterprise.

Sheilah wanted the goddess to help her recover from tuberculosis, which she understood as a sign that the mother goddess was angry at her for some fault. Thus her motive for vow fulfillment was a desire to prove herself morally worthy of the goddess's love and protection. This is why Sheilah's experience of vow fulfillment was disrupted by unconscious conflicts deriving from her belief that her anger at her mother and the goddess was "bad." The social and economic factors that led to changes in ritual vow fulfillment to the goddess—particularly the turning away from worship of an Amman goddess in an estate temple in favor of worship of the goddess in Bukit Mertajam—reflect the rejection of the hierarchical social order of the estate as a good, just, or ethical social order. These moral conceptions give ritual both its psychological meaning and its political significance.

This interpretation of Sheilah's actions rests on a description of culturally given understandings (such as the image of the hostile mother goddess and the idea that she punishes by inflicting suffering), which shape the conscious and unconscious experience of an individual so that a person may be said to "enact" culture. This interpretation also links the actions of those who fulfill vows to the society in which they live, showing the significance of their preference for vow fulfillment to the goddess of the Bukit Mertajam temple. There is nothing that guarantees the interpretation is correct, as Sheilah herself could not reflectively articulate the reasons for all her actions. Rather, this interpretation is of the sort that we make every day in our interactions with others. Such interpretations are contingent in the sense that they may be altered in the face of further interactions and greater knowledge. At base, such interpretations always involve the projection of motivations and conceptions onto the acts of others.

Wittgenstein points out that we recognize ceremonies or rites that we call religious in the cultures of other people, and he argues that "the religious actions or the religious life of the priest-king are not different in kind from any genuinely religious action today, say a confession of sins" (1979, 3–4e). He points out that Frazer can describe the ritual practices of others in language that is natural to him and familiar to his readers, although he treats their rituals as a primitive form of superstitious magic. He protests that Frazer failed to see that

> there is something in us too that speaks for those modes of action of the savages. . . . If I believed (which I don't) that there are human-superhuman beings somewhere that one can call Gods—if I say: "I fear the wrath of the Gods," then this shows that I (can) mean something by it, or can give expression to a sentiment which has nothing to do with that belief (. . . which is not necessarily bound up with that belief). (1979, 5e; Tambiah 1990, 62)

"What narrowness of spiritual life we find in Frazer!" laments Wittgenstein. "And as a result, how impossible for him to understand a different way of life from the English one of his time!" (5e).

What did Wittgenstein mean by *religious* and *spiritual*? Those who knew Wittgenstein describe him as deeply serious, rigorously ethical, and religious, but his religiosity was not conventional and did not rest on belief in a superior or supernatural being. To a friend, Wittgenstein said, "If you and I are to live religious lives, it mustn't be that we talk a lot about religion, but that our manner of life is different," and, "I can well imagine a religion in which there are no doctrinal propositions, in which there is thus no talking" (quoted in Monk 1990, 305).[13] Wittgenstein's religiosity appears to have consisted in a profound respect for human spirituality as manifest in the capacity to construct and sustain moral commitments and to live for a higher purpose, capacities that rest on a symbolic mode of thought.

### What Is Ritual?

Wittgenstein teaches that there is no essential quality (or set of characteristics) that can be found in all uses of a concept such as ritual.[14] In his comments on Frazer's description of the fire festivals of Europe, he notes that there are similarities but also differences among the festivals described, and it is something like a family resemblance among them that strikes one:

> The most noticeable thing seems to me not merely the similarities but also the differences throughout all these rites. It is a wide variety of faces with common

> features that keep showing in one place and in another. And one would like to draw lines joining the parts that various faces have in common. (1979, 13e)

Like members of a family, some events that we call rituals share some characteristics; other ritual events share different ones. All rituals do not have the same essential characteristic(s), but rather ritual is a concept with various applications. We can use the concept of ritual to call attention to a particular characteristic of an event in one context and to a quite different characteristic in another context.[15] For example, the word *ritualistic* can be used to evoke the image of perfunctory, meaningless routine.[16] On the other hand, rituals such as confession, absolution, or vow fulfillment embody conceptions that can give a life moral depth and meaning.

Recognizing the diversity of practices that may be called ritual protects one from reductionist explanations of human actions. As Wittgenstein wrote, in criticism of Freud's essentialism, "It is probable that there are many different sorts of dreams, and that there is no single line of explanation for all of them. Just as there are many different sorts of jokes. Or just as there are many different sorts of language" (1972, 42). In the following discussion, therefore, I do not intend my argument to apply to all possible events that might be described as rituals. Rather, I have in mind rituals that instantiate ethical relations among people through promises, oaths, vows, and other gestures that give expression to ethical conceptions.

### The Symbolic Origins of Language and Ritual

In *Philosophy in a New Key: A Study in the Symbolism of Reason, Rite, and Art* (1942), Susanne Langer suggests that ritual—in the form of dance and ritual gestures that had come to have conventional meanings for a group—antedated the evolution of language, and that the origin of language was to be found in the propensity of primates to symbolize; that is, the "transformation of experience into concepts, not the elaboration of signals and symptoms, is the motive of language" (126). The first symbolic objects represented relationships of emotional significance.[17]

Drawing from the work of the ethologist Wolfgang Kohler, Langer provides an example of proto-symbolic behavior among the great apes, which shows how the first symbols represent emotional relationships and helps us see how symbolic thought differs from expressive and instrumental communication:

> [The chimpanzee Gua], who was so attached to Mr. Kellogg that she went into tantrums of terror and grief whenever he left the house, could be comforted by being given his pair of coveralls. "This she would drag around with her," . . . "as a fetish of protection until his return." . . . Occasionally, if it was necessary for him to go away, the leave-taking could be accomplished without emotional display on the part of Gua if the coveralls were given her before the time of departure. (1942, 113)

Gua's attachment to Mr. Kellogg's trousers is reminiscent of a dog's recognition of his master's clothing, yet Langer's conception of symbolic thought helps us distinguish between the dog's recognition of his master's smell and Gua's use of Mr. Kellogg's trousers. If Gua were clinging to Mr. Kellogg's trousers because she felt anxious, angry, and sad when her trainer disappeared, her behavior would be a symptom or expression of emotion. But Langer points out that Gua appeared to use a conventional expression of feeling (the trousers) to anticipate an event and deal with the emotions evoked by it. The symbolic object represents Gua's apprehension of a state of affairs (the anticipated departure of her trainer). Therefore, Langer describes Gua's behavior as the "performance of a symbolic act" (114).

The use of a conventional object to stand for a complex of ideas and emotions, Langer notes, occurs naturally in dreams.[18] When an ordinary object or event—say, a fish or a stairway—appears in a dream and inspires incomprehensible terror or seems fraught with significance, we are inclined to reassure the dreamer, "It's just a fish . . . (or whatever)" (1942, 149). Like the chimpanzee Gua, we may be unable to articulate the meaning of such a symbol.

To see what Langer is getting at, it is helpful to turn to the work of object relations psychologists who have written on early symbol formation in human infants.[19] The pediatrician-turned-psychoanalyst D. W. Winnicott first pointed out the importance of the symbols that small children seem to invent quite naturally. He called a child's first preverbal symbols its "transitional objects."[20] They are objects, like Linus's security blanket, that appear to stand for the relationship between the child and the primary caretaker. They do not reflect the actual relationship at any particular moment; rather they are a conception of the positive or ideal relationship of love and security that in reality is disrupted by the caretaler's departure (or failure to meet the infant's needs). Here Winnicott draws on the work of Melanie Klein (1984), who argues that, before infants are able to identify others as whole persons with good and bad characteristics and subject to good and bad feelings, they split their experience of others (and of the self) into good (pleasurable) and bad (frustrating or pain-causing) objects. A developmentally later example of this kind of primitive splitting of the world into good and bad is found in fairy tales, which abound in evil stepmothers and fairy godmothers, along with evil monsters and princes charming. Thus the child is able to preserve the image of the all-good parent in contrast to one who is bad and frustrating. In the transitional object the child gives representation to an illusory experience of complete security and thereby is able to conceive or hold on to an idea and to learn to regulate emotions. As the object relations theorist Hanna Segal puts it, "the symbol is used not to deny but to overcome loss" (1988, 116–17). Winnicott says that such transitional phenomena are essential to the child's development of a self. He points out that the conception of a desired situation, symbolically represented, is the basis of the ability to envision a possibility and bring it into being. Thus the development of the capacity to symbolize is a prerequisite for the development of agency in relation to others who might satisfy one's desires.[21] In this way symbolic thought provides the basis for autonomy (self-rule on the basis of one's own desires).

According to Winnicott, the further development of the child's relationship to others is (in part) determined by the response of the primary caretaker to the child's first symbolic objects. The first symbolic objects provide a bridge between the inner world of inarticulate desires, fears, and emotions and the outer world in which the child must relate to others symbolically. When the caretaker recognizes the significance of the child's first symbolic object or provides the words or phrases that represent the infant's experience, the shared symbolic world that links mind to mind is founded.[22] Segal, like Langer, argues that the development of symbolic thought is a precursor of the development of language: "The capacity to communicate with oneself by using symbols is, I think, the basis of verbal thinking—which is the capacity to communicate with oneself by means of words. Not all internal communication is verbal thinking, but all verbal thinking is an internal communication by means of symbols—words" (169). She illustrates the role of symbolic thought in the development of language with Helen Keller's account of her rediscovery of language. For a long time Helen's teacher tried to communicate by writing on Helen's hand, but there was no acknowledgment. Helen continued to break and smash things in emotional outbreaks of frustration. Then, one day Helen broke a doll and for the first time cried about what she had done. Helen's reaction suggests that the doll was symbolic; it was not just an object but had been full of meaning to her. That same afternoon, when the teacher wrote the word *water* on Helen's hand, Helen grasped the sign as meaningful, as a representation of her experience of the water. We could say that, rather than learning the name of a thing in the world, Helen learned to use the sign for water to represent her conception of water and understood that this sign would be recognized by her teacher.

Segal calls the child's first symbols "symbolic equations" (164), because they connect something in the child's internal world with something in the external world. They could be said to be primitive symbols, because the symbol is not clearly connected to what it symbolizes. Children do not have the words to articulate the meaning of their first symbolic objects. We often must guess at the meaning to a child of a treasured object and wonder why another object seems to inspire fear, and why yet another is deliberately destroyed. Langer points out that such primitive symbolization sometimes appears as a symptom in a patient. She gives the example of a schizophrenic patient who had given up playing the violin because he equated it with masturbating in public. In this way, the chimpanzee Gua's symbolic trousers and the first symbols of the child are like the symbols that appear in dreams and inspire fear (1988). In normal development, primitive symbolization persists in dreams, fantasy, and creative work.

The acquisition of language binds experience in cultural forms, and the later development of language as an instrument of communication involves a growing shift away from subjective associations and the symbolic (which combines emotional and cognitive elements) to an emphasis on practical distinctions and discursive forms of knowledge. Langer contrasts the "linear, discrete, successive order" of the discursive presentation of ideas in language to the presentation of ideas in visual and musical forms, symbolic forms that involve ambiguity and ambivalence and a multiplicity of meanings represented "simultaneously so the relations . . . are grasped in one act" (1942, 75).

In summary, Langer argues that language grows from the propensity to represent concepts symbolically rather than from a need to relieve and express feelings or an instrumental, practical need to communicate wants. For Langer, ritual as a cultural form "'expresses feelings' in the logical rather than the physiological sense." It is "not a free expression of emotions, but a disciplined rehearsal of right attitudes" (153).[23] Feelings might well accompany the performance of a ritual because symbols that appear in rituals evoke feelings, but the point of the ritual is not the expression of feeling but rather "the communication of an idea of the feelings that begot their prototypes" (152). For Langer and for Winnicott, there is a continuity between the child's first use of symbolic objects and the meaning that adults give to religious symbols and cultural products, such as works of art. Through shared understanding of a conception that is symbolized, of gestures that "mean," rituals connect people and create awareness of the society to which one belongs and the values that people in the society share.

### The Magical Power of Ritual

In *Confucius: The Secular as Sacred* (1972), the philosopher Herbert Fingarette shows how rituals instantiate ethical social relations:

> What we have come to see . . . is how vast is the area of human existence in which the substance of that existence *is* the ceremony. Promises, commitments, excuses, pleas, compliments, pacts, these and so much more are ceremonies or they are nothing. It is thus in the medium of ceremony that the peculiarly human part of our life is lived. (1972, 14)

Indeed, he writes, "Human life in its entirety finally appears as one, vast, spontaneous and holy Rite: the community of man" (17).

According to Fingarette, Confucius wanted to show that the spirits evoked in ritual are not superhuman beings but, rather, the shared values that connect people to one another, shared values that are invoked through ceremonies and conventions.

> Confucius saw, and tried to call to our attention, that the truly, distinctively human powers have, characteristically, a magical quality. . . . What is necessary . . . is that one come upon this "obvious" dimension of our existence in a new way, in the right way. . . . Confucius found the path: we go by way of the notion of *li*. (6)

The word *li* is usually translated as "holy ritual" or "sacred ceremony," but Fingarette says that Confucius used the language and imagery of *li* to talk about the entire body of the mores—the customs, traditions, and conventions of society.

Fingarette uses examples of rituals and conventions from our own culture to show the enormous subtlety and complexity of ritual forms and how they are used to establish relationships between people.

> I see you on the street; I smile, walk toward you, put out my hand to shake yours. And behold!—without any command, stratagem, force, special tricks or tools, without any effort on my part to make you do so, you spontaneously turn toward me, return my smile, raise your hand toward mine. We shake hands—not by my pulling your hand up and down or your pulling mine, but by spontaneous and perfect cooperative action. Normally we do not notice the subtlety and amazing complexity of this coordinated "ritual" act. This subtlety and complexity become very evident, however, if one has had to learn the ceremony only from a book of instructions, or if one is a foreigner from a non-handshaking culture. (1972, 9)

In this example, we see that, although society dictates the form of a convention, the convention becomes a medium for spontaneous and natural self-expression. A handshake may be performed apathetically, enthusiastically, nervously, coolly—the form of the social convention does not restrict individual expressiveness but, rather, provides a medium for the expression of unique and personal affects. Second, as Fingarette emphasizes, the use of ritual or convention indicates the willingness of a person to abide by socially established rules. Think of the significance of the handshake before a contest or fight, and then the handshake between victor and vanquished after the contest. These gestures imply that both contestants will observe the rules during the conventionally limited period of conflict and will maintain a civil relation thereafter.

Fingarette also illustrates the "magical" power of convention with an example from our own society:

> The effortless power of *li* can also be used to accomplish physical ends, though we usually do not think of it this way. Let us suppose I wish to bring a book from my office to my classroom. . . . I turn politely, i.e., ceremonially, to one of my students in class and merely express in appropriate and polite (ritual) formula my wish that he bring me the book. This proper ceremonial expression of my wish is all; I do not need to force, threaten him, trick him. (Fingarette 1972, 10–11)

Of course, conventions grant more power to some people than to others. As Fingarette points out, "I cannot effectively go through the ceremony of bequeathing my servant to someone if, in our society, there is no accepted convention of slavery" (1972, 12). Yet, rituals that encode (and embody) relations of domination also involve the substitution of symbolic forms of action for the use of force or violence. Even animals employ symbolic forms of dominance and deference behavior—such as the chest beating of gorillas—to avoid a physical struggle to determine a relationship. What is different about the symbolic forms that human beings develop is that these ritual forms may also embody principles of social justice and moral accountability.

Fingarette argues that the substitution of symbolic or ritual acts for violence provides the framework for moral order. In our willingness to abide by rules, we act as moral agents and treat others as similarly oriented moral agents, rather than as creatures to be threatened, forced, manipulated, or maneuvered. Fingarette puts it like this:

> In general, what Confucius brings out in connection with the workings of cere-mony is not only its distinctively human character, its linguistic and magical character, but also its moral and religious character. . . . Rite . . . brings out . . . the moral perfection implicit in achieving one's ends by dealing with others as beings of equal dignity, as free co-participants in *li*. . . . It is in this beautiful and dignified, shared and open participation with others who are ultimately like one-self that man realizes himself. (1972, 15–16)

This perspective helps us see that the social relations encoded in ritual are not simply relations of domination; rituals also represent conceptions of respect and communality and moral obligations that those of high status may have to care for their dependents.

### Ritual as Ethical Life

The characteristic qualities of a ritual may be said to reflect the spirit of a peo-ple, the values of their culture. Take, for example, the handshake, the bow, the embrace and the kiss on both cheeks, and the bringing together of the hands with a nod of the head. Each of these symbolic forms of greeting reflects a different conception of social hierarchy and embodies a different degree of physical close-ness. For example, compared to a deferential bow or kissing of the hand of a su-perior, the handshake is distinctively egalitarian (although it may be used to dom-inate or intimidate).

In his later comments on *The Golden Bough* (which were written in the 1940s), Wittgenstein gave further thought to the spirit of a ritual as he read Frazer's description of the Beltane fire festival. He points out that, to interpret a ritual, we must see it in a context that shows its meaning.

> When I speak of the inner nature of the practice I mean all those circumstances in which it is carried out that are not included in the account of the festival, be-cause they consist not so much in particular actions which characterize it, but rather in what we might call the spirit of the festival: which would be described by, for example, describing the sort of people that take part, their way of behav-ior at other times, i.e. their character, and the other kinds of games that they play. And we should then see that what is sinister lies in the character of these people themselves. (1979, 14e)

These remarks are vague but suggestive. If we see the monumental rallies of the Nazi party in the context of fascism, then their spirit becomes clear. We cannot simply take their glorification of the nation as a ritual celebration of community.

Frazer suggests that the Beltane festival as it was performed by children in eighteenth-century Scotland might have originated as a ritual of human sacrifice. But the suggestion that the festival had a sinister import is not borne out by the context of the ritual. Wittgenstein objects that Frazer's hypothesis only *seems* to explain the Beltane festival.

> What I want to say is: What is sinister, deep, does not lie in the fact that is how the history of this practice went, for perhaps it did not go that way. . . .
>
> What makes human sacrifice something deep and sinister anyway? Is it only the suffering of the victim that impresses us in this way? All manner of diseases bring just as much suffering and do *not* make this impression. No, this deep and sinister aspect is not obvious just from learning the history of the external action, but *we* impute it from an experience in ourselves. (1979, 16e)

Wittgenstein suggests that we may explain a ritual in a way that reflects our own psychological needs and that in picturing the participants in a ritual as alien or primitive, we can avoid recognizing something about ourselves and our own practices.

In his essay "The Sheep and the Ceremony," Richard Wolheim also considers the question of how we are to judge the ethical implications of a ritual (Wolheim 1993, 1–21).[24] He begins by showing how rituals are like moral acts:

> They are felt to be obligatory, though not necessarily unconditionally so, and certainly not by all; they admit of being well done or being badly done, or at any rate of being variably done; they, like all actions, have consequences, but they are not to be done for, nor do they derive their values from these consequences; the value that they have is best thought of as their capacity to give value or meaning to a life—to the life, that is, of the person who performs them. (2)

He emphasizes that the meaning of a ritual is not intrinsic to the performance of the ritual but depends on the sincerity and subsequent acts of the participant. He reminds us that sometimes a person is judged to be merely going through the motions.

> Ritual on this view subjects a particular kind of life to much the same sort of ordeal as autobiography subjects a particular life. In each case what the ordeal amounts to is exposure to the light of day, and it is no small matter, no mere coincidence, whether what is exposed can stand up to the test. (1993, 9)

Like Fingarette, Wolheim uses the *Analects* of Confucius to frame his discussion of ritual. He begins with Book 3 where Confucius deplores the mere outward observance of forms and teaches the importance of a return to the sincere and reverent performance of the ancient ceremonies. His disciple raises a question about the ritual in which the new moon is announced to the Ancestors, suggesting that the practice of sacrificing a sheep should be done away with. Confucius replies, "You care for the sheep, I care for the ceremony" (Wolheim 1993, 1).

According to Wolheim, Confucius was deeply impressed by the power of ceremony and ritual to govern even the innermost recesses of human nature. Wolheim suggests that the concern of Confucius for the ceremony rather than for the sheep reflects the danger that, when people no longer have a reverent and sincere attitude toward the rituals of their society, they will lose respect for the moral principles that order social relations. When rituals are no longer seen to embody moral conceptions, they are emptied of meaning. People are then likely to take a cynical view of the values represented in rituals and to see rituals and cultural ideals as simply camouflage for forms of oppression, as Thracymachus saw the concept of justice in his dialogue with Socrates (see Pitkin 1972). Wittgenstein struggles to avoid such cynicism. He writes in the preface to his *Philosophical Remarks*:

> I should like to say "This book is written to the glory of God," but nowadays that would be chicanery, that is, it would not be rightly understood. It means the book is written in good will, and in so far as it is not so written, but out of vanity, etc., the author would wish to see it condemned. He cannot free it of these impurities further than he himself is free of them. (1975, preface; see McGuinness 1982, 92)

In the draft of this preface, he adds, "Everything ritual (everything high-priestly, as it were) must be strictly avoided, because it immediately turns bad. A kiss, to be sure, is also a ritual, and does not go bad—but the only allowable ritual is what is as genuine as a kiss" (McGuinness 1982, 92).

Wolheim objects to "the optimistic conclusion [of Confucius] . . . that every ritual, or every social phenomenon, that has stood up to the test of time is all right, and we have no reason to look for improvement" (1993, 9–10). He points out that the human ability to conceptualize—to project meaning in a symbolic form—reflects "natural movements of the psyche which do not themselves require reference to morality either to describe or explain them" (9). Wolheim suggests that evaluation of a ritual—like appreciation of a work of art—involves a judgment of its authenticity. Returning to the ceremony of the new moon and the sacrifice of the sheep, Wolheim shows what it means to judge the sincerity of a ritual rather than the sincerity of the individual performing the ritual.

> The ritual in itself denies, and derivatively those who perform it deny, the fact . . . of aggression as a human motive. The denial is effective in much the following way: First, the end to which this motive inherently moves—that is, the taking of a life—is isolated; it is bracketed; then it is ordained that this end should be enacted, should be repeated, over and over again, but always, on each enactment, at each repetition, the life is to be taken out of a motive as far

removed from aggression as possible—in the case of the ancient rites, from piety, or decency, or reverence for higher authority, and in the case of blood sports, out of high spirits or in a mood of stern endurance. (15)

According to Wolheim, a ritual is pathological when it mystifies or denies motives that are satisfied by the ritual (even when the ritual is said to satisfy other motives), as when the ritual sacrifice of the sheep is treated as an act of piety and isolated from association to motives of aggression. He suggests that a ritual may allow people to rationalize or justify practices that might otherwise be objectionable. So, we must ask: Does the ritual allow for the expression of self-knowledge with consequences of self-change or reparation, or does it represent an effort to deny complicity in the forms of evil embodied in a way of life—evils resulting from irresponsibility, inequity, neglect, greed, or other unacknowledged motives?

Wolheim helps us to understand the significance of ritual vow fulfillment on Thaipusam. At first encounter, one can hardly fathom why people would pierce their bodies as some devotees of Murugan do. Yet, when one understands the symbolic meaning of piercing the body—of subduing the inner demons—one sees that ritual vow fulfillment can be a transformative experience. Such rituals in which violence is turned upon the self, rather than directed at a scapegoat or sacrificial victim, reveal the human spirit as striving for ethical self-mastery. Ritual vow fulfillment speaks eloquently of people's need to find modes of moral redemption that will bring them into harmony with a conception of the good represented by the symbols of a religious system and of the power of ethical conceptions in people's lives.

9

## RITUAL, POWER, AND MORAL REDEMPTION

Anthropologists Clifford Geertz (1973, 1983) and Stanley Tambiah (1985, 1990) draw upon Wittgenstein's later philosophical writings, applying his insights into language to the concept of culture. They aspire to resolve a tension in the social sciences between theories that emphasize structure (that is, the ways in which the behavior of people is shaped by culture and language) and theories that emphasize human agency and show how people act upon the world with intentionality and try to reshape it to reflect their values and interests. Taken to one extreme, the social sciences hope to produce knowledge that would fulfill the promise of agency, allowing people to control their destiny. Taken to the opposite extreme, human agency disappears and the behavior of people is seen as determined by social structures and culturally given constructs.

This tension between structure and agency appears already in the work of Durkheim, who made the study of ritual central to anthropological theory. In his foundational work on religion, *The Elementary Forms of the Religious Life* (1915), Durkheim argues that structures of thought—organized as the classification of things in the world—are fundamentally reflections of the hierarchical structures of a society:

> A classification is a system whose parts are arranged according to a hierarchy
> . . . and men would never have thought of arranging their knowledge in this way
> if they had not known beforehand what a hierarchy was. . . . The hierarchy is ex-
> clusively a social affair. . . . We have taken [these ideas] from society, and pro-
> jected them into our conceptions of the world. It is society that has furnished the
> outlines which logical thought has filled. (Durkheim 1915, 173)

Durkheimians Robert Hertz ("The Pre-eminence of the Right Hand: A Study in
Religious Polarity" 1909, in Needham 1973) and Marcel Mauss ("Techniques of
the Body" 1936) showed how socially constructed cognitive categories encoded
in ritual are inscribed in physical movements (such as a cultural preference for the
right hand over the left) or embodied in practices so that the social hierarchy these
categories map and the social control that is engendered by them is, in general,
beyond the grasp of consciousness and articulation. This study of the Thaipusam
festival provides another illustration of the role ritual plays in symbolically ordering both the inner, psychological world and the outer, social world.

Van Gennep (1960) followed in the Durkheimian tradition in his analysis of
rites of passage, showing how they provided a structure consisting of three
stages—separation, transition (or a liminal stage), and reincorporation—that
moved individuals from one social status or role to another. When Victor Turner
(1969) applied Van Gennep's analysis of rituals of transition to rituals more commonly found in post-tribal societies, such as festivals and pilgrimages, he observed that many rituals involved the suspension of the normal social order so
that hierarchical distinctions were replaced by equality and symbolic poverty.
This created an egalitarian ethos of social solidarity. Thus, Turner showed that
people could also use ritual to contest the legitimacy of social and political hierarchies. The Thaipusam festival also illustrates how a ritual may implicitly challenge the legitimacy of dominant political hierarchies.

From the Durkheimian perspective, one of the most important functions of ritual is to legitimate and maintain a political order. However, at the same time that
ritual shapes people and the social world they live in, people use ritual forms to act
in pursuit of both individual and collective interests, and they may change rituals to
pursue these interests. In this chapter I begin by exploring these two aspects of ritual as developed in the theoretical approaches of Michel Foucault (1977, 1980) and
Talal Asad (1993) on the one hand and Pierre Bourdieu (1977, 1990b) and Catherine Bell (1992) on the other. This leads to a discussion of the ways in which Clifford Geertz (1973, 1983) and Stanley Tambiah (1985, 1990) draw on Wittgenstein's insights into language to formulate a theory of culture that acknowledges the
centrality of structures of thought and social organization in shaping human experience and behavior while showing how human agents create new cultural forms
and act upon the world to reshape it to accord with their values and interests.

The full significance of Wittgenstein's conception of language and non-
linguistic forms of thought and communication, like ritual, only appears, however,
if we set the work of Geertz and Tambiah alongside the work of the philosophers

discussed in the previous chapter, who write about ritual in a Wittgensteinian vein. This dual perspective shows the significance of ritual in the ethical underpinnings of collective life and the political significance of ritual—that is how ritual constructs forms of power. What this study of ritual vow fulfillment adds to this synthesis is insight into the way rituals shape the gestures that people can use to find moral redemption and realize moral conceptions in the creation of a self. Through sincere participation in rituals that give symbolic representation to ethical principles, people give their values concrete form and show the power of ethical constructs in human forms of life.

## What Rituals Do to People: Ritual as Discipline

From the perspective of theories that emphasize structures that establish hierarchies of power, ritual appears to be a form of social control. For example, in the view of Michel Foucault ritual is a formalized and routinized technology for marking and disciplining the body, which is "the place where the most minute and local social practices are linked up with the large scale organization of power" (Dreyfus and Rabinow 1983, 111).[1] In *Discipline and Punish: The Birth of the Prison* (1977) and "Body/Power" (1980, 55–62), Foucault describes the "meticulous rituals of power," the "penal ceremonies," and "rituals of execution" that are characteristics of Western societies and shows how these new (ritual) technologies emerged in the late seventeenth century in association with the social sciences. From the Foucaultian perspective, humans appear to be the passive vehicles of abstract agents, such as power (or concepts), as in this formulation: "The individual . . . is not the *vis-à-vis* of power; it is one, I believe, of its prime effects. The individual is an effect of power, and at the same time, or precisely to the extent to which it is that effect, it is the element of its articulation. The individual which power has instituted is at the same time its vehicle" (Foucault 1980, 98). Knowledge, from a Foucaultian perspective, does not empower people but is, rather, a primary form of power, which abstractly extends its control: "All this means that power, when it is exercised through these subtle mechanisms [procedures for collecting information and apparatuses of control], cannot but evolve, organise and put into circulation a knowledge, or rather apparatuses of knowledge" (Foucault 1980, 102).

Like Foucault, Talal Asad describes ritual as a prescribed practice of discipline:

> Ritual is therefore directed at the apt performance of what is prescribed, something that depends on intellectual and practical discipline but does not itself require decoding. In other words, apt performance involves not symbols to be interpreted but abilities to be acquired according to rules that are sanctioned by those in authority: it presupposes no obscure meanings, but rather the formation of physical and linguistic skills. (1993, 62)

In *Genealogies of Religion* (1993), Asad observes that the English word *ritual* once referred exclusively to a script or a pattern of sacred practices, with emphasis being placed on the correct performance of this script. He points to parallels between this conception of ritual, found in the Christian monasticism of medieval Europe, and the understanding of ritual practitioners in other cultures who resist when anthropologists ask about the meaning of a ritual.[2] For example, Sperber (1974) writes of the ritual of the Dorze:

> In a general way, the Dorze, who utilize a large number of symbols in connection with multiple, lively and complex rituals, do not explain them, and restrict their comments to the rules of use. . . . The few bits of exegesis that I gathered were improvised by good-natured informants in response to questions that no Dorze would have dreamed of asking. . . . All this goes to show that a complex symbolic system can work very well without being accompanied by any exegetic commentary. (18)

Asad argues that this conception of ritual—in which emphasis is placed on correct performance rather than on the meaning of the text—is common in many societies. He calls for greater attention to the ways in which religious practices and ideologies reflect and legitimate structures of power:

> Instead of approaching religion with questions about the social meaning of doctrines and practices, or even about the psychological effects of symbols and rituals, let us begin by asking what are the historical conditions (movements, classes, institutions, ideologies) necessary for the existence of particular religious practices and discourses. In other words, let us ask: how does power create religion. (1983, 258)

As we have seen in this study of the Thaipusam festival, Asad is correct in emphasizing that the introduction of a capitalist market economy has profound effects on the religious practices and institutions of a society. The working class Tamils of Malaysia have increasingly turned away from the institution of the estate Amman temple as they have entered the labor market and migrated to urban areas. Asad's conception of ritual as a practice of moral discipline is also helpful in suggesting how the myths and legends of Hindu tradition provide models of moral and physical self-discipline and images of the relationship of virtue to power that legitimate the power of those of high-caste status.

### What People Do with Rituals: Practice Theory

Pierre Bourdieu (1977) describes ritual performances as practices that people engage in for conscious and unconscious reasons, with the intention of satisfying "material and symbolic interests and organized by reference to a determined set of economic and social conditions" (36). He adopts from Marcel Mauss the concept of a *habitus,* or the socially given and culturally structured environment within which people act in pursuit of material and symbolic interests (Bourdieu 1990a, 52–65; see also Asad 1993, 75n.20). But he rejects the conception of cultural structures or rules that was central to the Durkheimian perspective, formulating a theory of *practice* that emphasizes human agency. Bourdieu's conception of practice refers to strategies that people develop in pursuit of their interests, which include reshaping the social world in terms of their values. These strategies tend to produce patterns of behavior that resemble social structures, but Bourdieu argues that to understand such patterns as determined by structures nullifies human agency. Thus, while rituals may encode relations of domination, they also are a venue for class struggle: "The different classes and class fractions are engaged in a symbolic struggle properly speaking, one aimed at imposing the definition of the social world that is best suited to their interest" (1991, 167).

In *Ritual Theory, Ritual Practice* (1992), Catherine Bell applies Bourdieu's practice theory to ritual. She finds that the concept of practice advances ritual theory beyond "the view that ritual is a functional mechanism or expressive medium in the service of social solidarity and control" (197). In Bell's view, "practice theory shows how ritualization as a strategic mode of practice produces nuanced relationships of power, relationships characterized by acceptance and resistance, negotiated appropriation, and redemptive reinterpretation of the hegemonic order" (196).

According to Bell, practice theory highlights four features of ritual: "Practice is (1) situational; (2) strategic; (3) embedded in a misrecognition of what it is in fact doing; and (4) able to reproduce or reconfigure a vision of the order of power in the world, or . . . *redemptive hegemony*" (1992, 81). Bell acknowledges that people are generally unaware of the political significance of their ritual acts. She describes this as *misrecognition*—a term she adopts from Bourdieu (Bell 1992, 108–10, 207). As we have seen, the devotees of Murugan who participate in vow fulfillment on Thaipusam do not see their acts as political. However, this does not necessarily mean that they are unaware of the political significance of bhakti devotional worship. As we have also seen, they resent the role of the Chettiars in the festival and fear the return of ritual forms that validate caste hierarchy. They also make judgments in their response to the efforts of reformers to eradicate forms of vow fulfillment that involve piercing the body and trance. They appear to understand that ritual vow fulfillment makes evident the moral worth of those at the bottom of the social hierarchies of class and caste who are filled with the power of Murugan when they fulfill vows by piercing their bodies. Their understanding of the political significance of vow fulfillment is implicit. By participating in rituals that give expression to their values, they make these ethical concepts part of the moral framework of collective life.[3]

### Agency and Structure

From the theoretical perspective represented by the work of Foucault and Asad, we see how ritual legitimates hierarchies of power and forms of domination and how people are shaped by the institutions of their society and the forms of knowledge that inform those institutions. The theoretical perspective of Bourdieu and Bell shows how people act through rituals in pursuit of material and symbolic interests, resisting forms of domination that they consider illegitimate. What these two perspectives share is a focus on structures of power and the role of ritual in legitimating and resisting forms of domination.[4] Recent writings by Clifford Geertz (1973, 1983) and Stanley Tambiah (1985, 1990) draw on Wittgenstein's later philosophical writings to present an interpretive approach to ritual that stands in contrast to the focus on the ways in which ritual both instantiates structures of power and provides a medium for resistance to structures of domination.

In "Thick Description: Toward an Interpretive Theory of Culture," Geertz adopts the expression *thick description* from Gilbert Ryle, a philosopher deeply influenced by the later writings of Wittgenstein (Geertz 1973, 6, 405n.). Geertz reads ritual as a cultural text, an exemplar of the culturally (and linguistically) given concepts that organize a society and make people's experience *meaningful*. For example, in the classic essay "Notes on the Balinese Cockfight," Geertz treats the Balinese cockfight as a "model," a "metaphor," a "fiction," an "image," a "means of expression," "a Balinese reading of Balinese experience, a story they tell themselves" (1973, 444, 448). He describes his theory as a semiotic theory of culture and argues (following Wittgenstein) that interpretation rather than explanation is required: "Believing with Max Weber that man is an animal suspended in webs of significance he himself has spun, I take culture to be those webs, and the analysis of it to be therefore not an experimental science in search of law but an interpretive one in search of meaning" (1973, 5). On the one hand, culture organizes human experience:

> Undirected by culture patterns—organized systems of significant symbols—man's behavior would be virtually ungovernable, a mere chaos of pointless acts and exploding emotions, his experience virtually shapeless. Culture, the accumulated totality of such patterns, is not just an ornament of human existence but—the principal basis of its specificity—an essential condition for it. (46)

On the other hand, culture is not a power that determines what people do, but rather a context within which people act:

> As interworked systems of construable signs (what . . . I would call symbols), culture is not a power, something to which social events, behaviors, institutions, or processes can be causally attributed; it is a context, something within which they can be intelligibly—that is, thickly—described. (14)

Geertz reminds us that the cockfight "does not kill anyone, castrate anyone, reduce anyone to animal status, alter the hierarchical relations among people or refashion the hierarchy; it does not even redistribute income in any significant way" (443). Rather, the cockfight "catches up [the] themes—death, masculinity, rage, pride, loss, beneficence, chance—and ordering them into an encompassing structure presents them in such a way as to throw into relief a particular view of their essential nature" (442).

In *Sherpas Through Their Rituals* (1978), Sherry Ortner applies a Geertzian perspective, with her own version of practice theory (1984), and shows how Sherpa rituals provide symbolic mechanisms for formulating personal and social problems and fashioning solutions for these problems by inducing "a transformation of subjective orientation to the 'facts' of [a] situation" (1978, 6). Similarly, Obeyesekere's case studies of the Hindu and Buddhist ascetics who are devotees of Skanda at Kataragama in Sri Lanka (1981) and his work on the cult of the Goddess Patini (1984) show how the collective representations of a religious tradition externalize the anxieties and deep motivations of a people in a particular society, presenting them in terms of a cosmic drama, giving them existential meaning, and providing "an avenue for self-reflection, communication with others, and in exceptional cases, for a radical transformation of one's being" (Obeyesekere 1990, 25).

In the theoretical perspective developed by Geertz (1973), ritual provides the medium for a resolution of individual problems in ways that give meaning to a human life. Geertz also shows how ritual forms change in response to social change (142–69), and he goes on to speak of "the politics of meaning" (311–26). The politics of meaning refers to the ways in which people "render . . . political life intelligible by seeing it, even at its most erratic, as informed by a set of conceptions—ideals, hypotheses, obsessions, judgments—derived from concerns which far transcend it" (312).

Ritual vow fulfillment can be taken as an exemplar of the politics of meaning. We learn what vow fulfillment means by listening to the stories about Murugan and the gods and goddesses of Hindu tradition. We see also how the ways in which people invoke the images and symbols of their tradition change in response to social, economic, and political changes, as in the shift from vow fulfillment to the Amman goddess to vow fulfillment to Murugan on Thaipusam. And, as Ortner and Obeyesekere point out, ritual vow fulfillment provides a means of psychological reorientation that potentially helps people harmonize their relations with others and find internal resolution to their conflicts.

In "A Performative Approach to Ritual" (1985, 87–166), Tambiah adopts the term *performative* from the ordinary language philosophy of J. L. Austin (1961, 1962). Austin examines statements in which the uttering of words is itself the execution of an act, as in "I give and bequeath my watch to my brother," or "I promise . . . ," "I choose . . . ," "I authorize . . . ," "I plead guilty," or the "I do" of a marriage ceremony. For Tambiah, ritual is performative in the sense that "saying something is also doing something" (1985, 128).[5]

Tambiah draws on the multiple meanings of *performative* to point to parallels between ritual performances and dramatic ones.[6] The comparison between ritual and dramatic performances emphasizes the ways in which the culturally given forms of ritual provide a script or medium for a performance. Furthermore, ritual performances, like dramatic ones, involve the use of multiple media—gestures, dance, music, and visual representations that evoke an emotional as well as cognitive response.

The analysis of ritual as performance (or text) has led to greater sophistication in discussion of the problem of agency and structure. The model of performance implies several different agents and different kinds of agency. There is the agency of the author(s) of the text, but also the agency of the performers who choose to perform a particular ritual or a particular variant of a ritual text and who may even revise the text or tradition in their performance. There is the agency of those who participate as audience (or readers of a text) and who more or less self-consciously interpret the text. The focus on hermeneutics has also led to greater (self-) awareness among anthropologists of their agency as interpreters of culture and authors of texts that represent cultural meanings (see Wagner 1981; Clifford and Marcus 1986; Marcus and Fischer 1986; Clifford 1988; Geertz 1988).

### Tambiah's Concept of Participatory Rationality

In *Magic, Science, Religion, and the Scope of Rationality* (1990), Tambiah develops a theory of human rationality based on the performative approach to ritual. He calls the form of rationality that underlies ritual performances *participatory* rationality. This is distinguished from instrumental rationality (or what Tambiah calls "the modality of *causality*"), which is applied in practical activities like boat-building, developed most self-reflectively as the methodology of science, and grounded in hypotheses about "natural laws" that are tested empirically. Instrumental rationality allows people to predict (within limits) an outcome determined by cause and effect, which is independent of our beliefs about what is happening.

Contrasted to this is the modality of *participation,* which invokes concepts that link people to one another and to the world in particular ways and which grounds action in a symbolic mode. The participatory modality of understanding, according to Tambiah, is most highly developed in religious and artistic traditions. He characterizes the rationality of participation as a way of relating to and constructing reality that occurs "when persons, groups, animals, places, and natural phenomena are in a relation of contiguity, and translate that relation into one of existential immediacy and contact and shared affinities" (1990, 107). Conceptions that describe how people are linked to one another and to the world—such as family, clan, nation, race, class, gender, and conceptions of the relation of humankind to God—allow people to predict (within greater limits) what people will do because they share certain beliefs or conceptions and *participate* in them. This is why anthropologists must introduce native concepts in their ethnographies and why they speak of people's reasons and motives rather than cause and effect. For example, if people believe that they share a certain identity based on clan membership, this will be the reason they do certain things, such as assist fellow members of the clan. However, if clan identity is no longer significant to them, clan rituals will die out. People will no longer assume that others will act in accord with the obligations of clan membership or that they can claim the rights belonging to members of a clan.

Unfortunately, no clear line demarcates causal and participatory modalities of rationality. All collective activities require that people employ instrumental (or

causal) rationality and that they participate in the social constructs that link people. These "participatory concepts" can be said to be used instrumentally to
achieve individual and collective ends. For this reason, there has been a tendency
in the social sciences to see all action as instrumental.

Tambiah's conception of a participatory modality of rationality is an important advance over earlier anthropological theories of symbolic action, because it
suggests a new paradigm for the rationality of symbolic acts and thereby also un-
dercuts the inclination to see an analogy between these acts and the obsessive acts
of someone who is troubled by internal psychological conflict. Tambiah's work
also shows why ritual acts that evoke participatory concepts connecting people to
one another are politically significant. They instantiate ethical and collective values that exist only through the commitments that people make and act upon.

### Ritual Acts and Ethical Life Reconsidered

Geertz and Tambiah show that agency and structure are opposite sides of the
same coin. Concepts embodied in ritual provide a structure that shapes and organizes individual experience and understanding so that human behavior is relatively predictable. Because social relations are relatively predictable, people can
be effective agents. They can use the medium of ritual to pursue both conscious
and unconscious aims; they can also revise traditional rituals and create new ones
in pursuit of such aims.

Geertz's emphasis on meaning, however, obscures the centrality of ethical
conceptions to the politics of meaning. And Tambiah's suggestive work on participatory rationality lacks an account of how participatory constructs are evalu-
ated and, when social and economic conditions permit, challenged—that is, how
participatory rationality is grounded in ethical concerns with mutual respect and
collective responsibility. This is peculiar, because rituals (and the words that
may accompany them) are the most important cultural forms used by people
when they renew their commitment to moral principles and bind themselves to
fulfill commitments to one another. For example, the inauguration of a president
involves the granting of powers in conjunction with the acceptance of moral responsibilities, as does the ritual that accompanies becoming a citizen. The moral
dimension of religious rituals is even clearer. Baptism names a child as a member of a Christian community and announces that the child will be raised as a
Christian and taught respect for the ethical principles of its community. In the
rite of confirmation, adolescents confirm their acceptance of Christian beliefs
and moral conceptions. In rituals like confession, atonement, penance, and vow
fulfillment, people express their acceptance of a moral code set forth in a religious tradition and renew their commitment to live in accord with this code.
These are moral acts in the sense that they are meant to bring a person's soul (an
internal identification with good) into harmony with collective representations
of the good. In this regard, the major difference between the moral conceptions

of a religious tradition and the rights and responsibilities represented in the rituals of secular political institutions is that the latter are recognized to be based on human agreement.

The philosophical essays of Fingarette and Wolheim show the significance of ritual in grounding the ethical forms of collective life. Object Relations psychologists show us that ethical symbols—like a child's first symbol, Winnicott's transitional object—represent an *ideal* relationship that is conceptualized from (but does not mirror) experience in the real world. These psychologists also provide insight into the ways that we use symbols in creating individual selves with particular aims and intentions. The later philosophy of Wittgenstein extends this insight, showing us that it is through symbolic acts, given form in rituals, that people seek moral redemption, renew their moral commitments, and strive to act with others to create a more just social order. If human beings did not have this capacity to represent symbolically ethical relationships—conceptions of a just social order based on mutual respect, collective responsibility, and individual autonomy—we would be no more than Hobbesian creatures, who seek only self-preservation and self-interest.

To understand rituals, two perspectives must be sustained. One perspective (developed by the philosophers considered in chapter 8) focuses on how individuals use ritual to constitute themselves as moral beings and how people collectively engage in rituals that construct a social order based on shared values. The second perspective (developed in anthropological studies of ritual) is a hermeneutics of suspicion that looks at how rituals—and the ethical concepts they embody—implicate people in relations of power. Taken alone, a theory that shows how ritual is used to construct forms of power fails to reflect the power of ritual in configuring a moral order and breeds cynicism, thereby eroding conceptions of moral autonomy and agency. What is necessary is a dual perspective that keeps in mind both the relations of domination that may be encoded in the cultural forms of a society and the ethical conceptions that are symbolically represented in rituals.

From this dual perspective, we see the asceticism and ritual vow fulfillment of the bhakti tradition and the Thaipusam festival as moral practices, and we also see how elites use the festival to legitimate their high status and to claim the loyal support of their clients. Attention to the ethical themes that run through the Thaipusam festival helps ensure that we do not simply adopt the view of elites, such as those upper-class reformers who dismiss the ritual vow fulfillment of working-class Tamils as primitive or irrational practices. Recognizing that the devotees of Murugan seek moral redemption and a more just social order reminds us that ritual potentially provides the foundation for non-violent, self-conscious, ethical reshaping of culturally given forms of life.

# GLOSSARY

In Malaysia there is a great deal of variation in the spelling of Tamil words, because several Tamil letters can be transcribed by two different English letters: //TAMIL// (k,g); //TAMIL// (s,c); //TAMIL// (t,d); and //TAMIL// (p,b), and also because there is no overarching social or political institution to provide a standardized spelling. In this text I use the traditional English spelling of the names of Hindu deities and other religious terms, following the most common spelling in the announcements of temple festivals in Malaysia—thus Murugan rather than Murukan, Shiva rather than Siva or Civam, Vishnu rather than Visnu, Krishna rather than Krsna, kavadi rather than kavati, and Brahmin rather than Brahman—but where local usage differs (for example, Muniswara rather than Muhishwara), I follow it. The Malay word *sakti* has been adopted from Tamil *shakti* (Skt. śakti), and Tamils in Malaysia spell it following Malaysian usage. When quoting from the work of other scholars, I follow the transcription used in the source. To make these inconsistencies easier to follow, alternative spellings of frequently used Tamil words are provided in this glossary (and in the text if the word appears only once). Tamil words that appear only once and are accompanied by an English translation do not appear in the glossary. Diacritical marks are used only in the glossary and in quotations. For Bahasa Malaysia, I have used the conventions of the reformed spelling.

**abhisheka (apiṣēkam, abhiṣēkam)** The ritual of anointing an icon with water or other fluid.

**Adi-Dravida (Ādi-Drāvida)** "Original Dravidian." A term applied to those of untouchable background.

**aḷaku (azhaku)** "Beauty." The needles or skewers used to perforate the body in ritual vow fulfillment.

**Amman (Ammaṇ)** Village goddess; generally a virgin mother.

**arōgarā (arokarā, harōharā) Skt.** "Praise him." [ Evocation of Shiva]

**aruḷ** "Grace" or "blessing." A trance that is experienced as an ecstatic contact with the divine.

**asura (Tamil acuran or cur)** Demonic beings who attempt to overthrow the gods.

**bāla** Male child, roughly between two and five years of age.

**bhakti**  A religious movement of devotional worship.

**Chettiar (Chettiyar)**  A money-lending caste.

**Chittirai (Chitthirai)**  Tamil month (April–May), famous for the temple festival at Madurai in Tamilnadu.

**dēva (dēvam, thēvam; pl. dēvankal or dēvanggal; thēvankal; also spelled with ei or ey)** God or gods.

**iccā**  Desire, passion.

**Idumban (Idumbaṇ)**  Devotee of Murugan and guardian of his temple.

**iṟaivaṇ**  A conception of divinity as eminence, absolute moral perfection.

**ishta dēvam (iṣṭa teyvam)**  A deity that is worshipped as an object of personal devotion.

**jāti**  A lineage subcaste.

**jñāna**  "Knowledge." Worship expressed as a search for knowledge of the divine.

**jutha (Tamil ecil or ecchel)**  Leavings of a meal that are polluted by saliva (Hindi).

**kangāni (kangāny)**  Overseer of a labor crew (now Malaysian English).

**karagam**  A pot decorated with flowers, strings, and vepellai (neem) leaves, symbol of the goddess.

**karma**  "Work." Deeds that cause rebirth in the world.

**kāvadi (kāvaṭi)**  A wooden arch borne on the shoulder of a devotee who fulfills a vow to Murugan.

**kirāni**  Clerical staff (of plantations).

**kōvil (kōil)**  A temple or shrine; literally "house of god."

**kriyā**  "Will" or "deed." Used to refer to worship as ritual properly observed.

**kulam**  Clan, lineage.

**kuṅkumam**  red powder (usually worn on the forehead); a sign of sakti (shakti), the power of the goddess.

**Mariamman (Māriammaṇ, Māriyammaṇ)**  Hot Goddess who brings both smallpox and rain.

**masukan (Bahasa Malaysia)**  Literally, "an entering." Possession by a supernatural spirit.

**migu**  Noble.

**mūrthi (mūrti in North India)**  Form, used to refer to a particular manifestation of a deity.

**Murugan (Murugaṇ, Murukaṇ)**  Son of Shiva and Parvati, best known in North India as the warrior god Skanda. As Murugan, this deity is especially identified with Tamils.

**nērttikaṭaṇ**  The fulfillment of a debt; used to refer to vow fulfillment.

**nōṇbu (nōṇpu)** Women's fasting rituals.

**pāca (pācam)** Worldly bonds.

**pacu** Soul.

**paṇḍāram (paṇṭāram)** A non-Brahmin priest, usually a hereditary caste occupation. Sometimes this title is applied to the apprentice of a Brahmin priest, who has the task of making garlands for the deity.

**Panguni Uttiram (Paṅguṇi Uttiram, Paṅkuṇi Uttiram)** A Shaivite festival celebrated in the Tamil month of Uttiram (March–April).

**pati** A transcendent conception of the deity in Shaiva Siddhantha.

**pēy (pei)** A ghost or demonic spirit that may possess people.

**prasād (prasādam)** Offerings to a deity that are returned to the worshipper.

**pūja** Worship.

**pūjāri (pūcāri)** One who performs pūja; title for a non-Brahmin priest.

**sakti (shakti, śakti)** "Power" or "energy." Especially the feminine form of divine energy.

**sāmiyāṭi (cāmiyāṭi, swāmiyāṭi, saamiyaa Di)** "God-dancer." A relatively low-caste person who is known to be possessed by a deity, often a hereditary role.

**Sangam (Cankam)** The period of Tamil history (first to third centuries A.D.) named after the poetic literature of the early Dravidian kingdoms.

**Subrahmanya (Subramañiya, Subrahmañiya, Subramañiyam, Subramañiam)** Epithet of Murugan, worshipped as the transcendent deity of Shaiva Siddhantha.

**tapas** Ascetic austerities and meditation.

**Thaipusam (Thaipūsam, Tai pūcam)** A Shaivite festival celebrated in the Tamil month of Tai (January–February).

**Thandayuthabani (Thaṇḍāyuthabāṇi, Dhaṇḍāyuthapāṇi)** One who bears the staff of an ascetic. Epithet of Murugan as worshipped at the Palani Temple.

**thaneer pandal (taneer, tannir pantal)** A shed constructed for a ceremonial occasion to shelter invited guests (literally, "water shed").

**vāhaṇam** Vehicle or mount of a god.

**vēl** Lance with a leaf-shaped head, weapon of Murugan.

**vibhūti (vipūti)** Sacred white ash (from burnt cow dung).

**Vinayagar (Vināyagar [Ganesh, Gaṇeśa])** The elephant-headed Hindu deity, son of Shiva and Parvati. He is usually addressed as Vinayagar or Pillaiyar by Tamils in Penang.

# NOTES

## CHAPTER 1: THE POWER OF MURUGAN'S LANCE

1. Norman Cohn, *The Pursuit of the Millennium: Revolutionary Messianism in Medieval and Reformation Europe and Its Bearing on Modern Totalitarian Movements* (1961).

2. Simon Elegant, "A Festival for the Fervent: A Hindu Celebration in Penang Is Full of Devotion and Self-Inflicted Suffering," *New York Times,* April 20, 1992.

3. This interpretation was provided by a non-Brahmin priest of the Sri Arul Maha Mariamman Temple. See chapters 3, 4, and 5 for further discussion of this important temple.

4. See Shulman (1980), who discusses the paradoxical relation between *mukti*, release or enlightenment, and *bhukti* or material reward (20–21; see also Diehl 1956, 255–56).

5. One way that some of these puzzling bits of information can be fitted together is through the conception that moments and places of conjunction are points where the divine—in both malevolent and benign forms—is most likely to manifest in the mundane world. Thus, for Hindus, crossroads are the haunts of demons and the confluence of rivers is sacred, as are the transitions between light and dark at sunset and dawn. The conjunction of astral forces with phases of the moon is considered to be an especially auspicious time, during which the deity associated with those constellations is most likely to be approachable (Stanley 1977).

6. As Sperber (1974) points out, "exegesis is not an interpretation but rather an extension of the symbol and must itself be interpreted" (34).

7. Also Durkheim writes, "A society is not simply constituted by a mass of individuals who compose it, by the territory they occupy, by the things they use and the actions they perform, but above all by the idea it has about itself. To be sure, it hesitates about the way it ought to see itself; it feels pulled in different directions. When these conflicts do break out, however, they do not take place between the ideal and the real but between different ideals, between the ideal of yesterday and ideal of today, between that backed by the authority of tradition and that which is only beginning to gain favor" (in Pickering 1975, 151–52).

8. See Peter Winch, "Understanding a Primitive Society" (1964); Wilson, *Rationality* (1970); and Stanley Tambiah, *Culture, Thought, and Social Action* (1985) and *Magic, Science, Religion, and the Scope of Rationality* (1990).

9. "The establishment of a single series thus creates *ex nihilo* a whole host of re-

lationships (of simultaneity, succession, or symmetry, for example) between terms and guide marks of different levels, which, being produced and used in different situations, are never brought face to face in practice and are thus compatible practically even when logically contradictory" (Bourdieu 1977, 107).

10. "A classification is a system whose parts are arranged according to a hierarchy . . . and men would never have thought of arranging their knowledge in this way if they had not known beforehand what a hierarchy was. . . . The hierarchy is exclusively a social affair. . . . We have taken (these ideas) from society, and projected them into our conceptions of the world. It is society that has furnished the outlines which logical thought has filled in" (Durkheim 1915, 173). Mary Douglas (1960, 1973) shows the relation of ritual to cognition.

11. "That an emblem is useful as a rallying-centre for any sort of a group it is superfluous to point out. By expressing the social unity in a material form, it makes this more obvious to all, and for that very reason the use of emblematic symbols must have spread quickly when once thought of" (Durkheim 1915, 262).

12. "Symbols and sentiments feed upon each other and their fruitful interplay lies at the heart of social behavior" (Lewis 1977, 2). This theme is developed in the work of Fernandez (in Geertz 1971) and Ortner (1978).

13. "It is in some sort of ceremonial form . . . that the moods and motivations which sacred symbols induce in men and the general conceptions of the order of existence which they formulate for men meet and reinforce one another. In a ritual, the world as lived and the world as imagined, fused under the agency of a single set of symbolic forms, turn out to be the same world" (Geertz 1973, 112).

## CHAPTER 2: MURUGAN AS METAPHOR

1. Shaivite ritual is based on agamic texts that prescribe sixteen acts of worship in the following order: offering hospitality, washing the feet, ablution, welcoming rites, enthronement, bathing or anointing the god, dressing the image, invocation, offering sandal paste, offering flowers, burning incense, burning oil lights, offering fruits and food, meditation, uttering mantras, and burning camphor. The ritual may be simplified to a sequence of offering sandal paste and flowers, burning incense and oil lamps, and offering fruit (Clothey 1969, 243).

2. Hart (1988) argues that a form of caste rooted in the sacred powers of women and ritual specialists is indigenous to southern India and provided a base for the introduction of the Vedic institution of caste.

3. "The medieval and modern South Indian temple expresses most perfectly the South Indian conceptions of sovereignty and community. . . . The realm itself was defined by the worship of the king and his tutelary as in the *Mahaïnavamiï* or *Navaraïtri* (festivals). Worship is constitutive of (it establishes or creates) community; the sovereignty of great humans (fathers, clan heads, kings) and gods is realized in worship events, or ritual performances, of a public kind in which all of any corporate whole (family to kingdom) express membership and in which all witness as well as compete for the honors which alone can be distributed by powerful personages and divinities" (Stein 1984, 320–21). However, see also Appadurai and Breckenridge (1976) and

Dirks (1993) for the way in which temple ritual reflects tensions and conflict within the community. Clifford Geertz's study of the traditional political system of Bali, *Negara: The Theatre State in Nineteenth-Century Bali* (1980), provides a comparable example of ritualistic authority.

4. Zvelebil (1981) believes that the deities associated with particular locations were the indigenous Dravidian gods and were associated with agriculture and therefore with the founding of villages (6). Daniel (1984) explains that in the view of Tamil villagers, the goddess, the soil of a place, and its inhabitants contain a common essence (61–67; see also Wadley 1975 and Shulman 1980).

5. It is worth remarking that the tradition by which Murugan has two wives, one light-skinned (of Brahmin caste) and one dark-skinned (of tribal or low caste), provides a metaphor for the relation of the ruler to high-caste groups and to tribal peoples and low-ranked castes.

6. An excellent film of the Chittirai festival entitled *Wedding of the Goddess* illustrates these points.

7. Translated with the assistance of Mr. Ramachandran, headmaster of the Ramakrishna Mission in Penang.

8. The *Paripatal* is one of the *Ettuttokai,* a collection of poems set to music. Of the twenty-four poems that have survived, eight are devoted to Murugan (Sastri 1966, 366; Zvelebil 1973b, 125).

9. In the seventh century, the first stone temples were built in southern India under the patronage of the Pallava kings. In Pallava sculpture, Murugan-Skanda is depicted as Somaskanda, the infant son of Shiva and Parvati. This image may represent the rulers of southern Indian kingdoms (and Dravidian deities who had been incorporated into the Vedic pantheon) as legitimate heirs of northern Indian traditions.

10. See A. K. Ramanujan, "The Indian Oedipus," in Edmunds and Dundes, eds. *Oedipus: A Folklore Casebook,* 1983. Notice that in the Indian tales with an oedipal theme, the son does not kill his father (see chapter 7 for further discussion of this point).

11. In Penang, Shiva is usually substituted for Brahma in this story, emphasizing oedipal tensions.

12. Hart (1978) attributes the *Tirumurukarruppatai* to the third century and Zvelebil (1973b) to the late third or fourth century, although it also contains interpolations from later periods (see Clothey 1978, 206–8).

13. The earliest mention of Valli in Tamil literature dates from the second or third century A.D. (Zvelebil 1981, 45, 54). The Valli story does not appear in the northern Indian *Skanda Purana.*

14. The Hindu kingdom of Vijayanagar was established in the Telegu-speaking area of southern India after the fall of the Cholas (13th c.) and the spread of Islam into the Deccan (14th c.). Vijayanagar extended its control into the Tamil plain in the fifteenth century. The revival in the worship of Murugan during this period has been attributed to the tendency toward democratization and Tamilization that resulted from the clearing of jungle lands and the incorporation of tribal peoples into the mainstream of Tamil culture (Clothey 1978, 107).

15. Guha is an epithet of Murugan, which means "Secret One."

16. The 1,367 poems attributed to Arunakiri are collected in the *Tiruppukal (Tirupuzh)*.

17. Today the priests of the Palani Murugan Temple are Brahmins. In the sixteenth century, a general of Tirumalai Nayak installed Adi-Shaiva priests in the temple (Clothey 1978, 229). However, the *Palani Sthalapurana* preserves the tradition that the original priests were the descendants of Pulippani, disciple of a Siddha Bhogar famed for his alchemical medicinal knowledge. Pulippani devised the magical amalgam from which the icon of Murugan at Palani is said to be made.

18. *Coolie* is derived from the Tamil word *kuli,* which refers to the hire or payment for occasional menial work *(Oxford English Dictionary)*.

19. Examples include the temple of Murugan at Palani; the shrine of Kataragama (where a form of Murugan is worshipped) in Sri Lanka; and the temples of Ayyappan at Sabari Malai in the hills of central Kerala, of Khandoba in the Deccan, and of Venkatesvara at Tirupati. See Alan Morinis (1984) for a description of the ways pilgrimage operates to maintain or undermine the existing social and political order.

20. The famed temple complex at Tirupati—described to visitors today as second in riches only to the Vatican—is one example of a major medieval temple that continues to be an important institution.

21. See Fuller (1984) for an account of the disputes over entry to the Minakshi Temple in Madurai.

22. After independence, the Hindu Religious and Charitable Endowments Act of 1951 placed Hindu temples under the direct control of the state governments.

23. The *Palani Sthalapurana* contains a legend that associates Murugan with worship in the vernacular Tamil. It begins with a competition between the followers of Shiva and those of Vishnu initiated by the sage Narada. The sage Agastya represents Shaivite doctrine and Vyasa represents Vaishnavite doctrine. Narada asks the other sages which of the two has attained the truth. As the sages debate, Agastya retires to worship Shiva. The god appears before the sage and teaches him a sacred mantra, saying, "This is sweet Tamil. Murugan will teach it all to you without leaving anything out" (Shulman 1980, 7). Agastya is credited with bringing from Murugan "the divine drink" of the Tamil language to southern India.

24. As Babb writes more generally of Hinduism,

> There are obvious differences between deities, but they tend to merge, and distinctions that seem obvious and sharp from one perspective often disappear when viewed from another. The resulting configuration is one that can maintain seemingly limitless diversity under an overarching unity. Ultimately, as the most casual student of Hinduism knows, all the gods and goddesses are "one." This is a doctrine of genuine significance, and not merely an extravagance of bookish philosophers. It is a doctrine that is reiterated frequently in the texts, but illiterate villagers are equally fluent in maintaining that although there are many deities, and although they have different and sometimes contradictory characteristics, in the end all are the same and all are "one." (Babb 1975b, 216)

25. Trawick (1990a) has shown how karma is understood to require a puritanical self-discipline that shapes child rearing in high-caste families: "Luxuries and soft

treatment should not become parakkam [habitual], they said. When a small child learned to deprive itself, to say no to a tempting sweet, this development was reported with glee to others as a significant advance" (103). "This family believed in karma, believed that everybody had committed some sins in the past for which they would eventually suffer punishment. It followed that if you wanted to contribute to someone's future happiness, the best way to do it was to make them miserable in the present and get the inevitable punishment over with. . . . One mother (not of this family) told me, it was wrong to make a child laugh because for every moment of laughter that the child enjoyed now he would have to suffer a moment of tears in the future" (104, see also 222).

26. In India, a Western visitor soon notices the centrality of dharma. When one tries to thank someone for a service rendered, the response is frequently, "It is my duty." In the formulation of Louis Dumont, "Hindu society is organized around the concept of dharma [duty] in a way roughly similar to modern society around that of the individual" (1967, 140).

27. Looking at southern Indian religion from a structuralist perspective, Dumont (1959b) has interpreted the relationship of the Amman goddess to the demonic warrior deities who guard her temple as a symbolic representation of the relation of the dominant landowning caste of the village to the low service castes.

28. As Washbrook (in Frankel and Rao 1989) notes:

> The chief relevance of the purity/pollution theory was at the very top and very bottom of the social order. Ritual purity was part of the *brahman's* mystique, a reason for the specialness of his religious skills, and groups seeking to associate themselves most directly with this mystique tended to emulate him and become purity conscious. (236)

29. George Hart argues that Brahmin ideas about purity and pollution mask ancient Tamil beliefs in a sacred power *(ananku)* that is wild and capricious and may cause undeserved suffering if not controlled. This power—the obverse of purity—inheres in demons, untouchables, and women, as well as in the king. Hart suggests that the object of ritual is the creation of an artificial but effective structure around dangerous objects or persons to neutralize the threat that they represent. He notes that low and stigmatized groups may manipulate people of higher castes by evoking their fear of the innate, dangerous power of untouchables and women (1973; 1975b, 81–137; 1978, 11–13).

30. See Kolenda 1976, 1978; Berreman 1979; and in response, Tambiah 1990, 126–27. As Washbrook observes, "Given the existence of inequalities in the distribution of wealth, power and status, the question of how far these are to be understood as the products of an 'illegitimate' domination as opposed to a 'legitimate' order imposed by nature, culture or society depends very much on the eye of the analyst-beholder and his informing ideology" (in Frankel and Rao 1989, 210). Washbrook surveys and comments on the extensive anthropological literature on caste in southern India, in the context of a discussion of how caste and class have played out in the politics of twentieth-century Tamilnadu. *Dominance and State Power in Modern India,* edited by Frankel and Rao (1989), contains contributions to a reconceptualization

of caste from the perspective of subaltern studies. Especially significant is the role of colonial administration in turning caste into a rigid system supported by law.

31. Similarly, Guha (1983) shows how the peasant insurgencies in colonial India reflected an "elementary" rebel consciousness.

32. The term "dominant caste" was used by M. N. Srinivas (1987) to describe a caste of relatively high rank that forms a sizable proportion of the local population and politically and economically dominates an area because it controls most of the land.

33. Moffatt (1979) notes that the Tamil villagers he studied participate in both collective rituals and individual devotion: "Every Harijan and every other villager . . . has at least five distinct gods to whom he gives regular devotion. The first of these is the 'chosen god,' the divine being whom an individual worshiper decides is paramount for himself or herself. The second and third are the 'household god' and the 'lineage god,' divine beings shared by the worshiper with the kin of his immediate family and of his patrilineage. And the fourth and fifth are the 'hamlet god' (depending on the worshiper's caste) and the 'village god,' beings shared by the worshiper with those with whom he or she has a common territory—hamlet or village" (221). Moffatt reports that the chosen deity most popular with the untouchable villagers he studied was Murugan.

## CHAPTER 3: THE HINDU TAMILS OF PENANG

1. As one scholar has commented, the Chettiars "have a reputation for sanctity and a ritual status almost as impressive as their bank balances" (Baker 1975, 72). See Dirks (1993) for a discussion of how the Nattukottai Chettiars used the wealth accumulated in colonial Malaya, Burma, and Ceylon, to enhance their status in Tamilnadu, translating wealth into status through religious ritual (370–74).

2. Swami Ramadasar attempted to establish another school in 1955, but this effort was not successful.

3. The relatively pure goddess of the "clean caste" hamlet *(uur)* does not actually enter the settlement of untouchable castes *(koloni)* when she is taken in procession. Untouchable worshippers must bring their offerings out to her (Moffatt 1979). Similarly, Alagar, deity of the rural hinterland, does not actually enter the city of Madurai when he is taken on procession during the Chittirai festival. His low-caste and untouchable worshippers come to meet him on the banks of the river at the edge of the city (Hudson 1977).

4. The Naduthurai Karumariamman Temple stands back from the main road in one of the rural hamlets that has been enveloped by George Town and turned into a kind of slum.

5. Converts to Christianity generally came from low-caste or untouchable groups.

6. Another important reform group that emerged from the anti-Brahmin movement is Vallalan Momran.

7. Maloney's description of the English-speaking elite of the Jaffna District in Sri Lanka could be applied to the English-speaking professional community of Malaysian Indians in Penang: "the English-knowing elite (2.5 percent of the popula-

tion) have a 'doctrine' of development, economic growth, casteless society, and socialism, by which they legitimize their position and authority. Villagers do not particularly share these views, but the urban elite believe that they have a moral obligation to 'pull' the whole population, while at the same time they are careful to keep the English language as a symbol of their elevated position so that few villagers can attain it" (Maloney 1975, 170).

8. Temples not owned by a caste lineage would include important pilgrimage temples and temples established by communities that have fragmented under the pressures of urbanization. See chapter 5 for further discussion of the Sri Arul Maha Mariamman Temple.

9. This temple is popularly known as the Queen Street Mariamman Temple. "Sri" and "Maha" are honorifics that have been added to the name of the goddess of the temple, which represent her as the goddess of Penang as a settlement. "Arulmigu" echoes the title of the Thandapani avatar of the Penang Hill Murugan Temple, which is the venue of vow fulfillment on Thaipusam. The title acknowledges the goddess of the Queen Street temple as a deity who graces her worshippers with divine trance, that is, as a deity associated with the egalitarian tradition of bhakti devotionalism.

10. Tamil dockworkers were politically more sophisticated than other Tamil laborers, because they had witnessed and even participated in protests organized by Chinese laborers before the Depression. In the late 1930s Tamil stevedores and warehouse workers mounted a successful campaign to improve wages and conditions (Arasaratnam 1979, 78–81).

11. Despite the fact that the Chitraparvam is celebrated as the annual festival of the Mariamman Temple, supporters of the festival insist that it honors Murugan. Some say that after defeating the asura demon Surapadma, Murugan declared a day of rest and celebration on Chitraparvam; others say that the festival marks the day Murugan was reconciled with his parents after quarreling with them and leaving home.

12. Similarly McGilvray (1983) notes of Tamils in Sri Lanka: "the sponsorship of local temple festivals is a dynamic arena of shifting status-dramatizations, both for castes and for matriclans" (106).

13. The term "dominant caste" was first used by M. N. Srinivas: "A caste may be said to be 'dominant' when it preponderates numerically over the other castes, and when it also wields preponderant economic and political power. A large and powerful caste group can more easily be dominant if its position in the local caste hierarchy is not too low" (Srinivas 1987, 4). Dumont (1966) argued that ownership of land is the source of dominance and that the relative size of the dominant caste is irrelevant.

14. I thank Professor Eugene Irschick for pointing out to me the significance of the Malay Reservation Act.

15. Lawsuits over the management of temple funds are common also in India (see Mines and Gourishankar 1990, for example; also Dirks 1993, 358–83).

16. The major ethnic groups of Malaysia are Malay (57.7 percent) and Chinese (31.8 percent). The minority community of Indian origin has declined in size relative to the other groups; in 1980 Malaysian Indians composed 10.5 percent of the popula-

tion. These statistics are from the *Far Eastern Economic Review (FEER)* of June 7, 1990.

17. On the politics of caste and class in twentieth-century Tamilnadu, see Washbrook (in Frankel and Rao 1989). For comparison with overseas Indians in Fiji, Sri Lanka, and East Africa, see Brown 1984; Brenneis 1984, 1987; Kelly 1991; Obeyesekere 1978; and Bharati 1976.

18. In general, 5 percent of Malaysian children attend Tamil-language primary schools. Theoretically, Bahasa Malaysia and English are taught in these schools. However, Tamil-educated pupils find it difficult to switch to Bahasa Malaysia at the secondary school level, in preparation for national examinations that would ensure a better job and future prospects of an improved standard of living (*FEER,* June 7, 1990).

19. The poor working conditions on plantations have led to labor shortages, which have been filled by illegal immigrants from Indonesia. Most recently, managers of rubber and oil palm estates have replaced the system of direct employment with contract labor, thereby freeing management from legal responsibility for workers (*FEER,* June 7, 1990).

20. For an analysis of changes in attitudes toward caste in Tamilnadu, see Barnett 1975.

21. However, in the late 1980s and the 1990s, young Tamils began to study Tamil as a third language in school. Malay students usually choose Arabic as a third language, and Chinese Malaysians choose Mandarin.

## CHAPTER 4: THAIPUSAM IN PENANG

1. *Pandaram* also refers to garland makers, but in Penang the term is generally used for a hereditary caste of non-Brahmin priests. A pandaram or pujari performs the puja in Tamil, following the teaching of his father, whereas a Brahmin priest would be expected to perform the puja in Sanskrit.

2. The purpose of this swing may be, as some suggest, to protect the image from being jolted as the chariot passes over ruts in the roads; but others say that the deity is being entertained—treated like a child—by being placed in the swing. The image of the infant or child-god will be discussed in chapter 7.

3. The jobs associated with the procession of Murugan are distributed by lot, indicating the equality that is perceived to exist among members of the same jati sub-caste.

4. In addition to the ceremonial escort, the Department of Public Works provides an escort of laborers with long poles to lift telephone and electric wires out of the procession's way. Murugan's chariot is followed by the vehicles of the local police and special units of military police, who are assigned to direct traffic and control the crowds that line the route of the chariot.

5. Describing the competition among middle level jati (lineage groups or localized caste groups) that characterized the traditional polities of Tamilnadu from precolonial times, Washbrook notes that a primary mode of justifying honor and privilege was through donation to temples: "The rewards for making donations consisted

of rights to participate in certain ceremonies in certain ways and to receive gifts and honours from the gods. These, in turn, established the position of the recipient families and jati groups in the local social hierarchy and underwrote their relative positions of privilege" (in Frankel and Rao 1989, 234; see also Appadurai and Breckenridge 1976, and Dirks 1987).

6. These flying dolls may be derived from the custom of hook-swinging. The dolls, like a hook-swinger, often carry a sword and a shield. See note 16 below.

7. The lotus is also a womb symbol.

8. There are girl kolattam troops, although in Penang boy troops are more common (on the kolattam in Tamilnadu, see Chettiar 1973, 159–60).

9. Formerly, as soon as the police turned away, gangs of small Chinese boys and beggars carrying large burlap bags would scramble forward to collect the coconut shards. These they sold to Chinese merchants, who dried them to make copra and *srikaya* (a kind of coconut jam). In 1985, the small boys and beggars seemed to have become guards of the coconut for employers who came in the evening with trucks to collect the piles of coconut shards that had been swept to the edge of the road by their small hirelings.

10. In Singapore, the Thaipusam procession goes to the Ganesha Temple on Keong Saik Road, where Murugan is said to visit his elder brother. This procession is sponsored by the Nattukottai Chettiars of Singapore. On the following day, ritual vow fulfillment takes place at the Perumal Temple (on Serangoon Road) where Vishnu is the presiding deity (see Mialaret 1969).

11. In fact, no marriage ceremony is performed in the Nattukottai Chettiar Temple on Thaipusam.

12. Unlike temples in India, Malaysian Hindu temples do not ordinarily publish a legendary history. Information about temples must be collected from priests and those who attend the temple for worship services. Paperback songbooks published in India are sold in stalls set up for the Thaipusam festival, and literature of the Divine Life Society and Tamil Youth Bell Club is distributed.

13. Nowhere in the hillside temple is Murugan depicted with his wives, because the tradition of ascetic vow fulfillment requires chastity.

14. Thus, the Arulmigu Bala Thandayuthabani Hill Temple celebrates its annual festival on Thaipusam Day in just the manner that the Nattukottai Chettiar Murugan Temple had celebrated its annual festival beginning the day before.

15. Yellow is associated with chastity and purity. Those who fulfill a vow wear yellow, just as celibate Buddhist monks wear robes of a saffron (yellow, orange, brownish-red) color. Yellow substances such as turmeric are believed to have a protective effect.

16. This description of hook-swinging (or pole-swinging) is given by Dubois and Beauchamp in *Hindu Manners, Customs, and Ceremonies* (1906): "At many of the temples consecrated to this cruel goddess [Mariamman] there is a sort of gibbet erected opposite the door. At the extremity of the crosspiece, or arm, a pulley is suspended, through which a cord passes with a hook at the end. The man who has made a vow to undergo this cruel penance places himself under the gibbet, and a priest then beats the fleshy part of the back until it is quite benumbed. After that the hook is fixed

into the flesh thus prepared, and in this way the unhappy wretch is raised in the air. While suspended he is careful not to show any sign of pain; indeed he continues to laugh, jest and gesticulate like a buffoon in order to amuse the spectators, who applaud and shout with laughter. After swinging in the air for the prescribed time the victim is let down again, and, as soon as his wounds are dressed, he returns home in triumph" (598). They add in a footnote: "'Hook-swinging,' as this is called is still practised in the Madura district. . . . Though the magistracy have orders to do all they can to prevent it, by dissuading men from offering themselves as victims, still, as it is not under ordinary circumstances a criminal offence, it cannot be prevented by legal process." In a pictorial essay on religious penance in India, Zumbro (1913) includes photographs of "pole-swinging" (1205, 1310, 1211). See also Thurston 1907, 487–501, and Elmore 1915, 31–32. Hook-swinging is known as *tukkam* among the Tamils of Sri Lanka. The practice is also found in Bengal, where it is associated with the Carak festival (see Gouranga Chattopadhyay, "Carak Festival in a West Bengal Village," in Harper, ed., 1964). This festival also includes tongue-piercing and trance dancing, and these practices are said to be gaining in popularity.

17. I was told that, before the war, devotees did not use long spears to pierce their cheeks in ritual vow fulfillment. I do not know how to assess this report as the practice certainly was known in India before this time.

18. Filmmaker David Griffin features one of these Chinese devotees of Murugan in the video he has made of the Thaipusam festival in Penang.

19. On the symbolism of color, see Beck (1969). The sakti (heat or energy) of the goddess in both its creative and destructive manifestations is symbolized by red. In ritual, red is counteracted and controlled by "white" substances thought to have cooling properties, such as milk, water, and vibhuti (sacred ash that remains after the heat of the fire has devoured everything else).

20. The identification with a fierce warrior spirit contrasts with an identification with Hanuman, suggesting resistance to hierarchy rather than an unswerving loyalty to one's master (see chapter 7).

21. Limes are also used in rituals of exorcism because they are believed to absorb demonic energy (see Babb 1975b, 233; Yalman 1964, 115–50). Perhaps the sacred ash (cool and white) counteracts the "heating" state of possession.

22. A member of the committee appointed to manage the Arulmigu Bala Thandayuthabani Hill Temple, which oversees the Thaipusam festival, commented that, should the Chettiars ever attempt to restrict those who entered the temple, "They would be slaughtered!"

23. The wounds in the cheeks are bound with a cloth that is wrapped under the chin and over the top of the head. I have occasionally seen blood stains on these cloths.

## CHAPTER 5: RITUALS AND POLITICS

1. According to the *Straits Echo,* January 19, 1946, Thaipusam was celebrated without incident immediately after the war.

2. In 1985, newspapers reported that an estimated 160,000 Hindu Tamils came to

Penang from plantations in the surrounding states to celebrate Thaipusam (*National Echo,* February 5, 1985). The total number of people who come to the festival includes Penang Chinese and tourists.

3. See Arunachalam (1980, 228) and Clothey (1978, 113–16) on the increasing popularity of Murugan in Tamilnadu over the same period.

4. Also relevant here is the work of James Scott on Malaysia—*Weapons of the Weak: Everyday Forms of Peasant Resistance* (1985) and *Domination and the Arts of Resistance: Hidden Transcripts* (1990)—and the writings of Indian historians, following the lead of Ranajit Guha, who have created the field of subaltern studies. Subaltern originally referred to a low-ranking officer in the British colonial army in India. These officers were typically colonial subjects who identified with the oppressor. However, scholars use the term to describe all people who are defined as subordinate by relations of domination constructed through a variety of means, linguistic, economic, social, and cultural. They have undertaken to rewrite history from the perspective(s) of non-elite colonial subjects, showing how they attempt to shape their own destinies.

5. The Indian National Army was disbanded after the war. INA officers either were sent to India to be tried for treason or were interned in Malaysia, until 1946, when protests by the Indian National Congress convinced the British not to proceed with prosecution (Arasaratnam 1979, 112).

6. According to Jain (1970), the NUPW continues to accommodate estate management because of the extreme dependency of laborers upon the company and management (353).

7. Mines and Gourishankar (1990) describe how rights and privileges are transformed into forms of power: "[The political big man] uses his control over the Kanchi temple and rights in other Kamakshi temples as a political resource in much the same manner that dominant men use their control of temples in local communities. First, [he] employs the Kanchi temple as a stage where he receives his most important symbolic honors, marking his preeminence among his followers. Next, . . . he attracts subordinate leaders to his constituency by granting them the right to sponsor worship and festivals for which they are also publicly awarded ritual honors. . . . These dominant men, in turn, use [him] to establish their individual public reputations as charitable persons dedicated to the public good" (770).

8. As it happens, this same businessman succeeded in becoming the patron of the Mariamman Temple in Bukit Mertajam (see chapter 8).

9. There are five Amman temples in Penang where the annual festival of goddess continues to be celebrated with rituals that include fire-walking.

10. Temple histories were collected with the assistance of Ramasamy Nagappan.

11. The Japanese are said to have profaned mosques by cutting pigs in them. By contrast, Hindu temples were left relatively undisturbed. Because of the war in China, the Chinese of Malaysia were treated even more harshly than the other ethnic groups. Consequently, some Chinese sought sanctuary in Hindu temples.

12. The secretary of the temple committee says that the temple committee includes members from different "medium and low" castes.

13. Worshippers often refer to the goddess of this temple as Mariamman. They

seem unaware of (or undisturbed by) this seeming inconsistency. One old man said there was a subsidiary altar for Mariamman in the temple and that the fire-walking festival was held in her honor.

14. Some members of the committee favored building a new temple where the Rajaji Tamil School now stands, because in their view the land still belongs to the temple. Another faction did not want to lose the Tamil school. The Lorong Kulit Mariamman Temple committee and the Karumariamman Temple committee have also been involved in ongoing disputes with the state government over ownership of the land on which their temple is built.

15. Continuity between the tradition of Amman worship and worship of Murugan is reflected in myths. For example, Murugan is given his implement of power, the vel (lance), by his mother, the goddess. The vel is often referred to as sakti, which is also a way of referring to the goddess. The festival of Skanda Sasthi, which celebrates Murugan's victory over the demon Surapadma, takes its name from Sasthi, goddess of fertility. In this context the goddess was sometimes said to be the spouse or attendant of Murugan (Clothey 1983, 57–58). Other legends say that Murugan was originally thought to be the son of Korravai, the goddess of war, and that he had no father (Zvelebil 1981, 8).

16. The Tamil word for vow fulfillment, *nerttikatan,* is derived from the Tamil root *ner,* meaning what is appropriate, just, or straight, and the word *katan* or debt, which refers to the debt one has incurred in the promise of the vow. *Nerttikatan* refers both to the vow made to a deity and to the offering made in fulfillment of a vow (Diehl 1956, 256–59). Arunachalam (1980) writes, "*nerttikatan,* or *vrata* (Sanskrit) is a single concept which, however, calls for several connotations in English: it is a penance, a sacred vow to observe certain austerities, including fasting, occasional vigils, continence, etc." (40–41). Other southern Indian festivals characterized by ritual vow fulfillment include Skanda Shasti, Karttikai, Ekadasi, and Shivaratri.

17. In Tamilnadu, the Madras Assembly banned the sacrifice of animals in 1950 (Barnett 1975, 169; Maloney 1975, 187).

18. Hindu festivals are traditionally associated with fairs.

19. Obeyesekere (1978) has noted that upper-class Hindu Tamils in Sri Lanka also find the ecstatic trance rituals of lower-class Tamils embarrassing. He suggests that they may see possession trance as a threat to the defenses they have erected against their own unconscious impulses (473).

20. The MIC was founded in 1946 by English-speaking Indians from northern India. Since 1955 the leadership has been Tamil.

21. Efforts to found multiethnic, class-based parties have failed under government policies designed to restrict the possibilities for multiethnic cooperation in the working class. For example, according to the Trade Unions Act, workers in pioneer industries such as the electronics industry are restricted to in-house unions. They are not allowed to form a nationwide union that might act effectively in the interests of the working class (*FEER,* July 22, 1993). The opposition Democratic Action party (DAP) is theoretically a multiracial party reflecting working-class interests, but in effect it is a predominantly Chinese party. In 1990 some Tamil politicians attempted to form a new political party, the All-Malaysia Indian Progressive Front, which was to

be allied to Semangat '46, a party that had broken away from UMNO. UMNO has been able to successfully counter this move and retain its dominance among Malays.

22. Mines and Gourishankar's description of the southern Indian "big-man" aptly fits the leadership style of MIC president, Datuk Samy Vellu: "Ideally, such men are altruistic leaders, dedicated to the service of their communities, but realistically they are commonly seen as masking their own venal interests with their role as benefactors. This conflict of individual and collective interests is a characterizing feature of big-man leadership and gives it a paradoxical quality: the more successful a big-man is as a benefactor, the more likely he is to be accused of self-interest" (1990, 783).

23. Washbrook notes that "while maintaining an egalitarian critique of the evils of the rich, DMK propaganda was inclined to attribute the evils to personal qualities of greed, which could be overcome by generosity, and not to suggest that wealth itself should be penalized" (Frankel and Rao 1989, 253–54).

24. In the October 1990 election, the Parti Islam (PAS) came to power in the state of Kelantan. This party is based in the Malay community and appears to provide another example of the use of religion to represent class protest: "PAS has . . . tried to make life easier for the very poor. Kelantan's 1,500 trishaw pullers are now exempt from the annual licensing fee, a small but welcome gesture to those on the margin of poverty" (*FEER,* January 31, 1991).

## CHAPTER 6: ARUL

1. See Bourguignon in Goodman, Henney, and Pressel 1974, introduction. Bourguignon reviews the anthropological literature on trance and develops the general thesis that trance behavior is subject to cultural norms (in Spindler 1978, 486). In addition I have drawn on studies by Yap (1960), Bourguignon (1965, 1974a, 1974b, 1989), Prince (1967), Walker (1972), Crapanzano and Garrison (1977), and Kapferer (1983).

2. As Wallace (1959) observed in one of the earliest studies of the cultural determinants of responses to hallucinatory experience, "despite the equivalence of process, that which is regarded as illness in one society may be regarded as merely one aspect of the normal and healthy life in another" (165).

3. From the *Rapport des commissaires chargés par le roi de l'examen du magnétisme animal, 1784,* quoted in Oughourlian (1991, 191).

4. The psychologist Milton Erickson devoted his career to the study of trance and the use of hypnotic trance in therapy. He was a master hypnotist who could be aptly described as a shaman, but he never developed a theory to explain hypnotic trance. He writes: "What hypnosis actually is can be explained as yet only in descriptive terms. Thus it may be defined as an artificially enhanced state of suggestibility resembling sleep wherein there appears to be a normal, time-limited, and stimulus-limited dissociation of the 'conscious' from the 'subconscious' elements of the psyche. This dissociation is manifested by a quiescence of the 'consciousness' simulating normal sleep and a delegation of the subjective control of the individual functions, ordinarily conscious, to the 'subconsciousness.' But any understanding of hypnosis beyond the descriptive is purely speculative" (1980, 4:8).

5. *The Encyclopedic Dictionary of Psychology* defines dissociation as "an unconscious defense mechanism in which a group of mental processes are separated (or split) from the remainder of the person's activity." It explains that in lectures given at Harvard (published in 1907 as *Symptoms of Hysteria)* Janet accepted William James' term *dissociation* as a translation of what he had described as *disaggregation* (Harre and Lamb 1983, 159).

6. However, when trance behavior does not accord with cultural patterns, it is generally viewed as a form of pathology, if not madness. The individual may be tolerated or restrained, depending on their behavior, but the trance experience of such a person will not play a role in maintaining or restructuring social relations.

7. Inglis provides another vivid description of the possession of the priest of an Amman temple (also called *camiyati*), as practiced by a lineage of Velar potters (in Waghorne and Cutler 1985). Diehl also describes a possession state called *kotanki* (named for the small drum beaten to induce the trance), which is entered by professional trancers who utter oracles (1956, 223–25; see also Moffatt 1979).

8. See Moreno for the story of another female *camiyati,* Valliyamma, who had a reputation for healing through the power of Murugan and had acquired a wide circle of devoted followers (in Waghorne and Cutler 1985, 113–19).

9. Erika Bourguignon points out that in demonic possession the "split-off parts of the personality" represented by the possessing spirit are felt to be alien and unacceptable to the individual, who thus concurs in society's judgment (in Spindler 1978, 486).

10. As in the case of Kia, Ayya's attacks of trance may have been precipitated by anger. He is described by his sister as "by nature a very angry person." Among Hindu Tamils the open expression of anger is appropriate only for certain individuals (and can only be expressed to a person of lower status), for example, men of the warrior caste or men of low status who are associated with the semi-demonic warrior deities. For others the direct or violent expression of anger is considered degrading. Ayya may also have felt that anger at a loved person was dangerous. His sister relates that his mother died when he was young. The boy was deeply affected and fell on top of the corpse, sobbing. Later episodes of *irraipattu* may have been precipitated by intensely angry feelings and fear that these feelings would harm a loved person.

11. In Western cultures, fear of hypnosis as a form of control by another person appears to be a major factor in the hypnotizability of a subject. In studies conducted after World War II, when there was a revival of interest in the use of hypnosis to treat battle trauma, about 20 percent of the population was categorized as easily hypnotizable and 20 percent as resistant, with the rest spread out in between. (There was considerable disagreement over whether hypnotizability was a positive or a negative personality trait.) In the late 1960s, there was renewed interest in hypnotism as a valuable technique for dealing with weight problems, addiction to smoking, and anxiety-producing situations. Hypnosis was redefined as "self-hypnosis" with the apparent consequence that the percentage of hypnotizable people increased. See H. Spiegel, *Trance and Treatment: Clinical Uses of Hypnosis* (1978), and Erika Fromm and Stephen Kahn, *Self-Hypnosis: The Chicago Paradigm* (1990).

12. The Chinese medium was possessed by the monkey god. Hilgard describes

photographs of the medium who had his cheeks pierced by sharpened sticks and other sticks thrust into his chest or back.

13. See Rouget, *Music and Trance: A Theory of the Relations Between Music and Possession* (1985).

14. Freud (1921) writes: "It is noticeable that, even when there is complete suggestive compliance in other respects, the moral conscience of the person hypnotized may show resistance" (S.E. 18:116; also see Erickson 1980, 1:498–530).

15. However, see Jensen and Suryani, *The Balinese People: A Reinvestigation of Character* (1992) for a critique of Mead and Bateson's work on Balinese character.

16. Freud (1921): "By the measures that he takes, then, the hypnotist awakens in the subject a portion of his archaic heritage which had also made him compliant towards his parents and which had experienced an individual re-animation in his relation to his father; what is thus awakened is the idea of a paramount and dangerous personality, towards whom only a passive-masochistic attitude is possible, to whom one's will has to be surrendered" (S.E. 18:127).

17. Ordinarily, Tamil devotees of Murugan do not practice going into trance. The people studied by Simons, Ervin, and Prince (1988) included a Punjabi girl (from northern India) and several Western-educated Malaysian Tamils of upper-caste background, for whom trance would be an alien experience identified with Tamils of lower-caste origin.

18. By the time of the Classical period, according to E. R. Dodds (1951), *ekstasis* (literally, "standing outside") was used to refer to an unusual mental and emotional state in which a person felt "not himself" (94–95, n.84).

19. Like Erickson, Hilgard does not think we can yet explain the physiology of such divided consciousness (1977, 247).

20. Similarly Freud (1921) writes: "The hypnotist avoids directing the subject's conscious thoughts towards his own intentions, and makes the person upon whom he is experimenting sink into an activity in which the world is bound to seem uninteresting to him; but at the same time the subject is in reality unconsciously concentrating his whole attention upon the hypnotist, and is getting into an attitude of *rapport*, of transference on to him" (S.E. 18:126).

21. For a critique of the Freudian model of the autonomous individual as a form of social control, see Lacan (1977) and Deleuze and Guattari (1983).

22. Ego identity is "more than the sum of the childhood identifications. It is the accrued experience of the ego's ability to integrate all identifications with the vicissitudes of the libido, with the aptitudes developed out of endowment, and with the opportunities offered in social roles. The sense of ego identity, then, is the accrued confidence [of] the inner sameness and continuity of one's meaning for others" (Erikson 1950, 253).

23. For a critical assessment of this formulation by an anthropologist, see Spiro 1993.

24. Dumont traces the evolution of the Western conception of the individual in relation to the ideology of egalitarianism in *From Mandeville to Marx: The Genesis and Triumph of Economic Ideology* (1977).

25. For a critical application of this view of Indian culture and Indian personal-

ity, see Mines 1988. There is no doubt that individuals of certain status and in particular roles are expected to demonstrate autonomy and are seen as having character and personality. However, Mines also describes evidence to support the view that, in Indian society, there is considerable pressure to behave toward others in the way prescribed by one's social relation to them.

26. See also Ramanujan (1989) and Kakar (1981). Alan Roland (1988), a psychoanalyst who practiced psychotherapy in northern India, similarly describes the very different cultural expectations that define maturity and mental health in India and America: "In the American urban middle and upper-middle classes, it is usually expected that a youth will develop the intrapsychic structures and integrated identity necessary to function independently in a variety of social groups and situations apart from the family, eventually leaving the family nest. Many Indian psychiatric leaders view these mental health norms as inappropriate to Indian psychological development and functioning in the extended family and culture, and thus as not at all universal. They rather emphasize the emotional bounding of kinship that enables the Indian person to live in emotionally close and responsibly interdependent relationships, where the sense of self is deeply involved with others, where relationships are governed by reciprocal hierarchical principles and where there is a constant need for approval to maintain and enhance self-regard. Their idea of mental health is not a rational, socially autonomous and self-actualizing person, but rather that of a person centered in a spiritual consciousness and being, so that there is an inner calm amid the stresses and pulls of close familial and other group hierarchical relationships" (Roland 1988, 60). Kakar (1990) describes how psychoanalysis in India has been reshaped by the cultural expectations of analysts and patients, citing the "traditional child-rearing practices and ideology of social relations, which emphasize a demonstratively close 'symbiotic' mode of relating with significant others." He observes that the relationship of the analyst and patient "fits more with the model of the guru-disciple than the doctor-patient relationship" (Kakar 1990, 431).

27. One can see how this teaching of collective responsibility for the behavior of related individuals was reflected in the conception of the village Amman goddess, who was thought to punish an entire village with drought or disease for the faults of a particular person or family.

28. There are striking instances in ritual vow fulfillment of men identifying with women (see chapter 7).

29. See D. W. Winnicott's essay "Ego Distortion in Terms of True and False Self" (in Winnicott 1965).

30. Roland observes that "it is extremely difficult for an Indian to express anger openly and directly to a hierarchical superior, although 'blistering angry feelings' might be redirected and expressed toward a substitute hierarchical figure" (1988, 70). Similarly, Trawick tells us that it is not acceptable for Tamil women to express anger (1990a, 193–94).

## CHAPTER 7: SYMBOLIC ACTS

1. Freud used the story of Oedipus in this way, and many people in Western societies use legendary or historical heroic figures as models for constructing an ideal-

ized identity. Freud himself used Hannibal and Moses in this way.

2. One informant suggested that the metamorphosis of Surapadma could symbolize the concept of *samsara,* according to which the human being takes numerous births, in different forms, and finally attains *moksha* (liberation) through the conquest of Murugan.

3. Obeyesekere (1981) writes that, among the Hindu Tamils of Sri Lanka, the demon Kalu Kumara "appears in the dreams of young postpubertal girls awakening to the pressures of sexual needs but unable to give expression to them. When the priest diagnoses a woman's illness as Kalu Kumara *dosa* [sin], it almost invariably implies that the patient is afflicted by disturbing sexual impulses. By contrast, Mahasona, the demon of the cemetery, is related to problems of aggression" (121).

4. J. Masson (1976), who has a preference for literal interpretations of behavior (as in his critique of Freud's theory of oedipal fantasy), argues that behind every Indian ascetic who inflicts pain on himself is an abused child. See following sections for oedipal fantasies related to ritual vow fulfillment to Murugan.

5. At the festival of the goddess in Bukit Mertajam, devotees who spontaneously entered a trance and began to dance wildly were described as possessed by the spirits of jungle animals. These animal spirits have not been brought under control but, rather, drive their victims to violent displays. On the association of animals with forbidden behavior in the folk speech of other cultures, see Leach (1964) and Brandes (1984).

6. The double imagery of bird and snake also appears in the iconography of Vishnu, whose vehicle, the Garuda, is understood to be an implacable enemy of snakes.

7. See Eliade, *Patterns in Comparative Religion* (1958, 164–71, 288) and La Barre (1962).

8. In a footnote, Zvelebil provides this gloss for the iconography of the serpent in relation to Murugan: "[Murugan] rides on the peacock, the killer of serpents, (serpent = cycle of years; peacock = killer of Time, and Death; important image in tantric yoga!)" (1973a, 131), suggesting a link between immortality and spiritual mastery and the control of sexual energies.

9. La Barre (1962), Slater (1968), and Brandes (1980) offer excellent discussions of the complexity of the serpent as a symbol that can stand for both male and female sexuality. Slater (1968) writes: "Thus the snake with its yawning jaws is primarily a devouring, enveloping, swallowing, strangling creature. It can not only penetrate but also incorporate, be both inside and outside, phallus and sheath, and its ability to shed its skin only underlines further this bisexual quality" (87). Slater claims that the female genital symbolism is the more salient and that the snake appears more often in mythology as a devouring than as a penetrating being. This genital symbolism is overlaid on earlier oral symbolism so that the biting serpent also suggests the narcissistic infant's relation to the mother and specifically the nursing infant devouring the mother (89). While Slater emphasizes the significance of the serpent as a symbol for the orally aggressive mother, La Barre (1962) notes that the widespread (false) folk belief that snakes drink mammalian milk suggests the importance of the snake as a symbol for the aggressive infant self (94).

10. In Western culture, the image of the intertwined serpents appears on the staff of Hermes Trismegistus who, as bringer and restorer of life, presided over coitus. The snakes are said to be male and female. The image, however, probably is derived from a fighting encounter between two male snakes (see La Barre 1962, 71).

11. The scorpion with its erect tail—which in Tamilnadu is sometimes depicted on the tongue of the demonic deities invoked to ward off the evil eye of envious neighbors—repeats the cobra imagery without evoking sexuality. La Barre notes the symbolic equivalence of snake and scorpion as representing both oral and phallic aggression in other cultures as well (1962, 62, 69).

12. This tale appears in the *Ramayana,* the *Mahabharata,* the *Markandeya Purana,* the *Harivamsa,* and the *Yoga-vasishtha* (Narayan 1964, 64–84; Dowson 1961, 339–42, 364–67).

13. Menninger (1938) identifies three components of martyrdom and asceticism: the self-punitive, the aggressive, and the erotic (120–25).

14. For example, the legend of the goddess Pattini, who is widely worshiped in Sri Lanka, tells of her birth from a mango:

> A golden mango appeared in a tree in the orchard of the king of Pandi; the king wished to bring it down, but all attempts failed. Ultimately the king of the gods, Sakra, descended from heaven in the guise of a humpbacked beggar and said he could bring the mango down. The king and courtiers were amused, but they gave him permission. Sakra wielded his bow and shot at the mango, and it fell down to earth. The king looked up in wonderment; some juice from the stem fell on his middle eye, which was blinded. Frightened, the king placed the mango in a golden casket and floated it down the river Kaveri. It was recovered way downstream by a merchant prince and his wife who were bathing there. They took the casket home, and lo, after seven days they found an infant girl, whom they adopted as their daughter. The myth of the goddess's "birth" in the mango is enacted in a ritual drama known as the "shooting of the mango" (Obeyesekere 1990, 28–29).

15. See Dundes (1987) on the symbolic equivalence of allomolifs (167–77).

16. Also see Obeyesekere (1990, 121). In southern India, Vinayagar (Ganesh) is represented as a perpetual bachelor. In northern India, however, Ganesh is said to have seven wives. This reversal of roles takes place also with regard to Murugan (Skanda), who is represented as a divine lover in southern India and as a celibate warrior in northern India.

17. For an in-depth discussion of the myths accounting for the birth of Ganesh, see Paul Courtright, *Ganesa: Lord of Obstacles, Lord of Beginnings* (1985).

18. In the *Mahabharata,* Ganesh is said to have broken off the tip of his tusk to use as a writing implement when he took down the story told by the sage Vyasa.

19. Kakar (1990) discusses Ganesh and Skanda as "personifications of the two opposing wishes of the older child on the eve of Oedipus" (441). See Obeyesekere (1990) for an extensive comparison of Ganesh and Skanda (Murugan) as cultural paradigms for oedipal conflict in Sri Lanka and southern India (114–21).

20. Chaudhuri (1956) argues that this strengthens the bond of affection between father and son (142).

21. Ramanujan writes: "We see that the Indian and the Greek tales, where they differ, do not differ in the basic pattern: (a) like sexes repel, (b) unlike sexes attract, across generations. But they do differ in the direction of aggression or desire. Instead of sons desiring mothers and overcoming fathers (e.g. Oedipus) and daughters loving fathers and hating mothers (e.g. Electra), most often we have fathers (or father-figures) suppressing sons and desiring daughters, and mothers desiring sons and ill-treating or exiling daughters or daughter-figures" (in Edmunds and Dundes 1983, 252). He cites as an example a Tamil tale (Type 706), in which a stepmother desires her stepson, Kunalan, who rejects her advances. She accuses him of making improper advances to her (Potiphar's Wife motif, K 2111.1), and his father punishes him by blinding him. Here we have an oedipal tale in which the symbolic blinding of the son is the act of the father (Ramanujan in Edmunds and Dundes 1983, 252).

22. Devereux has called this pattern, which emphasizes the father's hostility toward the son, the "Laius Complex" (in Edmunds and Dundes, 1983, 215–33).

23. Trawick (1990a) suggests that much of the erotic tension between mother and child is also transferred to siblings: "For the boy, a younger sister, being female offspring to his mother, could be seen as a duplicate of the mother, only being smaller, she would be less threatening, more accessible, and more amenable to control by him. For the girl, an elder brother, being a protector, could also be seen as a form of the mother, only, being male and other, he would possess added fascination" (171).

24. In the family studied by Trawick the father, Ayya, was relatively uninvolved with his son and did not participate in his everyday care (1990a, 225). Freeman's account of the life of Muli (1979) also illustrates this pattern. Muli portrayed his father "as an authoritarian critic who continually found fault with [his son's] behavior" (379). After the death of his grandfather, Muli's life history is a tale of his continual search for a more powerful male (due to caste or age) who will replace the benevolent grandfather. Thus, Muli especially valued his relationship with his "teacher," the leader of the village drama troupe, and his high-caste clients who used him to arrange liaisons with untouchable women. Although these people failed to fulfill Muli's expectations, he continued to court them. Muli, like his father, seemed singularly uninvolved with his son, whom he abandoned during a two-year affair. Even when his son became the first untouchable child in the village to enter high school, Muli resisted his wife's pleas that they sacrifice for the boy's school fees.

25. David Griffith, a filmmaker who has made a video of the Thaipusam festival in Penang, collected this story.

26. By contrast, in northern India, Durga is portrayed as a gentle young wife and daughter in need of family protection. See Kinsley (1986) on Durga Puja (95–115).

27. See Babb (1974, 1975a, 1975b) and Brown (1984) on the sexual imagery associated with the fire-walking festival of the goddess.

28. See Freud (1922) on Medusa's head (S.E. 18:273–74).

29. The theme of the aggressive, devouring mother also appears frequently in Indian folktales. In a corpus of tales analyzed by Beck, mothers are depicted as more hostile and aggressive toward their offspring than fathers. About half the tales that feature the mother-son relationship depict a mother's aggression or hostility toward her son: a mother is shown to be a party to her own son's sacrifice, or

is forced to eat him to avoid starvation, or comes to believe that he is an ogre. Twenty-four out of twenty-seven stories that describe mother-daughter relationships involve a mother who (inadvertently) eats the flesh of her own female offspring (in Blackburn and Ramanujan 1986, 76–102). The corpus represented in the various indexes of Indian folktales contains more tales from northern India than from southern India.

30. Sita takes on the form of Kali in order to subdue the demon. She does this out of love for her subjects, like a mother who is willing to go to any lengths to protect her children.

31. A devotee might then unconsciously see the lance of Murugan, symbol of his power, as a phallic implement that brings the devotee into sexual union with the god.

32. See Dinnerstein (1976), Chodorow (1978), Greenson (1978), and Benjamin (1988). Kakar has described the strong early identification of the Indian boy child with his mother (1981, 101). For an anthropologist's reflections on the construction of masculinity, see Gilmore, *Manhood in the Making: Cultural Concepts of Masculinity* (1990).

33. Trawick says that some of the men who attended Ayya's teaching sessions expressed an open homosexual interest in him. One of them said to him, "You are so attractive it's a shame you weren't born a woman" (74). Perhaps, reacting to the frightening possibility that a woman might become the angry, devouring goddess, men seek a safer version of the feminine in other men. In Freeman's life history of Muli, a similar pattern of feminine identification can be observed. Muli takes a feminine role in relation to the high-caste men for whom he procures prostitutes, and he is always eager to eat and flirt with them. He assumes the role of nurse for the Brahmin who has contracted a venereal disease, washing his clothes, preparing his food, and cleansing his body (1979, 153–64). Muli also enjoys the company of transvestites, with whom he seems to identify (383).

34. Kakar notes that the founding father of Indian psychoanalysis, Girindrashekhar Bose, wrote to Freud in 1929 about the cultural relativity of the forms of the oedipus complex: "Of course, I do not expect that you would accept offhand my reading of the Oedipus situation. I do not deny the importance of the castration threat in European cases; my argument is that the threat owes its efficiency to its connection with the wish to be female. The real struggle lies between the desire to be a male and its opposite, the desire to be a female. . . . The desire to be a female is more easily unearthed in Indian male patients than in European" (1990, 435).

35. As Fenichel notes, feminine masochistic behavior may serve to conceal the fantasy of seizing the invincible phallic vel, symbol of potency, from the powerful and ideal lord who is the object of one's love and with whom one identifies in the hope that one will get from this model the strength one lacks oneself (1953, 145).

36. Tamil anxiety about the sexuality of women is expressed succinctly in the following proverb: *Avatum pennale* (That which comes is through women), *Alivatum pennale* (That which destroys is through women), or "Through woman is being, and through woman is downfall" (Wadley 1980, 153).

37. See the novel *Chemeen* by Thakazhi S. Pillai.

38. Arivaraci was more religious than the other children, and each morning she

performed the daily worship to Ganesh, but her confidence in her own virtue was not great, and "under her breath she would curse herself for tiny mistakes" (Trawick 1990a, 235).

39. Kakar believes that because Hindu women turn aggression back against the self (in culturally approved ways through fasts and self-sacrifice) in a diffuse hostility of self-blame, they come to feel worthless, inferior, and bad (1981, 59).

40. Ayya explained that, "if people would not do what he said, then what he said must have been wrong. Then he had to punish himself because it would not be right to expect others to punish him" (Trawick 1990a, 194–95, 225).

41. At the Palani Temple, the traditional offering is sugar (Moreno, in Waghorne and Cutler 1985, 113). Sugar is traditionally brought as a gift to a newborn child. The sugar is touched to the lips of the child, with the wish that he or she should have sweet food and a sweet and pleasing life.

42. Referring to the appeal of the child-god Krishna, Kakar comments, "This particular theme reveals the child's primary need to be central to his world, rather than exist forlornly at its outskirts, to cause a glow in the eyes of adults rather than be looked at with indifference" (1981, 204).

43. La Barre has suggested that in both the Dionysian rituals of ancient Greece and the Eucharist, oral incorporative symbolism is used to transfer immortality from the god to his worshippers (1962, 89). Geza Roheim cites an Indian folk belief that a Brahmin seeking to be initiated by a magician must eat the excreta or blood of the magician. He also cites a Baiga myth from central India in which magical power is acquired by eating the father (1946, 503–8).

44. "When the fantasy in which one consumes the body (or bodily product) of a powerful being in order to enhance one's own supply of power has an aggressive form—the idea that the power of a mighty being or parent figure [has been] stolen or seized by force or that the powerful being [has been] damaged or devoured—a person may feel guilt and the fantasy will be repressed" (Fenichel 1953, 2:157). This observation is perhaps most aptly applied to the Eucharist.

45. Fenichel (1953) suggests that milk is a natural symbol for the relationship of human beings to others who are more powerful, such as deities: "The pattern of the very first object relation is that to the mother's breast and milk: 'I feel unpleasure—I swallow what is offered to me from the outside—the lost pleasure returns.' And in accordance with this we have the later sequence: 'I am helpless—I swallow the power which is in the external world—the lost pleasure returns'" (1953, 2:157). See De Vos and Suarez-Orozco (1987) for an application of these ideas by anthropologists. Also see Beals on the association of food and love in Indian culture (1962, 20–22).

## CHAPTER 8: A CEREMONIAL ANIMAL

1. Wittgenstein's *Remarks on Frazer's Golden Bough* (1979, first published in English in 1971) was written in two different periods, in 1931 and in the 1940s. In quoting from *Remarks on Frazer's Golden Bough* I have generally followed the translation of A. C. Miles, revised by Rush Rhees, as published by Brynmill Press (1979). However, where I thought Tambiah's translation in *Magic, Science, Religion, and the*

*Scope of Rationality* (1990) brought out Wittgenstein's thoughts more clearly, I have drawn on it.

2. "The description / representation [*Darstellung*] of a wish is, *eo ipso,* the description / representation of its fulfillment. And magic does give representation [*Darstellung*] to a wish; it expresses a wish" (Wittgenstein 1979, 4e).

3. Similarly, Sperber (1974) points out that understanding of the patterns of one's own culture is a tacit knowledge, and "tacit knowledge may in no case be acquired by rote; it must be reconstructed by each individual; it is therefore direct evidence of specific learning abilities, of a qualitatively determined creative competence" in all human beings (xi).

4. This critique is set forth in notes made by Rush Rhees from conversations with Wittgenstein in 1942–1943 (1972, 41–52).

5. "When we are studying psychology we may feel there is something unsatisfactory, some difficulty about the whole subject or study—because we are taking physics as our ideal science" (Wittgenstein 1972, 42). "Freud is constantly claiming to be scientific. But what he gives is *speculation*—something prior even to the formation of a hypothesis" (44).

6. But also, "For a *large* class of cases—though not for all—in which we employ the word 'meaning' it can be defined thus: the meaning of a word is its use in the language" (Wittgenstein 1968, #43).

7. "Wittgenstein is often believed to have taught that meaning and use are identical. But a careful reading shows that this is not a correct interpretation; he regards meaning and use as separate, but intimately related and interdependent" (Pitkin 1972, 84).

8. On turmeric used as a purifying and cooling potion and as a protective amulet when one fulfills a vow such as walking the fire, see Diehl (1956, 184, 252). On southern Indian fire-walking festivals, see Babb (1975b) and Brown (1984).

9. Loring Danforth, who has studied fire-walking as practiced by the Anastenaria of Greece and members of the American Firewalking Movement, summarizes research findings on the physics of fire-walking, drawing upon research by Albert Ingalls (sponsored by the University of London Council for Psychical Investigation), reported in *Scientific American* (1939), and research by Bernard Leikind and William McCarthy, reported in *The Skeptical Inquirer* (1985, 10). The ability of people to perform the fire-walk without being burned is attributed to the fact that, although the coals on which people walk are at a high temperature (1,000° to 1,200° F), the very low thermal conductivity of smoldering wood prevents damage to normal skin if the time of contact and the number of contacts with the coals are not too great. The researchers conclude that a specially induced mental state is not a prerequisite for a successful fire-walk (Danforth 1989, 286; see also Zilbergeld 1986). At large-scale fire-walking festivals, like the annual celebration at the Sri Mariamman Temple in Singapore (where seventeen hundred people crossed the fire pit in 1994), temple officials prepare for emergencies. An ambulance and doctors are present, and organizers report that between thirty and fifty people are treated for burns. There have been no fatalities since the festival began in 1840, and severe burns are extremely rare.

10. Kurtz (1992) interprets interactions such as this as examples of the ways in

which an Indian mother urges her child toward a more mature immersion in a larger and fundamentally benevolent group of mothers in an extended family.

11. Foster, writing of the Garifuna of Southern Belize, argues that possession is an attempt to coerce kin to supply support and nurturance through the threat of ancestral malevolence (1982, 18–23). I thank Walter Pitts for this reference.

12. The psychoanalyst Sudhir Kakar suggests that poisoned milk in this story may represent the poisoning effect of the mother's involvement with her son. He writes: "the fantasy of poisoned milk or poisoned breast resembles the 'double bind' in certain cases of schizophrenia in which the mother is perceived by the child to have given a contaminated love. That is, unconditional maternal love and empathy, responsive to the child's needs, are missing; the price of the mother's nurturing being that the child remain an extension of her person and a fulfiller of *her* needs" (1981, 148; see also 148–50).

13. Monk gives insight into Wittgenstein's understanding of religion in his discussion of Wittgenstein's reading of William James's *Varieties of Religious Experience,* Tolstoy's *Gospel in Brief,* and the works of Nietzsche (1990, chapter 6). See also Shields (1993).

14. Similarly Edmund Leach writes,

> In short, to understand the word *ritual* we must take note of the user's background and prejudices. A clergyman would probably assume that all ritual necessarily takes place inside a church in accordance with formally established rules and rubrics; a psychiatrist may be referring to the private compulsions of individual patients; an anthropologist will probably mean "a category of standardized behavior (custom) in which the relationship between the means and the end is not 'intrinsic'," but he will interpret this definition loosely or very precisely according to individual temperament. (1968, 521)

He concludes his encyclopedia article on ritual, "even among those who have specialized in this field there is the widest possible disagreement as to how the word ritual should be used and how the performance of ritual should be understood" (526).

15. Thus, studies of the ritual life of other peoples generally begin with several pages reviewing definitions of ritual and setting forth the characteristics that the author will treat as the central or essential characteristics of ritual. For example, Barbara Myerhoff writes, "Ritual has been defined variously, but there is a core of agreement as to its form and uses. It is prominent in all areas of uncertainty, anxiety, impotence and disorder" (1992, 161). For discussions of the defining characteristics of ritual, see Ortner (1978), G. Lewis (1980), Morris (1987), Wuthnow (1987, 97–144), and Kertzer (1988).

16. See Horace Miner's essay, "Body Ritual Among the Nacirema" (1956).

17. In Langer's words: "a genuine symbol can most readily originate where some object, sound, or act is provided which has no *practical* meaning, yet tends to elicit an emotional response, and thus hold one's undivided attention" (1942, 116–17).

18. Considering another instance of Gua's behavior, Langer quotes from Kohler to suggest that some symbolic gestures may be "natural" to a species. One gesture that we humans share with our primate relatives is kissing: "kissing is a natural demon-

stration on the part of chimpanzees, and has an emotional value for them. In her human surroundings [Gua] soon employed it in an unequivocally conscious way. She would kiss and offer her lips in recompense for small errors many times a day. . . . Thereafter she could be put down again and would play, but unless the ritual had been satisfactorily completed she would not be quiet or turn away until it had, or until some other climax superseded it" (1942, 115).

19. The term *object relation* is taken from Freud, who used it to refer to a person who is a loved object. In *Three Essays on the Theory of Sexuality* (1905), Freud writes, "Let us call the person from whom sexual attraction proceeds the *sexual object*" (135–36). The child's first object is the mother or primary caretaker, who is not initially perceived as a person but as a source of nurturance. Freud writes, "At a time at which the first beginnings of sexual satisfaction are still linked with the taking of nourishment, the sexual instinct has a sexual object outside the infant's own body in the shape of his mother's breast" (105, 222).

20. Winnicott, "Transitional Objects and Transitional Phenomena" (1951), in *Playing and Reality* (1971).

21. Segal points out that Melanie Klein also comes to the conclusion "that if symbolization does not occur, the whole development of the ego is arrested" (1988, 163).

22. Similarly, Marcia Cavell (1993) argues that the infant acquires symbolic capacities because its cry is taken as meaningful by others: "The infant is biologically programmed to do things that other people will interpret as meaningful signals for help. His cries are meaningful to us, but not to him. What is initially a cry without meaning to the crier, not a sign intended to be understood in a particular way, becomes meaningful in part through the behavior it produces in another. The child then begins to acquire concepts through that intercourse with other persons through which it acquires language" (223).

23. This formulation anticipates ideas developed by Talal Asad in his essay "On Discipline and Humility in Medieval Christian Monasticism," and in his other essays in *Genealogies of Religion: Discipline and Reasons of Power in Christianity and Islam* (1993).

24. This essay by Wolheim was first published in 1979 but was not easily available until reprinted in his *The Mind and Its Depths* (1993).

## CHAPTER 9: RITUAL, POWER, AND MORAL REDEMPTION

1. See also Block (1974, 1977), who describes ritual as a discipline in traditional society.

2. Asad cites A. Gell (1975, 211) on the Umedas of New Guinea: "Among my Umeda informants I found none willing to discuss the meaning of their symbols—to discuss their symbols *as* symbols 'standing for' some other thing or idea, rather than as concrete things-in-themselves. In fact I found it impossible even to pose the question of meaning in Umeda, since I could not discover any corresponding Umeda word for English 'mean,' 'stand for,' etc. Questions about symbols were taken by Umedas as questions about the *identity* rather than the *meaning* of a symbol: 'what is it?' not 'what does it mean?'" (quoted in Asad 1993, 61).

3. Pitkin has commented on the difference between the emic (or natives' point of view) and the etic (or outsiders' point of view) as follows: "The anthropologist may be able to see social, political, economic consequences and configurations of which the natives are not aware. It may seem obvious that the tribe could not be engaged in a war dance without knowing it, without intending to engage in a war dance and conceiving of what they are doing as a war dance. But would we feel that as decisively if the example were different? Suppose that the anthropologist said that they are 'reaffirming tribal norms' or 'reintegrating alienated members into the tribe' or 'permitting discharge of hostility in controlled and socially harmless ways' or 'demonstrating respect for the authority of tribal elders.' It seems to me that they might well be doing any of these things without knowing or saying that they are doing them. In such cases, of course, they are not doing what the anthropologist claims *instead of* what they say they are doing, but rather are doing both, doing the one *by way of* the other" (Pitkin 1972, 259).

4. On ritual and power, see Comaroff (1985), Kertzer (1988), Tambiah (1985), and Asad (1993).

5. J. L. Austin showed (1962) that many (perhaps *all*) descriptive or informative statements are in some essential way performative. Consider the statement of fact "It's hot in here." If a group of people are gathered in a small room, one of them is likely (to offer) to open a window, because people look for the intentions behind another person's words. There are conventions about how to get things done. We might even describe "It's hot in here" as a ritual remark, suggesting that it is a ritualized way of getting someone to open a window without resorting to a direct command or doing it oneself.

6. However, as Obeyesekere notes, one must also remember the essential differences between ritual performances and dramatic ones. The latter call for the "willing suspension of disbelief," while there cannot be any authentic ritual without belief (1990, 24). Erving Goffman's *Frame Analysis* (1986) is an early work that draws attention to the frame that sets both ritual and dramatic performances apart from ordinary social interactions. Goffman clarifies the role of the frame in determining how we interpret and respond to events: Must we take what is happening seriously? Or is this just a performance? Is it a comedy or a tragedy? A ritual, or an instance of psychotic behavior? See also Turner (1982), Kapferer (1983), and Grimes (1995).

# BIBLIOGRAPHY

Adigal, Prince Ilango
    1965    *Shilappadikaïram (The Ankle Bracelet).* Trans. Alain Danielou. New York: New Direction Books.

Anonymous
    n.d.    "Why Am I a Hindu." Published by the Penang Hindu Youth Organization.

Appadurai, Arjun, and Carol A. Breckenridge
    1976    "The South Indian Temple: Authority, Honour, and Redistribution." *Contributions to Indian Sociology* 10: 187–211.

Arasaratnam, Sinnappah
    1966    *Indian Festivals in Malaya.* Kuala Lumpur: Department of Indian Studies, University of Malaya.
    1979    *Indians in Malaysia and Singapore.* Kuala Lumpur: Oxford University Press.

Arunachalam, M.
    1980    *Festivals of Tamil Nadu.* Tiruchitrambalam (Tanjavur District, Tamilnadu, India): Gandhi Vidyalayam.

Asad, Talal
    1983    "Anthropological Conceptions of Religion: Reflections on Geertz." *Man* 18: 237–59.
    1993    *Genealogies of Religion: Discipline and Reasons of Power in Christianity and Islam.* Baltimore: Johns Hopkins University Press.

Austin, J. L.
    1961    *Philosophical Papers.* Oxford: Oxford University Press.
    1962    *How to Do Things with Words.* Cambridge, Mass.: Harvard University Press.

Aveling, Marian
    1957    "Hindu Temples in Penang: Ritual and Society." Revised version of a paper delivered to the Congress of the South Asian Studies Association, Canberra, Australia.

Ayyar, P. V. Jagadisa
    1982a    *South Indian Customs.* New Delhi: Asian Educational Services.
    1982b    *South Indian Shrines.* New Delhi: Asian Educational Services.

Aznam, Suhaini
    1984    "The Strength and Weakness of Being the Only Indian Party." *Far Eastern Economic Review* (July 26): 30.
    1990a  "Planter's Punch." *Far Eastern Economic Review* (Feb. 15): 24.
    1990b  "The Forgotten Ones," "New Motherland," "Cycle of Despair," "The Women's Burden," and "Breaking the Pattern." *Far Eastern Economic Review* (June 7): 15–21.

Babb, Lawrence
    1974    *Walking on Flowers: A Hindu Festival Cycle.* Singapore: University of Singapore Press.
    1975a  "Thaipusam in Singapore: Individualism in a Hierarchical Culture." Singapore: University of Singapore Press.
    1975b  *The Divine Hierarchy: Popular Hinduism in Central India.* New York: Columbia University Press.

Baker, Christopher
    1975    "Temples and Political Development." In *South India: Political Institutions and Political Change 1880–1940,* ed. C. Baker and D. Washbrook. Delhi: Macmillan.

Bakhtin, Mikhail
    1937    *The Dialogic Imagination: Four Essays.* Ed. Michael Holquist, trans. Caryl Emerson and Michael Holquist. Reprint, 1981. Austin: University of Texas Press.

Balint, Michael
    1959    *Thrills and Regressions.* New York: International Universities Press.

Banninga, J. J.
    1913    "The Marriage of the Gods." *National Geographic Magazine* 24: 1314–30.

Barnett, Stephen A.
    1975    "Approaches to Changes in Caste Ideology in South India." In *Essays on South India,* ed. Burton Stein. Honolulu: University of Hawaii Press.

Basham, A. L.
    1954    *The Wonder That Was India.* New York: Grove Press.

Bateson, G., and M. Mead
    1942    *Balinese Character: A Photographic Analysis.* Vol. 2. New York: The New York Academy of Sciences.

Beals, Alan R.
    1962    *Gopalpur: A South Indian Village.* New York: Holt, Rinehart and Winston.

Bean, Susan S.
    1975    "Referential and Indexical Meanings of *amma* in Kannada: Mother, Woman, Goddess, Pox, and Help!" *Journal of Anthropological Research* 31: 313–30.

Beck, Brenda
    1969    "Colour and Heat in South Indian Ritual." *Man* 4: 553–72.
    1972    *Peasant Society in Konku: A Study of Right and Left Subcastes in South*

*India*. Vancouver: University of British Columbia Press.

1975　"A Praise-Poem for Murugan." *Journal of South Asian Literature* 11: 95–116.

1976　"The Symbolic Merger of Body, Space, and Cosmos." *Contributions to Indian Sociology* 10: 213–43.

1981　"The Goddess and the Demon: A Local South Indian Festival and Its Wider Context." *Purusartha* 5: 83–136.

Bell, Catherine

1992　*Ritual Theory, Ritual Practice*. Oxford: Oxford University Press.

Benjamin, Jessica

1988　*The Bonds of Love: Psychoanalysis, Feminism, and the Problem of Domination*. New York: Pantheon Books.

Berkeley-Hill, Owen

1921　"The Anal-Erotic Factor in the Religion, Philosophy, and Character of the Hindus." *International Journal of Psycho-Analysis* 2: 306–38.

Berreman, Gerald D.

1979　*Caste and Other Inequities: Essays on Inequality*. Meerut, India: Folklore Institute.

Béteille, André

1965　*Caste, Class, and Power: Changing Patterns of Stratification in a Tanjore Village*. Berkeley and Los Angeles: University of California Press.

Bhagat, M. G.

1976　*Ancient Indian Asceticism*. New Delhi: Munshiram Manoharlal.

Bharati, Agehananda

1976　"Ritualistic Tolerance and Ideological Rigour: The Paradigm of the Expatriate Hindus in East Africa." *Contributions to Indian Sociology* 10: 317–39.

Blackburn, Stuart, and A. K. Ramanujan, eds.

1986　*Another Harmony: New Essays on the Folklore of India*. Berkeley and Los Angeles: University of California Press.

Bliss, Eugene

1986　*Multiple Personality, Allied Disorders, and Hypnosis*. Oxford: Oxford University Press.

Bloch, Maurice

1974　"Symbols, Song, Dance Features of Articulation: Is Religion an Extreme Form of Traditional Authority?" *European Journal of Sociology* 15: 55–81.

1977　"The Past and the Present in the Present." *Man* 12: 279–92.

1985　"From Cognition to Ideology." In *Power and Knowledge: Anthropological and Sociological Approaches*, ed. Richard Fardon. Edinburgh: Scottish Academic Press.

Bourdieu, Pierre

1977　*Outline of a Theory of Practice*. Trans. Richard Nice. Cambridge: Cambridge University Press.

1990a　*The Logic of Practice*. Trans. Richard Nice. Stanford: Stanford University Press.

1990b  *In Other Words: Essays Toward a Reflexive Sociology.* Trans. Matthew Adamson. Stanford: Stanford University Press.

1991  *Language and Symbolic Power.* Cambridge, Mass.: Harvard University Press.

Bourguignon, Erika

1965  "The Self, the Behavioral Environment, and the Theory of Spirit Possession." In *Context and Meaning in Cultural Anthropology,* ed. M. E. Spiro. New York: The Free Press.

1974a  "Cross-Cultural Perspectives on the Religious Uses of Altered States of Consciousness." In *Religious Movements in Contemporary America,* ed. I. Zaretsky and Mark Leone. Princeton: Princeton University Press.

1974b  *Culture and the Varieties of Consciousness.* Reading, Mass.: Addison-Wesley.

1989  "Multiple Personality, Possession Trance, and the Psychic Unity of Mankind." *Ethos* 17: 371–84.

Bourguignon, Erika, ed.

1973  *Religion, Altered States of Consciousness, and Social Change.* Columbus: Ohio State University Press.

Brandes, Stanley

1980  *Metaphors of Masculinity: Sex and Status in Andalusian Folklore.* Philadelphia: University of Pennsylvania Press.

1984  "Animal Metaphors and Social Control in Tzintzuntzan." *Ethnology* 13: 207–15.

1988  *Power and Persuasion: Fiestas and Social Control in Rural Mexico.* Philadelphia: University of Pennsylvania Press.

Brenneis, Donald

1984  "Straight Talk and Sweet Talk: Political Discourse in an Occasionally Egalitarian Community." In *Dangerous Words: Language and Politics in the Pacific,* ed. D. Brenneis and F. Myers. New York: New York University Press.

1987  "Performing Passions: Aesthetics and Politics in an Occasionally Egalitarian Society." *American Ethnologist* 14: 236–50.

Brown, Carolyn Henning

1984  "Tourism and Ethnic Competition in a Ritual Form: The Fire-Walkers of Fiji." *Oceania* 54: 229–44.

Carroll, Michael P.

1986  *The Cult of the Virgin Mary: Psychological Origins.* Princeton: Princeton University Press.

Carstairs, Morris

1958  *The Twice Born: A Study of a Community of High-Caste Hindus.* Bloomington: Indiana University Press.

Cavell, Marcia

1993  *The Psychoanalytic Mind: From Freud to Philosophy.* Cambridge, Mass.: Harvard University Press.

Chaudhuri, Arun Kumar Ray

1956 "A Psycho-Analytic Study of the Hindu Mother Goddess (Kali) Concept." *American Imago* 13: 123–46.

Chettiar, S. M. L. Lakshmanan
1973 *Folklore of Tamil Nadu*. New Delhi: National Book Trust, India.

Chodorow, Nancy
1978 *The Reproduction of Mothering: Psychoanalysis and the Sociology of Gender*. Berkeley and Los Angeles: University of California Press.

Clad, James
1984 "The Other Malaysians," "More and More Sink Below the Poverty Line," "Ancient Contacts and Colonial Exploitation," "The Primary Problem: Tamil School Failure," "The Cooperative Way to a New Economic Balance." *Far Eastern Economic Review* (July 26): 22–29.

Claus, Peter
1973 "Possession, Protection, and Punishment as Attributes of Deities in a South Indian Village." *Man in India* 53: 230–42.

Clifford, James
1988 *The Predicament of Culture: Twentieth Century Ethnography, Literature and Art*. Cambridge, Mass.: Harvard University Press.

Clifford, James, and George Marcus, eds.
1986 *Writing Culture: The Poetics and Politics of Ethnography*. Berkeley: University of California.

Clothey, Fred W.
1969 "Skanda-Sasti: A Festival in Tamil India." *History of Religions* 8: 236–59.
1978 *The Many Faces of Murugan: The History and Meaning of a South Indian God*. The Hague: Mouton.
1983 *Rhythm and Intent: Ritual Studies from South India*. Bombay: Blackie and Son.

Clothey, Fred W., ed.
1982 *Images of Man: Religion and Historical Process in South Asia*. Madras: New Era.

Cohn, Norman
1961 *The Pursuit of the Millennium: Revolutionary Messianism in Medieval and Reformation Europe and Its Bearing on Modern Totalitarian Movements*. New York: Harper Torchbooks.

Comaroff, Jean
1985 *Body of Power, Spirit of Resistance*. Chicago: University of Chicago Press.

Courtright, Paul B.
1985 *Ganesa: Lord of Obstacles, Lord of Beginnings*. New York: Oxford University Press.

Crapanzano, Vincent, and Vivian Garrison, eds.
1977 *Case Studies in Possession*. New York: Wiley.

Danforth, Loring M.
  1989   *Firewalking and Religious Healing: The Anastenaria of Greece and the American Firewalking Movement.* Princeton: Princeton University Press.
Daniel, E. Valentine
  1984   *Fluid Signs: Being a Person the Tamil Way.* Berkeley and Los Angeles: University of California Press.
Danielou, Alain
  1964   *Hindu Polytheism.* New York: Pantheon Books.
Darnton, R.
  1968   *Mesmerism and the End of the Enlightenment in France.* Cambridge, Mass.: Harvard University Press.
Deleuze, Gilles, and Felix Guattari
  1983   *Anti-Oedipus: Capitalism and Schizophrenia.* Minneapolis: University of Minnesota Press.
de Silva, Mervyn
  1990   "Arrogance of Power." *Far Eastern Economic Review* (7 June): 21.
De Vos, George A., and Marcelo M. Suarez-Orozco
  1987   "Sacrifice and the Experience of Power." *Journal of Psychoanalytic Anthropology* 10: 309–40.
Diehl, Carl Gustav
  1956   *Instrument and Purpose: Studies on Rites and Rituals in South India.* Lund, Sweden: Gleerups.
Dimock, Edward, E. Gerow, C. M. Naim, A. K. Ramanujan, Gordon Roadarmel, and J. A. B. van Buitenen
  1974   *The Literatures of India: An Introduction.* Chicago: University of Chicago Press.
Dinnerstein, Dorothy
  1976   *The Mermaid and the Minotaur: Sexual Arrangements and Human Malaise.* New York: Harper and Row.
Dirks, Nicholas B.
  1993   *The Hollow Crown: Ethnohistory of an Indian Kingdom.* New York: Cambridge University Press.
  1994   "Ritual and Resistance: Subversion as a Social Fact." In *Culture / Power / History: A Reader in Contemporary Social Theory,* ed. Dirks, Eley, and Ortner. Princeton: Princeton University Press.
Dodds, E. R.
  1951   *The Greeks and the Irrational.* Berkeley: University of California.
Douglas, Mary
  1960   *Purity and Danger.* New York: Praeger.
  1973   *Natural Symbols: Explorations in Cosmology.* New York: Random House.
Dowson, John
  1961   *A Classical Dictionary of Hindu Mythology and Religion, Geography, History, and Literature.* London: Routledge and Kegan Paul.

Dreyfus, Hubert, and Paul Rabinow
  1983 *Michel Foucault: Beyond Structuralism and Hermeneutics.* Chicago: University of Chicago Press.
Dubois, J. A., and Henry Beauchamp
  1906 *Hindu Manners, Customs, and Ceremonies.* Trans. H. K. Beauchamp. Reprint, 1959. Cambridge: Oxford University Press.
Dumont, Louis
  1959a "Possession and Priesthood." *Contributions to Indian Sociology* 3: 55–74.
  1959b "Structural Definition of a Folk Deity." *Contributions to Indian Sociology* 3: 75–87.
  1966 *Homo Hierarchicus: The Caste System and Its Implications.* Trans. Mark Sainsbury in 1970. Reprint, 1980. Chicago: University of Chicago Press.
  1967 "The Individual as an Impediment to Sociological Comparison and Indian History." In *Religion, Politics, and History in India: Collected Papers in Indian Sociology,* pp. 133–50. Paris: Mouton.
  1977 *From Mandeville to Marx: The Genesis and Triumph of Economic Ideology.* Chicago: University of Chicago Press.
Dumont, Louis, and David F. Pocock
  1958 "On the Different Aspects or Levels in Hinduism." *Contributions to Indian Sociology* 3: 31–44.
Dundes, Alan
  1962a "Earth-Diver: Creation and the Mythopoetic Male." *American Anthropologist* 64: 1032–105.
  1962b "From Etic to Emic Units in the Structural Study of Folktales." *Journal of American Folklore* 75: 95–105.
  1963 "Summoning Deity through Ritual Fasting." *American Imago* 20: 213–20.
  1980 *Interpreting Folklore.* Bloomington: Indiana University Press.
  1985 "The Psychoanalytic Study of Folklore." *Annals of Scholarship* 3: 1–42.
  1987 *Parsing Through Customs: Essays by a Freudian Folklorist.* Madison: University of Wisconsin Press.
Dundes, Alan, and Alessandro Falassi
  1975 *La Terra in Piazza: An Interpretation of the Palio of Siena.* Berkeley and Los Angeles: University of California Press.
Durkheim, Emile
  1915 *The Elementary Forms of the Religious Life.* Trans. Joseph Swain. Reprint, 1974. Glencoe: Free Press.
Eck, Diana
  1981 *Darśan: Seeing the Divine Image in India.* Chambersburg, Pa.: Anima Publications.
Edmunds, Lowell, and Alan Dundes, eds.
  1983 *Oedipus: A Folklore Casebook.* New York: Garland.
Elegant, Simon
  1992 "A Festival for the Fervent: A Hindu Celebration in Penang Is Full of Devotion and Self-Inflicted Suffering." *New York Times,* April 20, 1992.

Eliade, Mircea
    1958    *Patterns in Comparative Religion.* New York: New American Library.
    1969    *Patanjali and Yoga.* New York: Funk and Wagnalls.
Elmore, Wilbur T.
    1915    *Dravidian Gods in Modern Hinduism.* University of Nebraska Press.
Erickson, Milton H.
    1980    *The Collected Papers of Milton H. Erickson on Hypnosis.* 4 vols. New York: Irvington.
Erikson, Erik H.
    1950    *Childhood and Society.* London: Penguin Books.
Fairbairn, Ronald D.
    1952    *Psychoanalytic Studies of the Personality.* London: Routledge and Kegan Paul.
Fanon, Frantz
    1963    *The Wretched of the Earth.* New York: Grove Press.
Favazza, Armando, M.D.
    1987    *Bodies Under Siege: Self-Mutilation in Culture and Psychiatry.* Baltimore: Johns Hopkins University Press.
Fenichel, Otto
    1945    *The Psychoanalytic Theory of Neurosis.* New York: Norton.
    1953    *Collected Papers.* 2 vols. New York: Norton.
Fingarette, Herbert
    1967    *On Responsibility.* New York: Basic Books.
    1972    *Confucius: The Secular as Sacred.* New York: Harper and Row.
Foster, Byron
    1982    "Spirit Possession in Southern Belize." *Brazilian Studies* 10: 18–23.
Foucault, Michel
    1977    *Discipline and Punish: The Birth of the Prison.* Trans. Alan Sheridan. New York: Pantheon Books.
    1980    *Power/Knowledge: Selected Interviews and Other Writings, 1972–1977.* Ed. Colin Gordon. New York: Pantheon Books.
Frankel, Francine, and M. S. A. Rao, eds.
    1989    *Dominance and State Power in Modern India: Decline of a Social Order.* Vol. 1. Delhi: Oxford University Press.
Frazer, James George, Sir
    1922    *The Golden Bough: A Study in Magic and Religion.* (Abridged) Reprint, 1951. New York: Macmillan Co.
Freeman, James M.
    1979    *Untouchable: An Indian Life History.* Stanford: Stanford University Press.
Freud, Sigmund
    1895    *Studies on Hysteria.* Standard Edition. Vol. 2.
    1900    *The Interpretation of Dreams.* Standard Edition. Vols. 4 and 5.
    1905    *Three Essays on the Theory of Sexuality.* S.E. 7.
    1907    "Obsessive Acts and Religious Practices." S.E. 9: 117–27.

1910    *Leonardo da Vinci and a Memory of His Childhood.* S.E. 11: 63–137.
1913    *Totem and Taboo.* S.E. 13: 1–161.
1921    *Group Psychology and the Analysis of the Ego.* S.E. 18: 69–143.
1922    "Medusa's Head." S.E. 18: 273–74.
1923a   *The Ego and the Id.* S.E. 19: 3–68.
1923b   "A Neurosis of Demonical Possession in the Seventeenth Century." S.E. 19: 72–105.
1924    "The Economic Problem of Masochism." S.E. 19: 159–72.
1927    *The Future of an Illusion.* S.E. 21: 3–56.
1930    *Civilization and Its Discontents.* S.E. 21: 64–145.
1939    *Moses and Monotheism.* S.E. 23: 7–137.
Fromm, Erika, and Stephen Kahn
1990    *Self-Hypnosis: The Chicago Paradigm.* New York: The Guilford Press.
Fruzzetti, Lina, Akos Ostor, and Steve Barnett
1976    "The Cultural Construction of the Person in Bengal and Tamil Nadu." *Contributions to Indian Sociology* 10: 157–82.
Fuller, C. J.
1984    *Servants of the Goddess: The Priests of a South Indian Temple.* Cambridge: Cambridge University Press.
Geertz, Clifford
1973    *The Interpretation of Cultures.* New York: Basic Books.
1980    *Negara: The Theatre State in Nineteenth-Century Bali.* Princeton: Princeton University Press.
1983    *Local Knowledge: Further Essays in Interpretive Anthropology.* New York: Basic Books.
1984    "'From the Native's Point of View': On the Nature of Anthropological Understanding." In *Culture Theory: Essays on Mind, Self, and Emotion.* Ed. Richard Shweder and Robert LeVine. 123–36. Cambridge: Cambridge University Press.
1988    *Works and Lives: The Anthropologist as Author.* Stanford: Stanford University Press.
Geertz, Clifford, ed.
1971    *Myth, Symbol, and Culture.* New York: Norton.
Gennep, Arnold van
1960    *The Rites of Passage.* Trans. Monika Vizedom and Gabrielle Caffee. Chicago: University of Chicago Press.
Ghurye, Govind Sudashiv
1962    *Gods and Men.* Bombay: Popular Press.
Gill, M., and M. Brenman
1959    *Hypnosis and Related States: Psychoanalytic Studies in Regression.* New York: International Universities Press.
Gilmore, David D.
1990    *Manhood in the Making: Cultural Concepts of Masculinity.* New Haven: Yale University Press.

Goffman, Erving
1986  *Frame Analysis: An Essay on the Organization of Experience.* Boston: Northeastern University Press.
Goldman, Robert
1978  "Fathers, Sons, and Gurus: Oedipal Conflict in the Sanskrit Epics." *Journal of Indian Philosophy* 6: 325–92.
1985  "Karma, Guilt, and Buried Memories: Public Fantasy and Private Reality in Traditional India." *Journal of the American Oriental Society* 105: 413–25.
Goodman, Felicitas
1988  *How About Demons? Possession and Exorcism in the Modern World.* Bloomington: Indiana University Press.
Goodman, Felicitas, J. Henney, and E. Pressel
1974  *Trance, Healing, and Hallucination.* New York: Wiley Interscience Publication.
Greenson, Ralph
1978  "Disidentifying from Mother: Its Special Importance for the Boy." *Explorations in Psychoanalysis.* New York: International Universities Press.
Grimes, Ronald
1995  *Beginnings in Ritual Studies.* Rev. Ed. First edition, 1982. Columbia: University of South Carolina Press.
Guha, Ranajit
1983  *Elementary Aspects of Peasant Insurgency in Colonial India.* Delhi: Oxford University Press.
Guha, Ranajit, and Gayatri Chakravorty Spivak
1988  *Selected Subaltern Studies.* Oxford: Oxford University Press.
Gupta, Sankar Sen, ed.
1965  *Tree Symbol Worship in India.* Calcutta: Indian Publications.
Harper, Edward. B.
1957  "Shamanism in South India." *Southwestern Journal of Anthropology* 13: 267–87.
1959  "A Hindu Village Pantheon." *Southwestern Journal of Anthropology* 15: 227–34.
1964  "Ritual Pollution as an Integrator of Caste and Religion." *Journal of Asian Studies* 23: 151–97.
1967  "Fear and the Status of Woman." *Southwestern Journal of Anthropology* 25: 81–95.
Harper, Edward B., ed.
1964  *Aspects of Religion in South Asia.* Seattle: University of Washington Press.
Harre, Rom, and Roger Lamb, eds.
1983  *The Encyclopedic Dictionary of Psychology.* Cambridge, Mass.: MIT Press.

Hart, George L.

1973 "Woman and the Sacred in Ancient Tamilnad." *Journal of Asian Studies* 32: 233–50.

1975a "Ancient Tamil Literature: Its Scholarly Past and Future." In *Essays on South India,* ed. Burton Stein. Berkeley and Los Angeles: University of California Press.

1975b *The Poems of Ancient Tamil: Their Milieu and Their Sanskrit Counterparts.* Berkeley and Los Angeles: University of California Press.

1979a *Poets of the Tamil Anthologies.* Princeton: Princeton University Press.

1979b "The Nature of Tamil Devotion." In *Aryan and Non-Aryan in India,* ed. Madhav Deshpande and Peter E. Hook. Ann Arbor: University of Michigan Press.

1987 "Early Evidence for Caste in South India." In *Dimensions of Social Life: Essays in Honor of David B. Mandelbaum,* ed. Paul Hockings. Berlin: Mouton Gruyter.

Hatley, R.

1969 "The Overseas Indian in Southeast Asia: Burma, Malaysia, and Singapore." In *Man, State, and Society in Contemporary Southeast Asia,* ed. Robert Tilman. New York: Praeger Publishers.

Hilgard, Ernest

1977 *Divided Consciousness: Multiple Controls in Human Thought and Action.* New York: John Wiley and Sons.

Hiltebeitel, Alf

1988 *The Cult of Draupadi.* Vol. 1, *Mythologies: From Gingee to Kuruksetra.* Chicago: University of Chicago Press.

1989 *Criminal Gods and Demon Devotees: Essays on the Guardian of Popular Hinduism.* Albany: State University of New York.

Hudson, Dennis

1977 "Siva, Minaku, Visnu: Reflections on a Popular Myth in Madurai." *Indian Economic and Social History Review* 14: 107–18.

Hullet, Arthur

1978 "Thaipusam and the Cult of Subramaniam." *Orientations* 9: 27–31.

Irschick, Eugene F.

1969 *Politics and Social Conflict in South India: The Non-Brahman Movement and Tamil Separatism, 1916–1929.* Berkeley and Los Angeles: University of California Press.

Iyengar, P. T. Srinivas

1982 *History of the Tamils.* New Delhi: Asian Educational Services.

Jain, R. K.

1970 *South Indians on the Plantation Frontier.* Kuala Lumpur: University of Malaya Press.

James, William

1890 *The Principles of Psychology.* 2 vols. Reissued, 1950. New York: Dover Publications.

1906 *The Varieties of Religious Experience: A Study in Human Nature.* New York: Penguin. Reissued, 1982.

Jayaraman, R.
　　1966　"The Kaman Festival Among the Tamilian Estate Labourers in Ceylon."
　　　　　*Eastern Anthropologist* 19: 43–54.
Jensen, Gordon, and Luh Ketut. Suryani
　　1992　*The Balinese People: A Reinvestigation of Character.* Singapore: Oxford
　　　　　University Press.
Jha, Makhau
　　1969　"Spirit Possession Among the Maithil Brahmins." *Eastern Anthropolo-*
　　　　　*gist* 22: 361–68.
Jones, Ernest
　　1929　*Psycho-Myth, Psycho-History: Essays in Applied Psychoanalysis.* Vol.
　　　　　2. Reprint, 1974. New York: Hillstone.
Kakar, Sudhir
　　1981　*The Inner World: A Psychoanalytic Study of Childhood and Society in In-*
　　　　　*dia.* Delhi: Oxford University Press.
　　1990　"Stories from Indian Psychoanalysis: Context and Text." In *Cultural*
　　　　　*Psychology: Essays on Comparative Human Development,* ed. James
　　　　　Stigler, Richard Shweder, and Gilbert Herdt. Cambridge: Cambridge
　　　　　University Press.
Kapferer, Bruce
　　1983　*A Celebration of Demons: Exorcism and the Aesthetics of Healing in Sri*
　　　　　*Lanka.* Bloomington: Indiana University Press.
Karthigesu, R.
　　1980　"The Image of God." In Thaipusam Souvenir Program. Penang: Tamil
　　　　　Youth Bell Club.
　　n.d.　"Thaipusam in Malaysia." Unpublished essay in author's possession.
Kelly, John D.
　　1991　*A Politics of Virtue: Hinduism, Sexuality, and Countercolonial Discourse*
　　　　　*in Fiji.* Chicago: University of Chicago Press.
Kelly, John D., and Martha Kaplan
　　1990　"History, Structure, and Ritual." *Annual Review of Anthropology* 19:
　　　　　119–50.
Kertzer, David
　　1988　*Ritual, Politics, and Power.* New Haven: Yale University Press.
Keyes, Charles, and Valentine Daniel, eds.
　　1983　*Karma: An Anthropological Inquiry.* Berkeley and Los Angeles: Univer-
　　　　　sity of California Press.
Kinsley, David R.
　　1975　*The Sword and the Flute: Kali and Krishna.* Berkeley and Los Angeles:
　　　　　University of California Press.
　　1986　*Hindu Goddesses: Visions of the Divine Feminine in the Hindu Religious*
　　　　　*Tradition.* Berkeley and Los Angeles: University of California Press.
Kirkup, James
　　1963　*Tropic Temper.* London: Collins.
Klein, Melanie
　　1984　*Envy and Gratitude and Other Works, 1946–63.* London: The Hogarth
　　　　　Press.

Kolenda, Pauline Mahar
  1964    "Religious Anxiety and Hindu Fate." In *Religion in South Asia,* ed. Edward Harper. Seattle: University of Washington Press.
  1976    "Seven Kinds of Hierarchy in *Homo Hierarchicus.*" *Journal of Asian Studies* 35: 581–96.
  1978    *Caste in Contemporary India: Beyond Organic Solidarity.* Menlo Park, Calif.: Benjamin/Cummings.
Kracke, Waud H.
  1967    "The Maintenance of the Ego: Implications of Sensory Deprivation Research for Psychoanalytic Ego Psychology." *British Journal of Medical Psychology* 40: 17–28.
Kris, Ernst
  1952    *Psychoanalytic Explorations in Art.* New York: International Universities Press.
Kurtz, Stanley
  1992    *All the Mothers Are One: Hindu India and the Cultural Reshaping of Psychoanalysis.* New York: Columbia University Press.
La Barre, Weston
  1962    *They Shall Take Up Serpents: Psychology of the Southern Snake-Handling Cult.* Minneapolis: University of Minnesota Press.
Lacan, Jacques
  1977    *Ecrits: A Selection.* New York: W.W. Norton & Co.
Langer, Susanne
  1942    *Philosophy in a New Key: A Study in the Symbolism of Reason, Rite, and Art.* Cambridge, Mass.: Harvard University Press.
Lawson, Thomas, and Robert McCauley
  1990    *Rethinking Religion: Connecting Cognition and Culture.* Cambridge: Cambridge University Press.
Leach, E. R.
  1958    "Magical Hair." *Journal of the Royal Anthropological Institute* 88: 147–64.
  1964    "Anthropological Aspects of Language: Animal Categories and Verbal Abuse." In *New Directions in the Study of Language,* ed. E. Lenneberg, 23–63. Cambridge, Mass.: Harvard University Press.
  1968    "Ritual." *International Encyclopedia of the Social Sciences.* Vol. 13, 520–26. Ed. David Sills. New York: Macmillan Co. and the Free Press.
Lewin, Bertram D.
  1950    *The Psychoanalysis of Elation.* New York: Norton.
Lewis, Gilbert
  1980    *Day of Shining Red: An Essay on Understanding Ritual.* Cambridge: Cambridge University Press.
Lewis, I. M.
  1971    *Ecstatic Religion: An Anthropological Study of Spirit Possession.* (Revised 1989) London: Penguin.
  1977    Introduction. In *Symbols and Sentiments,* ed. I. M. Lewis, 1–24. London: Academic Press.

Longanathan, K.
  1985   "Why Thaipusam?" In Thaipusam Souvenir Program. Penang: Tamil
         Youth Bell Club.
Lukes, Steven
  1985   *Emile Durkheim, His Life and Work: A Historical and Critical Study.*
         Stanford: Stanford University Press.
Lynch, Owen M., ed.
  1990   *Divine Passions: The Social Construction of Emotion in India.* Berkeley
         and Los Angeles: University of California Press.
Lynn, Steven Jay, and Judith Rhue, eds.
  1991   *Theories of Hypnosis: Current Models and Perspectives.* New York:
         Guilford Press.
Maloney, Clarence
  1975   "Religious Beliefs and Social Hierarchy in Tamil Nadu, India." *American Ethnologist* 2: 169–92.
Mandelbaum, David G.
  1964   "Introduction: Process and Structure in South Asian Religion." In *Religion in South Asia,* ed. Edward Harper. Seattle: University of Washington Press.
Maniam, K. S.
  1984   "The Climb to Nowhere." *Far Eastern Economic Review* (July 26):
         30–31.
Marcus, George, and Michael Fischer
  1986   *Anthropology as Cultural Critique: An Experimental Moment in the Human Sciences.* Chicago: University of Chicago Press.
Masson, J. Moussaieff
  1974   "The Childhood of Krsna: Some Psychoanalytic Observations." *Journal of the American Oriental Society* 94: 454–59.
  1976   "The Psychology of the Ascetic." *Journal of Asian Studies* 35: 611–26.
Mauss, Marcel
  1936   "Les Techniques du corps." *Journal de la Psychologie* 32
         (March–April).
Mayer, Adrian C.
  1961   *Peasants in the Pacific: A Study of Fiji Indian Rural Society.* London:
         Routledge and Kegan Paul.
McGilvray, Dennis B.
  1983   "Paraiyar Drummers of Sri Lanka: Consensus and Constraint in an Untouchable Caste." *American Ethnologist* 10: 97–115.
  1988   "Sex, Repression, and Sanskritization in Sri Lanka?" *Ethos* 16: 99–127.
McGuinness, Brian, ed.
  1982   *Wittgenstein and His Times.* Chicago: University of Chicago Press.
Menninger, Karl
  1938   *Man Against Himself.* New York: Harcourt, Brace.
Mialaret, Jean-Pierre
  1969   *Hinduism in Singapore.* Singapore: Asia Pacific Press.

Miner, Horace
    1956    "Body Ritual among the Nacirema." *American Anthropologist* 58: 503–7.

Mines, Mattison
    1988    "Conceptualizing the Person: Hierarchical Society and Individual Autonomy in India." *American Anthropologist* 90: 568–759.

Mines, Mattison, and Vijayalakshmi Gourishankar
    1990    "Leadership and Individuality in South Asia: The Case of the South Indian Big-Man." *Journal of Asian Studies* 49: 761–86.

Mischel, W., and F. Mischel
    1958    "Psychological Aspects of Spirit Possession." *American Anthropologist* 60: 249–60.

Moffatt, Michael
    1979    *An Untouchable Community in South India: Structure and Consensus.* Princeton: Princeton University Press.

Monk, Ray
    1990    *Ludwig Wittgenstein: The Duty of Genius.* New York: The Free Press.

Moore, Barrington
    1978    *Injustice: The Social Bases of Obedience and Revolt.* New York: Pantheon Books.

Morinis, E. Alan
    1984    *Pilgrimage in the Hindu Tradition: A Case Study of West Bengal.* Delhi: Oxford University Press.

Morris, Brian
    1987    *Anthropological Studies of Religion.* Cambridge: Cambridge University Press.

Myerhoff, Barbara
    1992    *Remembered Lives: The Work of Ritual, Storytelling, and Growing Older.* Ann Arbor: University of Michigan Press.

Nagata, Judith
    1979    *Malaysian Mosaic: Perspectives from a Poly-Ethnic Society.* Vancouver: University of British Columbia Press.

Narayan, R. K.
    1964    *Gods, Demons, and Others.* New York: Viking Press.

Needham, Rodney
    1972    *Belief, Language, and Experience.* Chicago: University of Chicago Press.

Needham, Rodney, ed.
    1973    *Right and Left: Essays on Dual Symbolic Classification.* Chicago: University of Chicago Press.

Niehoff, Arthur
    1959    "The Survival of Hindu Institutions in an Alien Environment." *Eastern Anthropologist* 12: 171–87.

Obeyesekere, Gananath
    1978    "The Fire-Walkers of Kataragama: The Rise of Bhakti Religiosity in

Buddhist Sri Lanka." *Journal of Asian Studies* 37: 457–78.

1981   *Medusa's Hair: An Essay on Personal Symbols and Religious Experience.* Chicago: University of Chicago Press.

1984   *The Cult of the Goddess Pattini.* Chicago: University of Chicago Press.

1990   *The Work of Culture: Symbolic Transformation in Psychoanalysis and Anthropology.* Chicago: University of Chicago Press.

Oesterreich, T. K.

1930   *Possession: Demoniacal and Other Among Primitive Races, in Antiquity, the Middle Ages, and Modern Times.* London: Kegan Paul, Trench, Trubner.

O'Flaherty, Wendy Doniger

1973   *Siva: The Erotic Ascetic.* Oxford: Oxford University Press.

Ong, Aihwa

1987   *Spirits of Resistance and Capitalist Discipline: Factory Women in Malaysia.* Albany: State University of New York Press.

Ortner, Sherry

1978   *Sherpas Through Their Rituals.* Cambridge: Cambridge University Press.

1984   "Theory in Anthropology Since the Sixties." *Comparative Studies in Society and History* 26: 126–65.

Ostor, Akos

1980   *The Play of the Gods: Locality, Ideology, Structure, and Time in the Festivals of a Bengali Town.* Chicago: University of Chicago Press.

Oughourlian, Jean-Michel

1991   *The Puppet of Desire: The Psychology of Hysteria, Possession, and Hypnosis.* Stanford: Stanford University Press.

Parsons, Anne

1969   *Belief, Magic, and Anomie: Essays in Psychosocial Anthropology.* New York: The Free Press.

Pfaffenberger, Bryan L.

1977   "Pilgrimage and Traditional Authority in Tamil Sri Lanka." Ph.D. diss., University of California, Berkeley.

1979   "The Kataragama Pilgrimage: Hindu-Buddhist Interaction and Its Significance in Sri Lanka's Polyethnic Social System." *Journal of Asian Studies* 38: 253–70.

1980   "Social Communication in Dravidian Ritual." *Journal of Anthropological Research* 36: 196–219.

1982   *Caste in Tamil Culture: The Religious Foundations of Sudra Domination in Tamil Sri Lanka.* Syracuse, N.Y.: Syracuse University Press.

Pickering, W. S. F., ed.

1975   *Durkheim on Religion: A Selection of Readings with Bibliographies and Introductory Remarks.* London: Routledge and Kegan Paul.

Pillai, Thakazhi Sivasankara

1968   *Chemmeen.* Trans. Narayana Menam. Bombay: Jaico Publishing House.

Pitkin, Hanna Fenichel

1972   *Wittgenstein and Justice: On the Significance of Ludwig Wittgenstein for*

Social and Political Thought. Berkeley and Los Angeles: University of California Press.

Prakash, Gyan
 1990  "Writing Post-Orientalist Histories of the Third World: Perspectives from Indian Historiography." *Comparative Studies in Society and History* 32: 383–408.

Prince, Raymond, ed.
 1968  *Trance and Possession States.* Montreal: Proceedings of the Second Annual Conference of the R. M. Bucke Memorial Society.

Ramanujan, A. K.
 1973  *Speaking of Siva.* London: Penguin.
 1983  "The Indian Oedipus." In *Oedipus: A Folklore Casebook,* ed. Lowell Edmunds and Alan Dundes. New York: Garland.
 1989  "Is There an Indian Way of Thinking?" In *India Through Hindu Categories, ed* McKim Marriott. New Delhi: Sage.

Ricoeur, Paul
 1970  *Freud and Philosophy: An Essay on Interpretation.* Trans. Denis Savage. New Haven: Yale University Press.
 1974  *The Conflict of Interpretations.* Ed. Don Ihde. Evanston, Ill.: Northwestern University Press.
 1991  *From Text to Action: Essays in Hermeneutics.* Vol. 2. Trans. Kathleen Blamey and John Thompson. Evanston, Ill.: Northwestern University Press.
 1992  "Guilt, Ethics, and Religion." In *Experience of the Sacred: Readings in the Phenomenology of Religion,* ed. Sumner Twiss and Walter Conser Jr. Hanover, N.H.: Brown University Press.

Roheim, Geza
 1946  "The Oedipus Complex and Infantile Sexuality." *Psychoanalytic Quarterly* 45: 503–8.
 1950  *Psychoanalysis and Anthropology.* New York: International Universities Press.

Roland, Alan
 1988  *In Search of Self in India and Japan: Toward a Cross-Cultural Psychology.* Princeton: Princeton University Press.

Rouget, Gilbert
 1985  *Music and Trance: A Theory of the Relations Between Music and Possession.* Chicago: University of Chicago Press.

Said, Edward
 1978  *Orientalism.* New York: Vintage Books.

Sandhu, K. S.
 1969  *Indians in Malaya.* Cambridge: Cambridge University Press.

Sargant, William
 1957  *Battle for the Mind: A Physiology of Conversion and Brain-Washing.* London: Heinemann.

Sarkar, Sarasi Lal
 1943  "A Study of the Psychology of Sexual Abstinence from the Dreams of an

Ascetic." *International Journal of Psycho-Analysis* 24: 170–75.

Sastri, Nilakanta
1966   *A History of South India.* Madras: Oxford University Press.

Schechner, Richard
1986   "Wrestling Against Time: The Performance Aspect of Agni." *Journal of Asian Studies* 45: 359–63.

Scheper-Hughes, Nancy, and Margaret M. Lock
1983   "The Mindful Body: A Prolegomenon to Future Work in Medical Anthropology." *Medical Anthropology Quarterly* 1: 5–41.

Scott, James C.
1985   *Weapons of the Weak: Everyday Forms of Peasant Resistance.* New Haven: Yale Univesity Press.
1990   *Domination and the Arts of Resistance: Hidden Transcripts.* New Haven: Yale University Press.

Segal, Hanna
1988   "Notes on Symbol Formation." In *Melanie Klein Today: Developments in Theory and Practice.* Vol. 1, 160–77. Ed. E.B. Spillius. London: Routledge.

Shaw, William
1975   *Aspects of Malaysian Magic.* Kuala Lumpur: Muzium Nagara.

Shields, Philip
1993   *Logic and Sin in the Writings of Ludwig Wittgenstein.* Chicago: University of Chicago Press.

Shulman, David Dean
1980   *Tamil Temple Myths: Sacrifice and Divine Marriage in South Indian Saiva Tradition.* Princeton: Princeton University Press.

Shweder, Richard, and Robert LeVine, eds.
1982   *Culture Theory: Essays on Mind, Self, and Emotion.* Cambridge: Cambridge University Press.

Shweder, Richard, and Joan B. Miller
1984   "The Social Construction of the Person: How Is It Possible?" In *The Social Construction of the Person,* ed. Gergen and Davis. Berlin: Springer Verlag.

Simons, Ronald, Frank Ervin, and Raymond Prince
1988   "The Psychobiology of Trance." *Transcultural Psychiatric Research Review* 25: 249–84.

Skorupski, John
1976   *Symbol and Theory: A Philosophical Study of Theories of Religion in Social Anthropology.* Cambridge: Cambridge University Press.

Slater, Philip E.
1968   *The Glory of Hera: Greek Mythology and the Greek Family.* Boston: Beacon Press.

Soepadmo, E., and Ho Thian Hua, eds.
1971   *A Guide to Batu Caves.* Kuala Lumpur: Malaysian Nature Society and

Batu Caves Protection Association.

Somalay
1975    *Palani: The Hill Temple of Muruga.* Palani, Tamilnadu: Arulmigu Dhandayuthapani Swamy Temple.

Sperber, Dan
1974    *Rethinking Symbolism.* Cambridge: Cambridge University Press.

Spiegel, Herbert
1978    *Trance and Treatment: Clinical Uses of Hypnosis.* New York: Basic Books.

Spindler, George, ed.
1978    *The Making of Psychological Anthropology.* Berkeley and Los Angeles: University of California Press.

Spiro, Melford E.
1982    *Oedipus in the Trobriands.* Chicago: University of Chicago Press.
1987    *Culture and Human Nature: Theoretical Papers.* Chicago: University of Chicago Press.
1993    "Is the Western Conception of the Self 'Peculiar' Within the Context of World Cultures." *Ethos* 21: 107–53.

Spivak, Gayatri
1990    "Gayatri Spivak on the Politics of the Subaltern." Interview by Howard Winant. *Socialist Review* 20: 81–97.

Srinivas, M. N.
1966    *Social Change in Modern India.* Berkeley and Los Angeles: University of California Press.
1987    *The Dominant Caste and Other Essays.* Delhi: Oxford University Press.

Stanley, John M.
1977    "Special Time, Special Power: The Fluidity of Power in a Popular Hindu Festival." *Journal of Asian Studies* 37: 27–43.

Stein, Burton
1978    *South Indian Temples: An Analytic Reconsideration.* New Delhi: Vikas.
1980    *Peasant, State, and Society in Medieval South India.* Delhi: Oxford University Press.
1984    *All the King's Mana: Papers on Medieval South Indian History.* Madras: New Era.

Stevenson, H. N. C.
1954    "Status Evaluation in the Hindu Caste System." *Journal of the Royal Anthropological Institute* 84: 45–65.
1961    "Caste." *Encyclopaedia Britannica* 4: 973–82.

Stigler, James, Richard Shweder, and Gilbert Herdt, eds.
1990    *Cultural Psychology: Essays on Comparative Human Development.* Cambridge: Cambridge University Press.

Stirrat, R. L.
1984    "Sacred Models." *Man* 19: 199–215.

Strenski, Ivan
1987    *Four Theories of Myth in Twentieth-Century History: Cassirer, Eliade,*

*Levi-Strauss, and Malinowski.* Iowa City: University of Iowa Press.

Stutley, Margaret, and James Stutley

1977 *Harper's Dictionary of Hinduism: Its Mythology, Folklore, Philosophy, Literature, and History.* San Francisco: Harper and Row.

Tambiah, Stanley J.

1985 *Culture, Thought, and Social Action.* Cambridge, Mass.: Harvard University Press.

1990 *Magic, Science, Religion, and the Scope of Rationality.* Cambridge: Cambridge University Press.

Tamil Lexicon

1982 Tamil Lexicon. Madras: University of Madras.

Tampy, K. P. Padmanabhan

1961 *"Kavadi:* A Form of Worship in South India." *Folklore* 2: 401–3.

Thompson, E. P.

1966 *The Making of the English Working Class.* New York: Vintage.

Thurston, Edgar

1907 *Ethnographic Notes in Southern India.* 2 vols. Madras: Government Press.

1909 *Castes and Tribes of Southern India.* 7 vols. Madras: Government Press.

Trawick, Margaret

1990a *Notes on Love in a Tamil Family.* Berkeley and Los Angeles: University of California Press.

1990b "The Ideology of Love in a Tamil Family." In *Divine Passions: The Social Construction of Emotion in India,* ed. Owen Lynch. Berkeley and Los Angeles: University of California Press.

Turner, Victor

1967 *The Forest of Symbols.* Ithaca: Cornell University Press.

1969 *The Ritual Process: Structure and Anti-Structure.* Chicago: Aldine.

1974 *Drama, Fields, and Metaphors: Symbolic Action in Human Society.* Ithaca: Cornell University Press.

1982 *From Ritual to Theatre: The Human Seriousness of Play.* New York: Performing Arts Journal Publications.

van der Walde, P. H.

1968 "Trance States and Ego Psychology." In *Trance and Possession States,* ed. Raymond Prince, 57–68. Montreal: Proceedings of the Second Annual Conference of the R. M. Bucke Memorial Society.

Van Gennep, Arnold

1960 *The Rites of Passage.* Trans. Monika Vizedom and Gabrielle Caffee. Chicago: University of Chicago Press.

Venkataraman, K. R.

1956 "Skanda Cult in South India." In *The Cultural Heritage of India.* Vol. 4, *The Religions.* Calcutta: The Ramakrishna Mission Institute of Culture.

Vogel, J. Ph.

1926 *Indian Serpent Lore.* Reissued, 1972. Varanasi: Prithivi Pra Kashan.

Wadley, Susan

1975 *Shakti: Power in the Conceptual Structure of Karimpur Religion.*

Chicago: University of Chicago Press.

Wadley, Susan, ed.

1980   *The Powers of Tamil Women.* Syracuse, N.Y.: Syracuse University Press.

Waghorne, Joanne Punzo, and Normal Cutler (with V. Narayanan), eds.

1985   *Gods of Flesh, Gods of Stone: The Embodiment of Divinity in India.* Chambersburg, Pa.: Anima Publications.

Wagner, Roy

1981   *The Invention of Culture.* Chicago: University of Chicago Press.

Walker, Sheila S.

1972   *Ceremonial Spirit Possession in Africa and Afro-America.* Leiden: Brill.

Wallace, Anthony R. C.

1959   "Cultural Determinants of Responses to Hallucinatory Experience." *AMA Archives of General Psychiatry* 1: 589.

Ward, Colleen

1984   "Thaipusam in Malaya: A Psycho-Anthropological Analysis of Ritual Trance, Ceremonial Possession, and Self-Mortification Practices." *Ethos* 12: 307–34.

White, Geoffrey, and John Kirkpatrick, eds.

1985   *Person, Self, and Experience: Exploring Pacific Ethnopsychologies.* Berkeley: University of California Press.

Whitehead, Henry

1916   *The Village Gods of South India.* Reissued, 1983. New Delhi: Asian Educational Services.

1921   *The Village Gods of South India.* 2nd ed. Reissued, 1983. New Delhi: Asian Educational Services.

Whorf, Benjamin Lee

1964   *Language, Thought, and Reality.* Boston: MIT Press.

Wiebe, Paul D., and S. Mariappen

1978   *Indian Malaysians: A View from the Plantation.* New Delhi: Manohar.

Williams, Raymond

1983   *Key Words: A Vocabulary of Culture and Society.* Glasgow: Fontana.

Wilson, Bryan R., ed.

1970   *Rationality.* New York: Harper & Row.

Winch, Peter

1958   *The Idea of a Social Science and Its Relation to Philosophy.* London: Routledge and Kegan Paul.

1964   "Understanding a Primitive Society." *American Philosophical Quarterly* 1: 307–24.

Winnicott, D. W.

1965   *The Maturational Processes and the Facilitating Environment: Studies in the Theory of Emotional Development.* New York: International Universities Press.

1971   *Playing and Reality.* New York: Tavistock Publications.

1988   *Human Nature.* New York: Schocken Books.

Wirz, Paul

1966   *Kataragama: The Holiest Place in Ceylon.* Ceylon: Gunasena.

Wittgenstein, Ludwig
    1922   *Tractatus logico-philosophicus.* Reprint, 1981. London: Routledge & Kegan Paul.
    1968   *Philosophical Investigations.* Trans. B. E. M. Anscombe. First published posthumously in 1953. New York: Macmillan.
    1972   *Lectures and Conversations on Aesthetics, Psychology, and Religious Belief.* Ed. Cyril Barrett, compiled from notes taken by Yorick Smythies, Rush Rhees, and James Taylor. Berkeley and Los Angeles: University of California Press.
    1975   *Philosophical Remarks.* Ed. Rush Rhees, trans. Raymond Hargreaves and Roger White. New York: Barnes and Noble.
    1979   *Remarks on Frazer's Golden Bough.* Ed. Rush Rhees. Doncaster: Brynmill Press.
    1980   *Culture and Value.* Ed. G. H. Von Wright. Chicago: University of Chicago Press.
Wolheim, Richard
    1993   *The Mind and Its Depths.* Cambridge, Mass.: Harvard University Press.
Wuthnow, Robert
    1987   *Meaning and Moral Order: Explorations in Cultural Analysis.* Berkeley: University of California Press.
Yalman, Nur
    1964   "The Structure of Sinhalese Healing Rituals." *Journal of Asian Studies* 23: 115–50.
Yap, Pow Meng
    1960   "The Possession Syndrome." *Journal of Mental Science* 106: 151–56.
Zeig, Jeffrey
    1980   *A Teaching Seminar with Milton H. Erickson.* New York: Brunner/Mazel.
Zilbergeld, Bernie
    1986   "Hypnosis and Fire-walking." *Hypnosis: Questions and Answers,* ed. Zilbergeld, Edelstein, and Araoz. New York: W. W. Norton.
Zumbro, Rev. W. M.
    1913   "Religious Penances and Punishments Self-Inflicted by the Holy Men of India." *National Geographic Magazine* 24: 1257–313.
Zvelebil, Kamil V.
    1973a  *The Poets of the Powers.* London: Rider and Company.
    1973b  *The Smile of Murugan: On Tamil Literature of South India.* Leiden: E. J. Brill.
    1981   *Tiru Murugan.* Madras: International Institute of Tamil Studies.

# INDEX